Lecture Notes in Computer Science   8241

Commenced Publication in 1973
Founding and Former Series Editors:
Gerhard Goos, Juris Hartmanis, and Jan van Leeuwen

For further volumes:
http://www.springer.com/series/7407

T0171848

Ralf Hinze (Ed.)

Implementation and Application of Functional Languages

24th International Symposium, IFL 2012
Oxford, UK, August 30–September 1, 2012
Revised Selected Papers

 Springer

Editor
Ralf Hinze
University of Oxford
Oxford
UK

ISSN 0302-9743 ISSN 1611-3349 (electronic)
ISBN 978-3-642-41581-4 ISBN 978-3-642-41582-1 (eBook)
DOI 10.1007/978-3-642-41582-1
Springer Heidelberg New York Dordrecht London

Library of Congress Control Number: 2013954020

CR Subject Classification F.3, D.3, D.2, F.4.1, D.1, D.2.4

Printed on acid-free paper

Springer is part of Springer Science+Business Media (www.springer.com)

Preface

This volume contains the selected peer-reviewed revised articles that were presented at IFL 2012, the 24th International Symposium on Implementation and Application of Functional Languages. IFL 2012 was held in Oxford, UK, during 30 August–1 September, 2012. The goal of the IFL symposia is to bring together researchers actively engaged in the implementation and application of functional and function-based programming languages. IFL is a venue for researchers to present and discuss new ideas and concepts, work in progress, and publication-ripe results related to the implementation and application of functional languages and function-based programming.

The call for papers generated 37 submissions, all of which were accepted for presentation. Participants are invited to submit either a draft paper or an extended abstract describing work to be presented at the symposium. These submissions are screened by the program chair to make sure they are within the scope of IFL. It should be stressed, however, that these contributions are not peer-reviewed publications. The submissions accepted for presentation appear in the *draft* proceedings distributed at the symposium, which also appeared as a Department of Computer Science technical report (RR-12-06).

After the symposium, authors are given the opportunity to consider the feedback received from discussions at the symposium and are invited to submit revised full articles to the formal review process. The revised submissions are reviewed by the Program Committee considering their correctness, novelty, originality, relevance, significance, and clarity. Of the 37 papers presented at IFL 2012, the Program Committee reviewed 28 revised submissions, and 14 papers were ultimately selected for this volume. Each submission was reviewed by four members of the Program Committee. Three papers had an additional round of "shepherding" by a member of the Program Committee in order to improve the presentation and tailor it for the IFL audience.

Fritz Henglein, from the Department of Computer Science at the University of Copenhagen, was the invited speaker of IFL 2012. He delivered a truly inspiring talk about generic sorting and partitioning in linear time and fully abstractly. Thank you Fritz for your contribution to IFL 2012.

Following the IFL tradition, IFL 2012 provided participants with an opportunity to get to know each other and to talk outside the formal setting of presentations with a social event on the second day of the symposium. This year, the participants embarked on a boat trip on the river Isis, followed by a banquet at Balliol College, one of Oxford's oldest colleges.

Carrying on a tradition started in 2003, the Program Committee selected a paper for the *Peter J. Landin Award*, given to the best article presented at the symposium. The recipients of the award for IFL 2012 are Kanae Tsushima and Kenichi Asai, from

Ochanomizu University, for their contribution entitled "An Embedded Type Debugger."

Putting together IFL 2012 was truly a team effort. I am grateful to the Department of Computer Science, Elizabeth Walsh in particular, for administrative support and to St. Anne's College for hosting the event. I would like to thank the members of the Program Committee and the external referees for their care and diligence in reviewing the submitted papers. A special thank you is due to the three shepherds, Andy Gill, Tim Sheard, and Peter Thiemann. Finally, I would like to thank Kwok-Ho Cheung, Tom Harper, Daniel James, José Pedro Magalhães, and Nicolas Wu, for their help with organizing the symposium and for distributing the call for papers. The review process and compilation of the proceedings were greatly helped by Andrei Voronkov's EasyChair system, which I can highly recommend.

I hope that the readers will enjoy this collection of selected papers from IFL 2012. Make sure to join us at a future version of IFL!

September 2013   Ralf Hinze

Organization

Program Committee

Edwin Brady	University of St. Andrews, UK
Andrew Butterfield	University of Dublin, Ireland
Matthew Flatt	University of Utah, USA
Andy Gill	University of Kansas, USA
Stephan Herhut	IntelLabs, Santa Clara, USA
Ralf Hinze	University of Oxford, UK
Zhenjiang Hu	National Institute of Informatics, Japan
Patrik Jansson	Chalmers University of Technology, Sweden
Mauro Jaskelioff	Universidad Nacional de Rosario, Argentina
Gabriele Keller	University of New South Wales, Australia
Simon Marlow	Microsoft Research, UK
Pablo Nogueira	Technical University of Madrid, Spain
Bruno Oliveira	Seoul National University, Korea
José Nuno Oliveira	University of Minho, Portugal
Rinus Plasmeijer	Radboud University Nijmegen, The Netherlands
Tom Schrijvers	Ghent University, Belgium
Tim Sheard	Portland State University, USA
Wouter Swierstra	University of Utrecht, The Netherlands
Peter Thiemann	University of Freiburg, Germany
Simon Thompson	University of Kent, UK
Steve Zdancewic	University of Pennsylvania, USA

Additional Reviewers

Kazuyuki Asada	Andrew Farmer	Steffen Michels
Clara Benac Earle	Álvaro Fernández Díaz	David Nowak
Jeroen Bransen	Lars-Ake Fredlund	Hugo Pacheco
Manuel Chakravarty	Fritz Henglein	Exequiel Rivas
Larry Diehl	Pieter Koopman	Neil Sculthorpe
Jonas Duregård	Trevor McDonell	John Van Groningen

Local Organizing Committee

Ralf Hinze   University of Oxford, UK
Nicolas Wu   University of Oxford, UK
José Pedro Magalhães   University of Oxford, UK

Contents

A Notation for Comonads

Dominic Orchard$^{(\boxtimes)}$ and Alan Mycroft

Computer Laboratory, University of Cambridge, Cambridge, UK
{dominic.orchard, alan.mycroft}@cl.cam.ac.uk

Abstract. The category-theoretic concept of a *monad* occurs widely as a design pattern for functional programming with effects. The utility and ubiquity of monads is such that some languages provide syntactic sugar for this pattern, further encouraging its use. We argue that *comonads*, the dual of monads, similarly provide a useful design pattern, capturing notions of context dependence. However, comonads remain relatively under-used compared to monads—due to a lack of knowledge of the design pattern along with the lack of accompanying simplifying syntax.

We propose a lightweight syntax for comonads in Haskell, analogous to the do-notation for monads, and provide examples of its use. Via our notation, we also provide a tutorial on programming with comonads.

Many algebraic approaches to programming apply concepts from category theory as design patterns for abstracting and structuring programs. For example, the category-theoretic notion of a *monad* is widely used to structure programs with *side effects*, encapsulating effects within a parametric data type [1,2]. A *monadic* data type M has accompanying operations which provide composition of functions with *structured output* of type $a \to M\,b$. Side effects can be seen as *impure output* behaviour, encoded by the data type M.

Monads are so effective as an abstraction technique that some languages provide a lightweight syntactic sugar simplifying programming with monads, such as the **do**-notation in Haskell and the *let!* notation in F# [3].

Comonads are the *dual* structure to *monads*, where a comonadic data type C has operations for the composition of functions with *structured input*, of type $C\,a \to b$. Whilst monads capture impure output behaviour (side effects), comonads capture impure *input* behaviour, often described as *context dependence*, encoded by the data type C. There are various examples of programming with comonads in the literature including dataflow programming via streams [4], attribute evaluation [5], array computations [6], and more [7]. However, despite these examples, comonads are less widely used than monads.

There are two reasons for this: one is that they are less well-known, the other, related reason is the lack of language support, which impedes the use of comonads as a design pattern. To remedy this, we propose a syntax which simplifies programming with comonads in Haskell, called the **codo**-*notation*, which also serves to promote the comonad design pattern.

R. Hinze (Ed.): IFL 2012, LNCS 8241, pp. 1–17, 2013.
DOI: 10.1007/978-3-642-41582-1_1, © Springer-Verlag Berlin Heidelberg 2013

In Haskell, comonads are defined by the following class[1]:

```
class Comonad c where
    extract :: c a → a
    extend :: (c a → b) → c a → c b
```

The contextual view of comonads is that values of type $c\ a$ encode context-dependent computations of values of type a, and functions $c\ a \to b$ describe *local operations* within some context. The *extract* operation defines a notion of *current context* and is a trivial local operation returning the value at this context; *extend* defines the range of *all possible contexts*, extending a local operation to a *global* operation by applying it at every context. Thus comonads abstract "boilerplate" code for extending an operation, defined at one context, to all contexts.

For example, arrays can be seen as encoding contextual computations, where a value depends on its position. An array paired with an array index denoting the current context – called the *cursor* – is a comonad. Its *extract* operation accesses the cursor element of the array; *extend* applies a local operation, which computes a value from an array at a particular cursor, to an array at each possible cursor index in its domain (i.e., globally), computing an array of results [6]. Local operations of this form, on arrays, are ubiquitous in image processing, scientific computing, and cellular automata.

The **codo**-notation simplifies programming with comonads. For example, the following **codo**-block defines a local operation for computing image contours:

$$contours :: CArray\ (Int, Int)\ Float \to Float$$
$$contours = \textbf{codo}\ x \Rightarrow y \leftarrow gauss2D\ x$$
$$z \leftarrow gauss2D\ y$$
$$w \leftarrow (extract\ y) - (extract\ z)$$
$$laplace2D\ w$$

where *CArray i a* is a cursored-array data type, with index type i and element type a, and $gauss2D, laplace2D :: CArray\ (Int, Int)\ Float \to Float$ compute, at a particular index, *discrete Gaussian* and *Laplace* operators on 2D arrays. A contour image can thus be computed by applying (*extend contours*) to an image.

The primary contribution of this paper is the **codo**-notation, introduced in detail in Sect. 1, continuing with arrays as an example. The notation desugars into the operations of a comonad (Sect. 3) which provides an equational theory for the notation following from the laws of a comonad (Sect. 2). The **codo**-notation is analogous to the **do**-notation for programming with monads in Haskell, but with some notable differences which are explained from a *categorical semantics* perspective in Sect. 4. Section 5 discusses related work, including a comparison of the **codo**-notation to Haskell's *arrow notation*.

This paper contributes examples (arrays, trees, and graphs), explanation, and notation to promote comonads in programming. A prototype of the notation,

---

[1] Available via Edward Kmett's `Control.Comonad` package.

as a macro-based library using quasi-quoting brackets, is provided by the codo-notation package.[2] An implementation as a GHC extension is in progress.

Array example. The array comonad is used throughout the next section to introduce **codo**. It is defined in Haskell by the following data type and instance:

> **data** $CArray\ i\ a = CA\ (Array\ i\ a)\ i$
>
> **instance** $Ix\ i \Rightarrow Comonad\ (CArray\ i)$ **where**
> $extract\ (CA\ a\ i) = a\ !\ i$
> $extend\ f\ (CA\ a\ i) = $ **let** $es' = map\ (\lambda j \rightarrow (j, f\ (CA\ a\ j)))\ (indices\ a)$
>   **in** $CA\ (array\ (bounds\ a)\ es')\ i$

where *extract* accesses the cursor element using the array indexing operation !, and, for every index j of the parameter array, *extend* applies f to the array with j as its cursor, returning an index-value pair list from which the result array is constructed. Note, the return and parameter arrays have the same size and cursor, i.e., *extend* preserves the incoming *context* in its result.

Many array operations can be defined as local operations $c\ a \rightarrow b$ (hereafter *comonadic operations*, sometimes called *coKleisli* arrows/morphisms in the literature) using relative indexing, e.g., the *laplace2D* operator, for approximating differentiation, can be defined:

> $laplace2D :: CArray\ (Int, Int)\ Float \rightarrow Float$
> $laplace2D\ a = a\ ?\ (-1, 0) + a\ ?\ (1, 0) + a\ ?\ (0, -1) + a\ ?\ (0, 1) - 4 * a\ ?\ (0, 0)$

where (?) abstracts relative indexing with bounds checking and default values[3]:

> $(?) :: (Ix\ i, Num\ a, Num\ i) \Rightarrow CArray\ i\ a \rightarrow i \rightarrow a$
> $(CA\ a\ i)\ ?\ i' = $ **if** $(inRange\ (bounds\ a)\ (i + i'))$ **then** $a\ !\ (i + i')$ **else** 0

(where Ix is the class of valid array-index types). Whilst *laplace2D* computes the Laplacian at a single context (locally), *extend laplace2D* computes the Laplacian at every context (globally), returning an array rather than a single float.

1   Introducing *codo*

The **codo**-notation provides a form of *let*-binding for composing comonadic operations, which has the general form and type:

$$(\textbf{codo}\ p \Rightarrow \overline{p \leftarrow e};\ e) :: Comonad\ c \Rightarrow c\ t \rightarrow t'$$

(where p ranges over patterns, e over expressions, and t, t' over types). Compare this with the general form and type of the monadic **do**-notation:

---

[2] http://hackage.haskell.org/package/codo-notation
[3] There are many alternative methods for abstracting boundary checking and values; our choice here is for simplicity of presentation rather than performance or accuracy.

$$(\mathbf{do}\ \overline{p \leftarrow e}; e) :: Monad\ m \Rightarrow m\ t$$

Both comprise zero or more binding statements of the form $p \leftarrow e$ (separated by semicolons or new lines), preceding a final result expression. A **codo**-block however defines a function, with a pattern-match on its parameter following the **codo** keyword. The parameter is essential as comonads describe functions with structured input. A **do**-block is instead an expression (nullary function). Section 4 compares the two notations in detail.

Comonads and codo-notation for composition. The *extend* operation of a comonad provides composition for comonadic functions as follows:

$$(\hat{\circ}) :: Comonad\ c \Rightarrow (c\ y \rightarrow z) \rightarrow (c\ x \rightarrow y) \rightarrow c\ x \rightarrow z$$
$$g\ \hat{\circ}\ f = g \circ (extend\ f) \tag{1}$$

The laws of a comonad are equivalent to requiring that this composition is associative and that *extract* is its identity (discussed further in Sect. 2).

The **codo**-notation abstracts over *extend* in the composition of comonadic operations. For example, the composition of two array operations:

$$lapGauss = laplace2D \circ (extend\ gauss2D)$$

(i.e., $laplace2D\ \hat{\circ}\ gauss2D$), can be written equivalently in the **codo**-notation:

$$lapGauss = \mathbf{codo}\ x \Rightarrow y \leftarrow gauss2D\ x$$
$$laplace2D\ y$$

where $lapGauss :: CArray\ (Int, Int)\ Float \rightarrow Float, x, y :: CArray\ (Int, Int)\ Float$.

The parameter of a **codo**-block provides the context of the whole block where all subsequent local variables have the same context. For example, x and y in the above example block are arrays of the same size with the same cursor.

For a variable-pattern parameter, a **codo**-block is typed by the following rule: (here typing rules are presented with a single colon: for the typing relation)

$$[\text{varP}]\frac{\Gamma; x : c\ t \vdash_c e : t'}{\Gamma \vdash (\mathbf{codo}\ x \Rightarrow e) : Comonad\ c \Rightarrow c\ t \rightarrow t'}$$

where $\vdash_c$ types statements of a **codo**-block. Judgments $\Gamma; \Delta \vdash_c \ldots$ have two sequences of variable-type assumptions: Γ for variables outside a block and Δ for variables local to a block. For example, variable-pattern statements are typed:

$$[\text{varB}]\frac{\Gamma; \Delta \vdash_c e : t \quad \Gamma; \Delta, x : c\ t \vdash_c r : t'}{\Gamma; \Delta \vdash_c x \leftarrow e; r : t'}$$

where r ranges over remaining statements and result expression i.e. $r = \overline{p \leftarrow e}; e'$.

A variable-pattern statement therefore locally binds a variable, in scope for the rest of the block. The typing, where $e : t$ but $x : c\ t$, gives a hint about **codo** desugaring. Informally, $(\mathbf{codo}\ y \Rightarrow x \leftarrow e; e')$ is desugared into two functions,

$$\boxed{\Gamma \vdash \textbf{codo } p \Rightarrow e : Comonad\ c \Rightarrow c\ t \to t'}$$ $$\boxed{\Gamma; \Delta \vdash_c \overline{p \leftarrow e}; e : t}$$

$$[\text{varP}]\ \frac{\Gamma; x : c\ t \vdash_c e : t'}{\Gamma \vdash (\textbf{codo } x \Rightarrow e) : c\ t \to t'}$$

$$[\text{varB}]\ \frac{\Gamma; \Delta \vdash_c e : t \quad \Gamma; \Delta, x : c\ t \vdash_c r : t'}{\Gamma; \Delta \vdash_c x \leftarrow e;\ r : t'}$$

$$[\text{tupP}]\ \frac{\Gamma; x : c\ t, y : c\ t' \vdash_c e : t''}{\Gamma \vdash (\textbf{codo } (x,y) \Rightarrow e) : c\ (t,t') \to t''}$$

$$[\text{tupB}]\ \frac{\Gamma; \Delta \vdash_c e : (t_1, t_2) \quad \Gamma; \Delta, x : c\ t_1, y : c\ t_2 \vdash_c r : t'}{\Gamma; \Delta \vdash_c (x,y) \leftarrow e;\ r : t'}$$

$$[\text{wildP}]\ \frac{\Gamma; \cdot \vdash_c e : t}{\Gamma \vdash (\textbf{codo } \_ \Rightarrow e) : \forall a.c\ a \to t}$$

$$[\text{letB}]\ \frac{\Gamma; \Delta \vdash_c e : t \quad \Gamma; \Delta, x : t \vdash_c r : t'}{\Gamma; \Delta \vdash_c \textbf{let } x = e;\ r : t'}$$

$$[\text{exp}]\ \frac{\Gamma \vdash e : t}{\Gamma; \cdot \vdash_c e : t} \qquad [\text{var}]\ \frac{\Gamma, v : c\ t; \Delta \vdash_c e : t'}{\Gamma; \Delta, v : c\ t \vdash_c e : t'}$$

Fig. 1. Typing rules for the **codo**-notation

the first statement as $\lambda y \to e$ and the result expression as $\lambda x \to e'$. These are comonadically composed, i.e., $(\lambda x \to e') \circ (extend\ (\lambda y \to e))$, thus $x : c\ t$.

Further typing rules for the **codo**-notation are collected in Fig. 1.

Non-linear plumbing. For the *lapGauss* example, **codo** does not provide a significant simplification. The **codo**-notation more clearly benefits computations which are not mere linear function compositions. Consider a binary operation:

$minus :: (Comonad\ c, Num\ a) \Rightarrow c\ a \to c\ a \to a$
$minus\ x\ y = extract\ x - extract\ y$

which subtracts its parameters at their respective current contexts. Using **codo**, *minus* can be used to compute a *pointwise* subtraction, e.g.

$contours' = \textbf{codo } x \Rightarrow y \ \leftarrow\ gauss2D\ x$
$\qquad\qquad\qquad z \ \leftarrow\ gauss2D\ y$
$\qquad\qquad\qquad w \leftarrow\ minus\ y\ z$
$\qquad\qquad\qquad laplace2D\ w$

(equivalent to *contours* in the introduction which inlined the definition of *minus*). The context, and therefore cursor, of every variable in the block is the same as that of x. Thus, y and z have the same cursor and *minus* is applied pointwise. The equivalent program without **codo** is considerably more complex:

$contours'\ x = \textbf{let } y = extend\ gauss2D\ x$
$\qquad\qquad\qquad w = extend\ (\lambda y' \to \textbf{let } z = extend\ gauss2D\ y'$
$\qquad\qquad\qquad\qquad\qquad\qquad\qquad \textbf{in }\ minus\ y'\ z)\ y$
$\qquad\qquad \textbf{in } laplace2D\ w$

where the nested *extend* means that y' and z have the same cursor, thus *minus* $y'\ z$ is pointwise. An alternate, more point-free, approach uses the composition $\hat\circ$:

$contours' = laplace2D \mathbin{\hat\circ} (\lambda y' \to minus\ y' \mathbin{\hat\circ} gauss2D\ \$\ y') \mathbin{\hat\circ} gauss2D$

This approach resembles that of using monads without the do-notation, and is elegant for simple, linear function composition. However, for more complex plumbing the approach quickly becomes cumbersome. In the above two (non-**codo**) examples, care is needed to ensure that *minus* is applied pointwise. An incorrect attempt to simplify the first non-**codo** *contours'* might be:

$$contour\_bad \; x = \textbf{let} \; y = extend \; gauss2D \; x$$
$$z = extend \; gauss2D \; y$$
$$w = extend \; (minus \; y) \; z$$
$$\textbf{in} \; laplace2D \; w$$

In the above, *extend* (*minus y*) *z* subtracts *z* at every context from *y* at a particular, fixed context, i.e., not a pointwise subtraction. An equivalent expression to *contours_bad* can be written using nested **codo**-blocks:

$$contour\_bad = \textbf{codo} \; x \Rightarrow y \leftarrow gauss2D \; x$$
$$(\textbf{codo} \; y' \Rightarrow z \leftarrow gauss2D \; y'$$
$$w \leftarrow minus \; y \; z$$
$$laplace2D \; w) \; y$$

where *y* in *minus y z* is bound in the outer **codo**-block and thus has its cursor fixed, whilst *z* is bound in the inner **codo**-block and has its cursor varying. Variables bound outside of the nearest enclosing **codo**-block are "unsynchronised" with respect to the context inside the block, i.e., at a different context.

A **codo**-block may have multiple parameters in an uncurried-style, via tuple patterns ([tupP], Fig. 1). For example, the following block has two parameters, which are Laplace-transformed and then pointwise added:

$$lapPlus :: CArray \; Int \; (Float, Float) \rightarrow Float$$
$$lapPlus = \textbf{codo} \; (x, y) \Rightarrow a \leftarrow laplace2D \; x$$
$$b \leftarrow laplace2D \; y$$
$$(extract \; a) + (extract \; b)$$

This block has a single comonadic parameter with tuple elements, whose type is of the form *c* (*a, b*). However, inside the block $x : c \; a$ and $y : c \; b$ as the desugaring of **codo** *unzips* the parameter (see Sect. 3). A comonadic tuple parameter ensures that multiple parameters have the same context, e.g., *x* and *y* in the above example have the same shape/cursor. Therefore, a pair of arguments to *lapPlus* must be *zipped* first, provided by the *czip* operation:

$$\textbf{class} \; ComonadZip \; c \; \textbf{where} \; czip :: (c \; a, c \; b) \rightarrow c \; (a, b)$$

For *CArray*, *czip* can be defined:

$$\textbf{instance} \; (Eq \; i, Ix \; i) \Rightarrow ComonadZip \; (CArray \; i) \; \textbf{where}$$
$$czip \; (CA \; a \; i, CA \; a' \; j) =$$
$$\textbf{if} \; (i \not\equiv j \lor bounds \; a \not\equiv bounds \; a') \; \textbf{then} \; error \; \texttt{"Shape/cursor mismatch"}$$
$$\textbf{else let} \; es'' = map \; (\lambda k \rightarrow (k, (a \; ! \; k, a' \; ! \; k))) \; (indices \; a)$$
$$\textbf{in} \; CA \; (array \; (bounds \; a) \; es'') \; i$$

Thus only arrays of the same shape and cursor can be zipped together. In the contextual understanding, the two parameter arrays are thus *synchronised* in their contexts. The example of *lapPlus* can be applied to two (synchronised) array parameters x and y by *extend lapPlus* (*czip* (x, y)).

Any data constructor pattern can be used for the parameter of a **codo**-block and on the left-hand side of a binding statement. For example, the following uses a tuple pattern in a binding statement (see [tupB], Fig. 1), which is equivalent to *lapPlus* by exchanging a parameter binding with a statement binding:

$$lapPlus = \textbf{codo}\ z \Rightarrow (x, y) \leftarrow extract\ z$$
$$a \leftarrow laplace2D\ x$$
$$b \leftarrow laplace2D\ y$$
$$(extract\ a) + (extract\ b)$$

Tuple patterns are specifically discussed here since they provide multiple parameters to a **codo**-block, as seen above. The typing of a general pattern in a statement, for some type/data constructor T, is roughly as follows:

$$[\text{patB}] \frac{\Gamma; \Delta \vdash_c e : T\,\bar{t} \quad \Gamma; \Delta, \Delta' \vdash_c r : t' \quad dom(\Delta') = var\text{-}pats(p)}{\Gamma; \Delta \vdash_c (T\ p) \leftarrow e;\ r : t'}$$

where $dom(\Delta')$ is the set of variables in a sequence of typing assumptions, and *var-pats* is the set of variables occurring in a pattern.

Example: labelled graphs. Many graph algorithms can be structured by a comonad, particularly compiler analyses and transformations on *control flow graphs* (CFGs). The following defines a labelled-graph comonad as a (non-empty) list of nodes which are pairs of a label and a list of their connected vertices:

```
data LGraph a = LG [(a, [Int])] Int   -- pre-condition: non-empty lists
instance Comonad LGraph where
    extract (LG xs c) = fst (xs !! c)
    extend f (LG xs c) = LG (map (λc' → (f (LG xs c'), snd (xs !! c')))
                           [0 .. length xs]) c
```

The *LGraph*-comonad resembles the array comonad where contexts are positions with a *cursor* denoting the current position. Analyses over CFGs can be defined using graphs labelled by syntax trees. For example, a *live-variable* analysis (which, for an imperative language, calculates the set of variables that may be used in a block before being (re)defined) can be written, using **codo**, as:

```
lva = codo g ⇒ lv0 ← (defUse g, [])   -- compute definition/use sets, paired
              lva' lv0                 -- with initial empty live-variable set

lva' = codo ((def, use), lv) ⇒
            live_out ← foldl union [] (successors lv)
            live_in  ← union (extract def) ((extract live_out) \\ (extract use))
```

$$lvp \qquad \leftarrow ((extract\ def, extract\ use), extract\ live\_in)$$
$$lvNext \ \leftarrow lva'\ lvp$$
$$\textbf{if}\ (lv \equiv live\_in)\ \textbf{then}\ (extract\ lv)\ \textbf{else}\ (extract\ lvNext)$$

where *union* and set difference ($\backslash\backslash$) on lists have type $Eq\ a \Rightarrow [a] \to [a] \to [a]$ and *defUse* :: *LGraph AST* $\to$ ($[Var], [Var]$) computes the sets of variables defined and used by each block in a CFG. The analysis is recursive, refining the set of live variables until a fixed point is reached.

The live variables for every block of a CFG can be computed by *extend lva*.

Costate, trees, and zippers. Arrays were used to introduce comonads and **codo** to aid understanding since the notion of *context* is made clear by the *cursor*. The above graph example has a similar form. Both are instances of a general comonad, often called the *costate* comonad, whose data type is a pair of a function from contexts to values and a particular context: $C\ a = (s \to a) \times s$.

For both arrays and labelled graphs, the type of contexts is a finite domain of integer, or integer-tuple, indices. For labelled graphs, the costate comonad is combined with *product comonad* (see [8]) pairing the label of a node with the list of its successors, thus the type is isomorphic to $C\ a = (s \to (a \times [s])) \times s$.

For *costate*, the notion of context is explicitly provided by a cursor acting as a *pointer* or *address*. This is not the only way to define a notion of context. Other data types encode the context structurally rather than using a cursor. For example, a comonad of labelled binary trees can be defined:

> **data** *BTree a* = *Leaf a* | *Node a* (*BTree a*) (*BTree a*)
>
> **instance** *Comonad BTree* **where**
> $\quad$ *extract* (*Leaf a*) = *a*
> $\quad$ *extract* (*Node a l r*) = *a*
>
> $\quad$ *extend f* (*Leaf a*) = *Leaf* (*f* (*Leaf a*))
> $\quad$ *extend f* t@(*Node a l r*) = *Node* (*f t*) (*extend f l*) (*extend f r*)

The action of *extend* is to apply its parameter function f to successive suffix trees, thus f can only access its children, not its parents. Thus *extend* not only defines what it means for a local (comonadic) operation to be applied globally, but also which contexts are *accessible* from each possible context.

A tree comonad that has a structural notion of context but whose comonadic operations can access any part of the tree can be defined using Huet's *zipper* data type, where trees are split into a path to the current position and the remaining parts of the tree [5, 9]. For a certain class of data types it has been shown that a zipper structure can be automatically derived by *differentiation* of the data type [10]. All container-like zippers are comonads [11] where the notion of context is encoded structurally, rather than by a *pointer*-like cursor. The **codo**-notation thus provides a convenient syntax for programming with zipper comonads.

2 Equational Theory

As shown in Sect. 1, *extend* provides composition for comonadic functions, Eq. (1). The laws of a comonad are exactly the laws that guarantee this composition is *associative* with *extract* as a *left* and *right unit*, i.e.

$$
\begin{array}{lllll}
\text{(right unit)} & f \mathbin{\hat{\circ}} extract \equiv f & \rightsquigarrow & extend\ extract \equiv id & \text{[C1]} \\
\text{(left unit)} & extract \mathbin{\hat{\circ}} f \equiv f & \rightsquigarrow & extract \circ (extend\ f) \equiv f & \text{[C2]} \\
\text{(associativity)} & h \mathbin{\hat{\circ}} (g \mathbin{\hat{\circ}} f) & \rightsquigarrow & extend\ g \circ extend\ f & \\
& \equiv (h \mathbin{\hat{\circ}} g) \mathbin{\hat{\circ}} f & & \equiv extend\ (g \circ extend\ f) & \text{[C3]}
\end{array}
$$

As there is no mechanism for enforcing such rules in Haskell the programmer is expected to verify the laws themselves.

Since **codo** is desugared into the operations of a comonad, the comonad laws imply equational laws for the **codo**-notation, shown in Fig. 2(a). Figure 2(b) shows additional **codo** laws which follow from the desugaring.

Comonads are functors. The category theoretic notion of a *functor* can be used to abstract *map*-like operations on parametric data types. In Haskell, functors are described by the *Functor* type class, of which *map* provides the list instance:

```
class Functor f where fmap :: (a → b) → f a → f b
instance Functor [] where fmap = map
```

(a) Comonad laws

[C1] **codo** $x \Rightarrow f\ x$
$\equiv$ **codo** $x \Rightarrow y \leftarrow extract\ x$
$\qquad f\ y$

[C2] **codo** $x \Rightarrow f\ x$
$\equiv$ **codo** $x \Rightarrow y \leftarrow f\ x$
$\qquad extract\ y$

[C3] (iff x is not free in e_1)
$\quad$ **codo** $x \Rightarrow y \leftarrow e_1$
$\qquad z \leftarrow e_2$
$\qquad e_3$
$\equiv$ **codo** $x' \Rightarrow z \leftarrow ($**codo** $x \Rightarrow y \leftarrow e_1$
$\qquad\qquad\qquad e_2)\ x'$
$\qquad e_3$
$\equiv$ **codo** $x' \Rightarrow y \leftarrow e_1$
$\qquad ($**codo** $x \Rightarrow z \leftarrow e_2$
$\qquad\qquad e_3)\ x'$

(b) Pure laws

(η) **codo** $x \Rightarrow f\ x \equiv f$

(β) **codo** $x \Rightarrow z \leftarrow ($**codo** $y \Rightarrow e_1)\ x$
$\qquad e_2$
$\equiv$ **codo** $x \Rightarrow y \leftarrow extract\ x$
$\qquad z \leftarrow e_1$
$\qquad e_2$

(χ) **codo** $p \Rightarrow e$
$\equiv$ **codo** $z \Rightarrow p \leftarrow extract\ z$
$\qquad e$

(c) Additional laws – if Eq. (2) holds

codo $x \Rightarrow f\ a\ b$
$\equiv$ **codo** $x \Rightarrow (a', b') \leftarrow extract\ (czip\ (a, b))$
$\qquad f\ a'\ b'$

codo $(b, c) \Rightarrow f\ (czip\ (b, c))$
$\equiv$ **codo** $(b, c) \Rightarrow z \leftarrow (extract\ b, extract\ c)$
$\qquad f\ z$

Fig. 2. Equational laws for the **codo**-notation

All comonads are functors by the following definition using *extend* and *extract*:

$$cmap :: Comonad\ c \Rightarrow (a \rightarrow b) \rightarrow c\ a \rightarrow c\ b$$
$$cmap\ f\ x = extend\ (f \circ extract)$$

While *fmap* applies its parameter function to a single element of a data type, *extend* applies its parameter function to a subset (possibly the whole) of the parameter structure. Thus *extend* generalises *fmap*.

Monoidal operation. The $czip :: (c\ a, c\ b) \rightarrow c\ (a, b)$ operation introduced in Sect. 1 corresponds to that of a *(semi)-monoidal functor* which may satisfy various laws with respect to the comonad (see the discussion of *(semi)-monoidal comonads* in [8]). The following property, which we call *idempotency* of a semi-monoidal functor, frequently holds of comonad/*czip* implementations:

$$czip\ (x, x) \equiv cmap\ (\lambda y \rightarrow (y, y))\ x \tag{2}$$

This property implies **codo** laws relating tuple patterns and *czip* (Fig. 2(c)). For every rule involving a tuple pattern there is an equivalent rule derived using the (χ) rule (Fig. 2(b)) which exchanges parameter and statement binders.

Shape preservation. The *shape* of a data structure is defined by its structure without any values, which can be computed as such: (where $const\ x = \lambda\_ \rightarrow x$)

$$shape = cmap\ (const\ ())$$

An interesting derived property of comonads is that, for any comonadic function f, $(extend\ f)$ preserves the shape of the incoming structure in its result. For example, *extend* of the array comonad preserves the size, cursor, and dimensions of the parameter array in the result. Appendix A gives a proof of this property, which is stated formally, for a comonad c and function $f :: c\ a \rightarrow b$, as:

$$shape \circ (extend\ f) \equiv shape \tag{3}$$

This property explains why all locally bound variables in a **codo**-block bind comonadic values which have the same context.

3   Desugaring *codo*

The desugaring of **codo** is based on Uustalu and Vene's semantics for a context-dependent λ-calculus [8]. It has two parts: translation of statements into composition via *extend*, and management of the environment for variables bound in a **codo**-block. The first part is explained by considering a restricted **codo**-notation, which only ever has one local variable, bound in the previous statement.

(1). *Single-variable environment.* For a comonad C, consider the **codo**-block:

$$foo1 = (\textbf{codo}\ x \Rightarrow y \leftarrow f\ x;\ g\ y) :: C\ x \rightarrow z$$

where $f :: C\ x \to y$, $g :: C\ y \to z$. The first statement $y \leftarrow f\ x$ can be desugared as a function with parameter x and body $f\ x$, the second, which is the final result expression, can be similarly desugared as a function from y to its expression, i.e. $(\lambda x \to f\ x)$ and $(\lambda y \to g\ y)$. Both are functions with structured input, thus the semantics of *foo1* is their comonadic composition (equivalent to $g \mathbin{\hat{\circ}} f$):

$$[\![foo1]\!] = (\lambda y \to g\ y) \circ (extend\ (\lambda x \to f\ x)) :: C\ x \to z.$$

(2). *Multiple-variable environment.* A **codo**-block may bind multiple variables, allowing the following example with binary function $h :: C\ x \to C\ y \to z$:

$$foo2 = (\textbf{codo}\ x \Rightarrow y \leftarrow f\ x;\ h\ x\ y) :: C\ x \to z$$

The first statement cannot be desugared as before since the second statement uses both x and y, thus the desugaring must return x with the result of $f\ x$:

$$(\lambda x \to (extract\ x, f\ x)) :: C\ x \to (x, y) \tag{#4}$$

Applying *extract* to x means that $extend$ (#4), of type $C\ x \to C\ (x, y)$, returns the parameter x and the result of $f\ x$ synchronised in their contexts.

The desugaring of the second statement is a function taking a value $C\ (x, y)$ and *unzipping* it, binding the constituent values to x and y in the scope of the result expression, where x and y are synchronised at the same context since *cmap* preserves the context encoded by the comonadic value:

$$(\lambda env \to \textbf{let}\ x = cmap\ fst\ env$$
$$y = cmap\ snd\ env\ \textbf{in}\ h\ x\ y) :: C\ (x, y) \to z \tag{#5}$$

The desugaring of *foo2* is therefore $[\![foo2]\!] = (\#5) \circ (extend\ (\#4))$.

3.1   General Construction

The desugaring translation traverses the list of binding statements in a **codo**-block, accumulating a comonadic environment of the local variables bound so far. The accumulated environment is structured by right-nested pairs terminated by a unit value (). Thus, the actual desugaring of *foo2* is:

$$[\![foo2]\!] = (\lambda env \to \textbf{let}\ y = cmap\ fst\ env$$
$$x = cmap\ (fst \circ snd)\ env\ \textbf{in}\ h\ x\ y)$$
$$\circ (extend\ (\lambda env \to (\textbf{let}\ x = cmap\ fst\ env\ \textbf{in}\ f\ x, extract\ env)))$$
$$\circ (cmap\ (\lambda env \to (env, ())))$$

For *foo2*, the environment in the first statement contains just x and has type $C\ (x, ())$, and in the second statement contains x and y and has type $C\ (y, (x, ()))$.

The top-level translation of a **codo**-block is defined:

$$[\![\textbf{codo}\ x \Rightarrow b]\!] = [\![x \vdash b]\!]_c \circ (cmap\ (\lambda x \to (x, ())))$$
$$[\![\textbf{codo}\ \_ \Rightarrow b]\!] = [\![\_ \vdash b]\!]_c \circ (cmap\ (\lambda x \to (x, ())))$$
$$[\![\textbf{codo}\ (x, y) \Rightarrow b]\!] = [\![x, y \vdash b]\!]_c \circ cmap\ (\lambda p \to (fst\ p, (snd\ p, ())))$$

where $[\![\Delta \vdash b]\!]_c$ is the translation of the binding statements b within a **codo**-block, with the scope of the local variables Δ. In the translation here, types are omitted for brevity. A translation with the types included can be found in the first author's forthcoming PhD dissertation [12].

The top-level translation generalises easily to arbitrary patterns. In each case, $[\![-]\!]_c$ is pre-composed with a lifted projection function, which projects values inside the incoming parameter comonad to right-nested pairs terminated by (). The translation of binding statements yields a Haskell function of type:

$$[\![\Delta \vdash \overline{b}; e]\!]_c : Comonad\ c \Rightarrow c\,(t_1, (\ldots, (t_n, ()))) \to t$$

where $e : t$ and $\Delta = v_1, \ldots, v_n$ where $v_i : c\ t_i$. The definition of $[\![-]\!]_c$ is:

$$[\![\Delta \vdash e]\!]_c = [\![\Delta \vdash e]\!]_{exp}$$
$$[\![\Delta \vdash x \leftarrow e; r]\!]_c = [\![x, \Delta \vdash r]\!]_c \circ extend\,(\lambda env \to ([\![\Delta \vdash e]\!]_{exp}\ env, extract\ env))$$
$$[\![\Delta \vdash (x, y) \leftarrow e; r]\!]_c = [\![x, y, \Delta \vdash r]\!]_c \circ extend\,(\lambda env \to (\lambda((x, y), \Delta) \to (x, (y, \Delta)))$$
$$([\![\Delta \vdash e]\!]_{exp}\ env, extract\ env))$$

where $[\![\Delta \vdash e]\!]_{exp}$ translates expressions on the right-hand side of a statement or for the result of a block. The last case translates tuple-pattern statements where $\lambda((x, y), \Delta) \to (x, (y, \Delta)))$ reformats results into the right-nested tuple format of the environment; this generalises in the obvious way to arbitrary patterns.

The translation of expressions unzips the incoming comonadic environment, binding the values to the variables in Δ with a local *let*-binding:

$$[\![v_1, \ldots, v_n \vdash e]\!]_{exp} = \lambda env \to \mathbf{let}\ [v_i = cmap\ (fst \circ snd^{i-1})\ env]_1^n\ \mathbf{in}\ e$$

where snd^k means k compositions of snd and $snd^0 = id$.

The next section compares **codo**-notation with **do**-notation, and explains why the desugaring of **codo**-notation is more complex.

4   Comparing do- and codo-notation

Whilst comonads and monads are dual, this duality does not appear to extend to the **codo**- and **do**-notation. Both provide *let*-binding syntax, for composition of comonadic and monadic operations respectively. However, **codo**-blocks are parameterised, of type $c\ a \to b$ for a comonad c, whilst **do**-blocks are unparameterised, of type $m\ a$ for a monad m. Since comonads abstract functions with structured input, the parameter to a **codo**-block is important. In the **do**-notation, expressions have implicit input via their free variables and Haskell's scoping mechanism is reused for handling local variables in a **do**-block.

The **codo**- and **do**-notation can be seen as internal domain-specific languages, for contextual and effectful computations respectively, with their semantics defined by translation to Haskell. This perspective is similar to the approach of *categorical* *semantics*, where typed programs are given a denotation as a morphism[4] in some category, mapping from the inputs of a program to the outputs. The disparity between **codo-** and **do**-notation is illuminated by this approach.

Categorical semantics. For the simply-typed λ-calculus, the traditional approach recursively maps the *type derivation* of an expression to a morphism [13]:

$$[\![\Gamma \vdash e : t]\!] : ([\![t_1]\!] \times \ldots \times [\![t_n]\!]) \longrightarrow [\![t]\!]$$

where $\Gamma = x_1 : t_1, \ldots x_n : t_n$. Thus, an expression $e : t$ with the free-variable typing assumptions Γ is modelled as a morphism from a *product* of the types for the free variables, as inputs, to the result type as the output.

Categorical semantics for effectful computations. Moggi showed that effectful computations can be given a semantics in terms of a *Kleisli* category [14,15], which has morphisms $a \to m\ b$ for a monad m, with denotations:

$$[\![x_1 : t_1, \ldots x_n : t_n \vdash e : t]\!] : ([\![t_1]\!] \times \ldots \times [\![t_n]\!]) \longrightarrow m\ [\![t]\!]$$

In Moggi's calculus, *let*-binding corresponds to a call-by-value (eager) evaluation of effects followed by substitution of a pure value, corresponding to composition of the denotations provided by the *bind* operation of a monad. The semantics of multi-variable environments requires a *strong monad*: a monad with an additional *strength* operation. The effectful semantics for *let*-binding is as follows (here $a \xrightarrow{f} b$ abbreviates $f : a \to b$ with arrow concatenation expressing composition; $[\![-]\!]$ brackets are elided on types in morphisms for brevity):

$$\frac{[\![\Gamma \vdash e : t]\!] = g : \Gamma \to m\,t \qquad [\![\Gamma, x : t \vdash e' : t']\!] = h : \Gamma \times t \to m\,t'}{[\![\Gamma \vdash \mathbf{let}\ x = e\ \mathbf{in}\ e' : t']\!] = \Gamma \xrightarrow{\langle id, g \rangle} \Gamma \times m\,t \xrightarrow{strength} m(\Gamma \times t) \xrightarrow{bind\ h} m\,t'} \quad (6)$$

where $\langle f, g \rangle$ is the function pairing: $\lambda x \to (f\ x, g\ x)$, *bind* is the prefix version of Haskell's ($\ggg$) :: *Monad* $m \Rightarrow m\ a \to (a \to m\ b) \to m\ b$ operator and *strength* provides distributivity of $\times$ over m:

$$strength : (a \times m\ b) \to m\ (a \times b)$$
$$bind : (a \to m\ b) \to (m\ a \to m\ b)$$

Whilst the **do**-notation provides a semantics for effectful *let*-binding embedded in Haskell, the translation is simplified by reusing Haskell's scoping mechanism since, in Haskell, all monads are *strong* with a canonical *strength*:

```
strength :: Monad m ⇒ (a, m b) → m (a, b)
strength (a, mb) = mb ⋙ (λb → return (a, b))
```

It is straightforwardly proved that this definition of *strength* satisfies the properties of a *strong monad* (see [14] for these properties). The standard translation of **do**

---

[4] *Morphisms* generalise the notion of function. Readers unfamiliar with category theory may safely replace 'morphism' with 'function' here.

can be derived from (6) by inlining the above *strength* and simplifying according to the monad laws:

$$\frac{\Gamma \vdash e : m\, t \qquad \Gamma, x : t \vdash e' : m\, t'}{\Gamma \vdash [\![\textbf{do } x \leftarrow e; e']\!] : m\, t' \ \equiv\ \Gamma \vdash e \ggg (\lambda x \to e') : m\, t'}$$

This gives a translation using just the monad operations and Haskell's scoping mechanism to define the semantics of multi-variable scopes for effectful *let*-binding. Thus the inputs to effectful computations are handled implicitly and so a **do**-block is an expression of type *m a*.

Categorical semantics for contextual computations. The dual of Moggi's semantics interprets expressions in a *coKleisli category*, with denotations:

$$[\![x_1 : t_1, \ldots x_n : t_n \vdash e : t]\!] : c\,([\![t_1]\!] \times \ldots \times [\![t_n]\!]) \longrightarrow [\![t]\!]$$

for a comonad *c*. Uustalu and Vene gave the semantics of a *context-dependent* calculus in this form [8].

For a comonadic semantics, the input of an expression – the values of the free variables – thus have a *comonadic* product structure rather than just a product structure as in the monadic approach. Therefore, Haskell's scoping mechanisms cannot be directly used since the variables local to a **codo**-block must have the same comonadic context and are therefore wrapped in a comonadic data type. The local environment of a **codo**-block is therefore handled manually in the desugaring of **codo** resulting in a more complicated translation than that of the **do**-notation. The desugaring of statements is equivalent to the semantics of *let*-binding in Uustalu and Vene's approach:

$$\frac{[\![\Gamma \vdash e : t]\!] = g : c\,\Gamma \to t \qquad [\![\Gamma, x : t \vdash e' : t']\!] = h : c\,(\Gamma \times t) \to t'}{[\![\Gamma \vdash \textbf{let } x = e \textbf{ in } e' : t']\!] = c\,\Gamma \xrightarrow{extend\langle extract, g\rangle} c\,(\Gamma \times t) \xrightarrow{h} t'}$$

The other parts of the desugaring manage projections from the (comonadic) environment, simulating application and variable access in a comonadic semantics.

5   Related Work and Conclusions

Arrow notation. In Haskell, various notions of computation can be encoded as a *category* structure, with additional *arrow* operations for constructing computations and handling environments, defined by the *Category* and *Arrow* classes:

```
class Category cat where            class Category a ⇒ Arrow a where
  id :: cat x x                       arr :: (x → y) → a x y
  (∘) :: cat y z → cat x y → cat x z  first :: a x y → a (x, z) (y, z)
```

A *Category* thus has a notion of composition and identity for its morphisms, which are modelled by the type *cat x y*. The *Arrow* class provides *arr* for promoting a Haskell function to a morphism and *first* transforms a morphism to take and return an extra parameter, used for threading an environment through a computation. Other arrow combinators can be derived from this minimal set.

Every comonad defines a *coKleisli category*, whose morphisms have structured input, where composition is defined as in Sect. 1. Furthermore, all coKleisli categories in Haskell are *arrows*:

data *CoKleisli c x y* = *CoK* { *unCoK* :: (*c x* → *y*) }

instance *Comonad c* ⇒ *Category* (*CoKleisli c*) **where**
    id = *CoK extract*
    (*CoK g*) ∘ (*CoK f*) = *CoK* (*g* ∘ (*extend f*))

instance *Comonad c* ⇒ *Arrow* (*CoKleisli c*) **where**
    arr k = *CoK* (*k* ∘ *extract*)
    first (*CoK f*) = *CoK* (λ*x* → (*f* (*cmap fst x*), *extract* (*cmap snd x*)))

where *arr* pre-composes a function with *extract*, and *first* is defined similarly to the handling of the local block environment in the desugaring of **codo**.

The *arrow notation* simplifies programming with arrows [16, 17], comprising: *arrow formation* (**proc** *x* → *e*), *arrow application* (*f* ≺ *x*) and *binding* (*x* ← *e*). Given the above coKleisli instances for *Category* and *Arrow*, comonadic operations can be written in the arrow notation instead of using the **codo**-notation. For example, the original *contours* example can be written as follows:

proc *x* → **do** *y* ← *CoK gauss2D* ≺ *x*
        z ← *CoK gauss2D* ≺ *y*
        w ← *returnA* ≺ *y* − *z*
        CoK laplace2D ≺ *w*

The *arrow* notation here is not much more complicated than **codo**, requiring just the additional overhead of the arrow application operator ≺ and lifting of *gauss2D* and *laplace2D* by *CoK*. One difference is that the variables here have a non-comonadic type, i.e., *Float* rather than *CArray* (*Int*, *Int*) *Float*.

The arrow notation is however more cumbersome than **codo** when plumbing comonadic values, for example when using comonadic binary functions (of type *c t* → *c t'* → *t''*). The alternate definition of *contours* using *minus* becomes:

proc *x* → **do** *y* ← *CoK gauss2D* ≺ *x*
        z ← *CoK gauss2D* ≺ *y*
        w ← *CoK* (λ*v* → *minus* (*fmap fst v*) (*fmap snd v*)) ≺ (*y*, *z*)
        CoK laplace2D ≺ *w*

where *v* :: *c* (*y*, *z*) must be deconstructed manually. Whilst *minus* can be inlined here and the code rewritten to the more elegant first example, this is only possible since *minus* applies *extract* to both arguments. For other comonadic operations, with more complex behaviour, this refactoring is not always possible.

Comparing the two, *arrow* notation appears as powerful as **codo**-notation, in terms of the computations which can be expressed. Indeed, from a categorical perspective, both notations need only a comonad structure (i.e., coKleisli category) with no additional *closed* or *monoidal* structure (see Paterson's discussion [17, Sect. 2.1]). However, whilst arrow notation is almost as simple as **codo** for some purposes, the syntax is less natural for more complicated plumbing of comonadic values (as seen above). We argue that **codo** provides the most elegant and natural solution to programming with comonads, with a cleaner applicative-style.

Other applications. There are many interesting comonads which have not been explored here. For example, the semantics of the Lucid dataflow language are captured by an *infinite stream comonad* [4], which was used by Uustalu and Vene to define an interpreter for Lucid in Haskell. Using **codo**-notation, Lucid can be embedded directly into Haskell as an internal domain-specific language.

Many comonadic data types are instances of the general concept of *containers*. *Containers* comprise a set of *shapes* S and, for each shape $s \in S$, a type of *positions* Ps, with the data type $C\,a = \sum_{s \in S}(Ps \to a)$, i.e., a coproduct of functions from positions to values for each possible shape [18]. Ahman et al. recently showed that all *directed containers* (those with notions of sub-shape) are comonads, where positions are contexts and sub-shapes define accessibility between contexts for the definition of *extend* [11]. The labelled binary-tree example in Sect. 1 can be described as a directed-container comonad. The *costate* comonad can be generalised to *cursored containers* with type $C\,a = \sum_{s \in S}(Ps \to a) \times Ps$.

Whilst the **codo**-notation was developed here in Haskell, it could be applied in other languages with further benefits. For example, a **codo**-notation for ML could be used to abstract laziness using a *delayed-computation* comonad with data type $C\,a = () \to a$, or defining lazy lists using the stream comonad.

Concluding remarks. Comonads essentially abstract boilerplate code for data structure traversals, allowing succinct definitions of *local* operations by abstracting their promotion to *global* operations. The **codo**-notation presented here simplifies programming with comonads. We hope this prompts the use of comonads as a design pattern and tool for abstraction, and promotes further exploration of comonads yielding new and interesting examples.

Whilst the **codo** keyword is used in the notation here, some may prefer an alternate keyword as **codo**-notation is not exactly dual to **do**-notation (Sect. 4). For example, using **context** as the keyword provides more intuition about its use, akin to **do**, but causes more serious namespace pollution.

Acknowledgements. We thank Jeremy Gibbons, Ralf Hinze, Tomas Petricek, Tarmo Uustalu, and Varmo Vene for helpful discussions, and to the anonymous reviewers for their comments on this paper and an earlier draft. This research was supported by an EPSRC Doctoral Training Award.

A Proof of Shape Preservation

To prove shape preservation we first prove the following intermediate lemma:

$$cmap\ g \circ extend\ f = extend\ (g \circ f) \tag{7}$$

$$cmap\ g \circ extend\ f$$
$$\equiv extend\ (g \circ extract) \circ extend\ f \qquad \text{definition of } cmap$$
$$\equiv extend\ (g \circ extract \circ extend\ f) \qquad \text{[C3]}$$
$$\equiv extend\ (g \circ f) \quad \square \qquad \text{[C2]}$$

The proof of shape preservation (3) is then:

$$shape \circ (extend\ f)$$
$$\equiv (cmap\ (const\ ())) \circ (extend\ f) \qquad \text{definition of } shape$$
$$\equiv extend\ ((const\ ()) \circ f) \qquad (7)$$
$$\equiv extend\ ((const\ ()) \circ extract) \qquad (const\ x) \circ f \equiv (const\ x) \circ g$$
$$\equiv (cmap\ (const\ ())) \circ (extend\ extract) \qquad (7)$$
$$\equiv cmap\ (const\ ()) \qquad \text{[C1]}$$
$$\equiv shape \qquad \text{definition of } shape$$

$\square$

References

1. Wadler, P.: The essence of functional programming. In: Proceedings of POPL '92, pp. 1–14. ACM (1992)
2. Wadler, P.: Monads for functional programming. In: Jeuring, J., Meijer, E. (eds.) AFP 1995. LNCS, vol. 925, pp. 24–52. Springer, Heidelberg (1995)
3. Petricek, T., Syme, D.: Syntax Matters: writing abstract computations in F#. Pre-proceedings of TFP (Trends in Functional Programming), St. Andrews, Scotland (2012)
4. Uustalu, T., Vene, V.: The essence of dataflow programming. In: Horváth, Z. (ed.) CEFP 2005. LNCS, vol. 4164, pp. 135–167. Springer, Heidelberg (2006)
5. Uustalu, T., Vene, V.: Comonadic functional attribute evaluation. Trends Funct. Program. **6**, 145–160 (2007)
6. Orchard, D., Bolingbroke, M., Mycroft, A.: Ypnos: declarative, parallel structured grid programming. In: DAMP '10, pp. 15–24. ACM, NY (2010)
7. Kieburtz, R.B.: Codata and Comonads in Haskell (1999) (unpublished)
8. Uustalu, T., Vene, V.: Comonadic notions of computation. Electron. Notes Theor. Comput. Sci. **203**, 263–284 (2008)
9. Huet, G.: The zipper. J. Funct. Program. **7**, 549–554 (1997)
10. McBride, C.: The derivative of a regular type is its type of one-hole contexts. Unpublished manuscript (2001)
11. Ahman, D., Chapman, J., Uustalu, T.: When is a container a comonad? In: Birkedal, L. (ed.) FOSSACS 2012. LNCS, vol. 7213, pp. 74–88. Springer, Heidelberg (2012)
12. Orchard, D.: Programming contextual computations (2013) Forthcoming PhD dissertation. http://www.cl.cam.ac.uk/techreports
13. Lambek, J., Scott, P.: Introduction to higher-order categorical logic. Cambridge University Press, Cambridge (1988)
14. Moggi, E.: Computational lambda-calculus and monads. In: Logic in Computer Science, LICS'89, pp. 14–23. IEEE (1989)
15. Moggi, E.: Notions of computation and monads. Inf. Comput. **93**, 55–92 (1991)
16. Hughes, J.: Programming with arrows. In: Vene, V., Uustalu, T. (eds.) AFP 2004. LNCS, vol. 3622, pp. 73–129. Springer, Heidelberg (2005)
17. Paterson, R.: A new notation for arrows. In: ACM SIGPLAN Notices, vol. 36, pp. 229–240. ACM (2001)
18. Abbott, M., Altenkirch, T., Ghani, N.: Containers: constructing strictly positive types. Theor. Comput. Sci. **342**, 3–27 (2005)

Iterating Skeletons
Structured Parallelism by Composition

Mischa Dieterle[1]([✉]), Thomas Horstmeyer[1], Jost Berthold[2], and Rita Loogen[1]

[1] FB Mathematik und Informatik, Philipps-Universität Marburg, Marburg, Germany
{dieterle, horstmey, loogen}@informatik.uni-marburg.de
[2] Department of Computer Science, University of Copenhagen,
Copenhagen, Denmark
berthold@diku.dk

Abstract. Algorithmic skeletons are higher-order functions which provide tools for parallel programming at a higher abstraction level, hiding the technical details of parallel execution inside the skeleton implementation. However, this encapsulation becomes an obstacle when the actual algorithm is one that involves iterative application of the same skeleton to successively improve or approximate the result. Striving for a general and portable solution, we propose a skeleton iteration framework in which arbitrary skeletons can be embedded with only minor modifications. The framework is flexible and allows for various parallel iteration control and parallel iteration body variants. We have implemented it in the parallel Haskell dialect Eden using dedicated stream communication types for the iteration. Two non-trivial case studies show the practicality of our approach. The performance of our compositional iteration framework is competitive with customised iteration skeletons.

1 Introduction

Modern hardware shows an increasing degree of parallelism at multiple levels. Graphics processing units (GPUs) and modern multicore CPUs offer numerous processing elements on one chip; cloud computing solutions promise to scale compute clusters up to previously inconceivable node counts with ease. It therefore becomes more and more difficult to effectively program these complex large-scale platforms at a convenient level of abstraction, especially when the programmer is not a parallelism expert. Research in parallel programming has developed a range of concepts and models for *skeleton-based parallel programming* to facilitate parallel programming and separate algorithm and parallelism concerns in this increasingly parallel computer landscape.

Algorithmic skeletons implement the parallel behaviour for applications of an algorithm class [4], represented directly as higher-order functions in functional languages. A concrete algorithm can be parallelised simply by applying the appropriate skeleton to function parameters which define the details of this algorithm, entirely hiding parallelism aspects in the skeleton implementation.

R. Hinze (Ed.): IFL 2012, LNCS 8241, pp. 18–36, 2013.
DOI: 10.1007/978-3-642-41582-1_2, © Springer-Verlag Berlin Heidelberg 2013

This approach of "parallel building blocks" constitutes a problem when the parallel algorithm involves iterations – applying the same skeleton repeatedly to successively improving data. Each skeleton incurs a certain overhead of thread and process creation, termination detection and communication/synchronisation. Repeatedly using one and the same skeleton leads to a repetition of this parallel overhead for every skeleton instantiation.

Example. Consider a simple *genetic algorithm* which computes the development of a population of individuals under some mutation until a termination criterion is met. The flowchart in Fig. 1 shows the iterated steps of the algorithm.

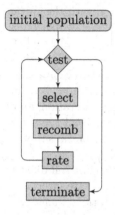

```
type Individual = (Genome, Rating)
test   ::  Individual → Bool        -- terminate?
select :: [Individual] → [(Genome, Genome)]
                            -- parents for next gen.
recomb ::  (Genome, Genome) → [Genome]
                            -- generate offspring
rate   ::  Genome → Individual    -- evaluation
```

A straightforward parallel version of the algorithm using recursion is listed beneath. It tests whether at least one individual of a given population fulfills the termination criteria. If not, genomes are `selected` based on their fitness (i.e. their relative rating) and paired as parents for the next generation. A parallel `map` implementation (`parMap`) is used to `recombine` the parents (already distributed into n sublists, one for each processing element (PE)) and `rate`

Fig. 1. Flowchart

the offspring – working on each sublist of the population in an own parallel process. The results of all processes are gathered and passed to a recursive call of the main function `ga`. The algorithm terminates when one of the new individuals passes the test.

```
ga :: [[Individual]] → Individual
ga pop = case (test_select pop) of
            Left  parentss → ga $ parMap recomb_rate parentss
            Right solution → solution
test_select :: [[Individual]]
              → Either [[(Genome, Genome)]] Individual
recomb_rate :: [(Genome, Genome)] → [Individual]
```

In this parallel implementation, new `parMap` processes are created for each recursive call of `ga`. However, it would be much better to reuse processes, initialisation data, and communication channels across the different `parMap` invocations, especially when running the parallel program in a distributed environment. Also, if processes were reused, they would work on localised data and could even share a local state across the entire computation.

As the parallel behaviour is encapsulated inside a skeleton's implementation, it is generally very hard to optimise the repeated use of a skeleton without modifying the skeleton itself. On the other hand, a solution that involves rewriting parallel skeletons for every concrete sequence of applications is not favourable; we seek a more general method to compose skeletons for iterative computations, which we call *skeleton iteration*[1] subsequently.

Our Approach. We propose a general functional iteration scheme `iter` which is a meta-skeleton (combinator) using an iteration control and an iteration body function as parameters, and streams for exchanging data between both. Specific control and body functionality can be freely combined to express a wide range of iterative algorithmic patterns. We show how to lift ordinary skeletons in a systematic way to work on communication streams such that they can be used as iteration bodies in our iteration scheme. The central idea is to replace the repeated instantiations of the same body skeleton in an iteration with the single instantiation of a lifted body skeleton, the *iteration body*, which works on a stream of input values instead and produces a stream of output values. The control function transforms the output stream into the input stream which thus depends on the output stream, yielding a circular program, i.e. a program which uses such a self-referential data structure [3]. Each value on the input stream corresponds to an instantiation of the original skeleton, i.e. to an iteration step.

To improve programming comfort and safety we introduce special types for the communication streams as these replace iterative processing. Special support is provided for iteratively processing distributed data structures.

We have implemented our iteration framework in the parallel Haskell dialect Eden [9,10]. The functional approach makes it easy to precisely state interfaces and to identify conceptional requirements from our implementation. Using two non-trivial case studies, K-means and N-body, we compare the performance of implementations using our framework to that of straightforward recursion-based implementations, and, for K-means, to a monolithic customised `parMap` iteration skeleton [13]. The K-means case study shows that our framework performs much better than a straightforward recursion-based version with repeated process instantiation, and that it is competitive with the specialised monolithic skeleton. In the N-body case study, the framework-based implementation scales better and reduces overhead compared to the recursive version. However, when run on a small number of processors, the latter has slightly better overall runtimes.

In total, our skeleton iteration framework allows for targeted optimisations of iterative algorithms, with respect to minimising data transfers and controlling dependencies. It drastically improves code structure and readability and provides an acceptable performance with low effort.

Plan of Paper. In the next section, we introduce the proposed skeleton iteration framework gradually, starting with the Haskell prelude function for iteration. The performance evaluation follows in Sect. 3. Sections 4 and 5 provide a discussion of related work and conclusions.

---

[1] *Skeleton iteration* should not be confused with *parallel for-loops* or *parallel map*, where a sequential block is executed in parallel by multiple threads, instead of several times. We focus on computations defined by algorithmic skeletons which are by themselves already parallel and will be executed several times in sequence.

2   Iterating Skeletons

The Haskell prelude function iterate defines the iteration of a parameter function
f, producing an infinite list (or: stream) of all intermediate results of the iteration:
[x, (f x), (f (f x)),...]. The same stream can be defined in a self-referential way,
using the map function and a feedback of the result stream instead of a recursive
function call (this technique of *circular programs* has been used by Bird [3] to
improve data structure traversals).

```
iterate :: (a → a) → a → [a]
iterate f x = x : iterate f (f x)

streamIterate :: (a → a) → a → [a]
streamIterate f x = xs
  where xs = x : map f xs
```

We are especially interested in the case where the parameter f of map, which we call
iteration body in the following, is a parallel skeleton, the *body skeleton*, i.e. when
evaluation of f involves the creation of threads or processes and communication
of data between them. Both the iterate function and the variant streamIterate
above would in this case repeatedly construct and destroy the parallel process
system evaluating f in every iteration step. As an illustrative example, consider
the case where the body skeleton is a parallel map (parMap), i.e. creates one parallel
process per input list element to apply a parameter function to it. The following
specialised version of streamIterate implements this:

```
iterateParMap0 :: (a → a) → [a] → [[a]]
iterateParMap0 g xs = xss
  where xss = xs : map (parMap g) xss
```

Note that, in the result type of iterateParMap0, type [[a]] denotes a *stream
of lists*, i.e. the outer list is infinite, while the inner lists are finite and computed
in parallel (by the iteration body parMap g of type [a] → [a]).

As the iteration body (parMap g) is always the same, it would be desirable
to use just one set of processes for all iterations, instead of creating a new set of
processes in each step. This can be achieved by first transposing the input into
a list of streams and then applying parMap (map g) to it; and finally restoring the
original order with a second transposition. The transposition function transposeS
fixes the length of its result list to the length of the first inner list of its input. This
guarantees that parMap is applied to a finite list.

```
iterateParMap1 :: (a → a) → [a] → [[a]]
iterateParMap1 g xs = xss
  where xss = xs : transposeS (parMap (map g) (transposeS xss))
```

Now the iteration via map takes place within the processes created by parMap
only once, saving the process creation overhead. In this simple example, it is sufficient to replace the iteration map (parMap g) with the composition

$$\text{transposeS} \circ (\text{parMap (map g)}) \circ \text{transposeS}.$$

It is by virtue of streaming and the use of map to express the iteration that we can lift the body skeleton parMap to work on streams and push the iteration (expressed by map) inside the processes. Just swapping map and parMap in the definition (leading to parMap (map g) xss) would instead lead to a pseudo-parallelisation over the *stream* instead of over the *lists*. In the absence of a distinction between lists (for parallelism) and streams (for iteration), types do not indicate this mistake. In the following, we will propose special types and mechanisms to generalise this approach and make a clear distinction between the iteration stream and the list of inputs to the parallel processes. We will also add special control functions for the iteration to improve locality and performance.

2.1   Iteration Type and Body

In this subsection, we introduce the iteration type used to distinguish between streams and lists and we show how to lift body skeletons, which can then be embedded in the iteration scheme discussed in the subsequent subsection.

Implementation Language and Process Types. We use the parallel Haskell dialect Eden to present our language-independent concept. Eden is geared towards distributed memory settings, but works equally well on shared memory system [10]. In Eden, the parMap skeleton

```
parMap :: (Trans b, Trans c) ⇒ (b → c) → [b] → [c]
```

creates a parallel process for every element of the input list, which eagerly evaluates the application of the parameter function (mapping input of type b to output of type c). Processes are distributed among the available processing elements (PEs) (i.e. cores of a multicore or nodes of a compute cluster); and their inputs (the list elements) and process outputs (elements of the result list) are sent implicitly to and from these processes.

Communication-related properties of Eden processes are determined by types, using overloaded communication functions in the type class Trans for transmissible data. As a principle, data transmitted between processes will be evaluated to normal form prior to sending, which introduces additional strictness into Haskell in favour of parallelism. Furthermore, instances for Trans determine different send modes: while the default mode is to fully evaluate and send data as a single item, product types (tuples) can be decomposed and sent concurrently, and recursive types (such as lists) can be transmitted as streams, element by element. The important aspect here is that the type of a process determines the communication mode for its input and output data.

Special Stream Type for Iteration. In our iterateParMap definitions above, streams were modeled as lists, leading to a potential pseudo-parallelisation of the algorithm when parallelisation is applied at the outer level. In order to have a clear distinction of the (sequential) iteration stream and the (parallel) input to the iteration body, we introduce a special iteration type Iter (see Fig. 2), which is isomorphic to lists but different with respect to the communication mode. This

```
newtype  Iter a = Iter {fromIter :: [a]}
instance Functor  Iter where
    fmap f = Iter ∘ map f ∘ fromIter

distribWith :: (a → [b]ᵏ) → Iter a → [Iter b]ᵏ
distribWith f = map Iter ∘ transposeS ∘ map f ∘ fromIter

combineWith :: ([b]ᵏ → a) → [Iter b]ᵏ → Iter a
combineWith f = Iter ∘ map f ∘ transposeS ∘ map fromIter
```

Fig. 2. Iter type and auxiliary functions

enables the programmer and the type checker to identify iteration inputs and outputs in type signatures and thereby increases readability and type safety. Furthermore, the intended streaming behaviour can be defined in a targeted manner by an appropriate `Trans` instance for `Iter`, while other lists can be communicated as single items.[2] The functor instance of `Iter` provides `fmap`, lifting a function of type a → b to iteration streams, `Iter a → Iter b`.

Aside from the new data type, Fig. 2 shows auxiliary functions for common uses of `Iter` data when defining efficiently iterable skeletons. Function `distribWith` splits a single iteration stream into many iteration streams, where the ith element of each output stream is generated from the ith element of the input stream. The function parameter `f` produces a list of output elements for each element of the input iteration stream; these lists are then distributed into a list of output streams using `map Iter ∘ transposeS`. Consider the special case of `f = id`, which implies a = [b] and merely interchanges an outer `Iter` and an inner list. One subtle detail here is that `f` must produce lists of identical length k for all its arguments (elements of the iteration stream) as indicated by the superscript k of the list result type of `f`.[3] The number of output streams, which defines the parallelism degree, is determined by the first incoming stream element and thus equal to the size of the result lists of `f`, again indicated by superscript k in the list type. Finally, the function `combineWith` defines the inverse transformation.

Lifting Body Skeleton parMap. With these tools at hand, it is easy to define the efficient iterable version of `parMap` in a more readable and type-safe way (see Fig. 3). The lifted skeleton `simpleParMapIter` transforms inputs of type $\text{Iter } [b]^k$, i.e. streams of fixed-length lists, element by element into outputs of type $\text{Iter } [c]^k$. It creates k `map` processes, each transforming a stream of values of type b into a stream of values of type c. The auxiliary functions `distribWith` and `combineWith` are applied to the identity function `id` and thus reduce to type conversions and transpositions. Consequently, the behaviour of

---

[2] The original Eden definition specifies that top-level lists are communicated as streams. In this work, we use a modified `Trans` class which gives programmers more control of streaming through separate stream types.

[3] The superscripts in our types are merely annotations to indicate implicit constraints on the list lengths. Fixed sized lists could however be implemented e.g. using the recent Haskell library `Vec`, see http://hackage.haskell.org/package/Vec

```
simpleParMapIter :: forall b c. (Trans b, Trans c)
                 ⇒ (b → c) → Iter [b]ᵏ → Iter [c]ᵏ
simpleParMapIter f bss = css where
  bss' = distribWith id bss    :: [Iter b]ᵏ
  css' = parMap (fmap f) bss'  :: [Iter c]ᵏ
  css  = combineWith id css'
```

Fig. 3. Parallel map as an iteration body

simpleParMapIter corresponds to the iteration body of iterateParMap1:
transposeS ○ (parMap (map g)) ○ transposeS.

In iterateParMap1, the output stream was simply fed back into the iteration
body. Instead, an iteration control function should be used to decide about termination. In the following, we propose an iteration scheme which combines an
iteration body, i.e. a lifted body skeleton, with such an iteration control.

2.2   Iteration Scheme and Iteration Control

A Generic Iteration Scheme. *Iteration control* links together the output and
input iteration streams of the body skeletons, to produce new input and decide
termination. The body skeleton's input stream must be started with initial data,
and the result stream must be conditionally fed back to the body skeleton, or
terminated by closing the input stream and returning a final result. This can be
defined in terms of the following generic iteration scheme:

```
simpleIter :: (a → Iter c → (Iter b,d))  --control
           → (Iter b → Iter c)   --body
           → a → d               --in/out
simpleIter control body a = d where
  (iterB,d) = control a iterC
  iterC     = body iterB
```

The meta-skeleton simpleIter takes two function parameters: an *iteration con-*
trol function which produces initial input and handles the two loose ends of the
iteration stream, also determining the final result, and an *iteration body* function.
While not restricted to it, the iteration body is typically an iterable skeleton like
simpleParMapIter. All parallelism is encapsulated in these two parameter functions, simpleIter only deals with the interconnection, and thereby provides a very
liberal interface to combine iteration control and body functions.

Iteration Control Functions. The iteration body is allowed to transform input
of type Iter b to a different type Iter c. Thus, output cannot be fed back directly
by the control function, but needs to be transformed back from Iter c to Iter b, in
an element-wise fashion. The *iteration control function* must be carefully defined
to ensure progress in the circular iteration scheme. It has to provide the initial
input for the iteration body, it needs to check a termination condition, and to
produce the final output from the iteration body's output upon termination. Two
common examples for iteration control functions are loopControl, which performs
exactly *n iterations* by forwarding *n* inputs without any transformation, and

whileControl, which takes a function parameter checkNext to transform the initial input and iteration output of type a to a new iteration input of type b (Left alternative). It stops the iteration with a result of type d (Right alternative). The lazy patterns ~(...:_) in both control functions are necessary because the corresponding pattern matching can only be performed after the final iteration step. Note that the rest stream matching the underscore pattern _ is empty. Both control functions ensure progress because they provide their second argument a as initial input and essentially pass the elements of the output stream (or at least parts of them) to the input stream until the number of iterations is reached or the termination condition is fulfilled.

```
loopControl :: Int → a → Iter a → (Iter a, a)
loopControl n a (Iter as) = (Iter as', a') where
  (as',~(a':_)) = splitAt n (a:as)

whileControl :: (a → Either b d) → a → Iter a → (Iter  b,d)
whileControl checkNext a (Iter as) = (Iter $ lefts bs, d) where
  (bs,~(Right d:_)) = (break isRight o map checkNext) (a:as)
```

In whileControl, the parameter function checkNext only considers the output of a single iteration step to decide termination or to compute the input for the next step. The general control function type in simpleIter is much more liberal, in fact it is not even required that the control function generates exactly one iteration body input for each iteration body output. Often, it appears more suitable to use a *state-based* control function like the one shown here:

```
whileControlS :: (a → State s (Either b d)) → s
                   → a → Iter a → (Iter b, d)
```

Its first parameter function is a state transformation for a single iteration step, thereby combining safety (i.e. guaranteed progress) and flexibility. We have implemented generic stateful control functions and used them in our measurements, but present our work in terms of the stateless interface due to space constraints.

Running Example. The genetic algorithm presented earlier is an example of a parallel map iterated with a conditional control function:

```
gaBody    :: Iter [[(Genome, Genome)]]^k → Iter [[Individual]]^k
gaBody    = simpleParMapIter recomb_rate

gaControl :: [[Individual]]^k → Iter [[Individual]]^k
             → (Iter [[(Genome, Genome)]]^k, Individual)
gaControl =  whileControl test_select

gaIter    :: [[Individual]]^k → Individual
gaIter    = simpleIter gaControl gaBody
```

The iteration body is constructed from `recomb_rate` by `simpleParMapIter`, and iteration control uses the `test_select` function inside `whileControl`. Function `simpleIter` combines `gaControl` and `gaBody` to implement the genetic algorithm with parallel recombination and rating.

2.3 Performance Tweaking

The main potential for optimisation of iteration steps lies in reducing communication overhead. One obvious bottleneck is that data is gathered in the control function and then redistributed to the iteration body in each step. One approach to optimise communication is to *keep all data distributed* between the iterations. In Eden, this can be done using remote data [6]. We can create a remote data handle from local data and fetch the data remotely using functions:

```
release :: Trans a ⇒ a → RD a
fetch   :: Trans a ⇒ RD a → a
```

When data is `released`, an intermediate data handle of type `RD` a is created, which can be forwarded between several processes at negligible communication cost, until the destination process `fetches` the real data. `release` and `fetch` establish a direct connection between a producer and a consumer process.

In our scenario of iterative algorithms, termination can often be decided from only a small fraction of data, while most of the data remains unmodified across several iteration steps. When the iteration body's inputs and outputs are lifted to remote data, data will be passed directly from the output of a process to its input for the following iteration step. It is straightforward to define a variant of the `simpleParMapIter` skeleton for remote data, by lifting its parameter function to the remote data interface:

```
parMapIterRD :: (Trans b, Trans c)
                ⇒ (b → c) → Iter [RD b]^k → Iter [RD c]^k
parMapIterRD f = simpleParMapIter (release ∘ f ∘ fetch)
```

This variant can now be combined with control function `loopControl n` to iterate a computation n times on input (already supplied as remote data), and data will never be gathered and re-distributed in-between the iteration steps. In every iteration step, input for each process will be `fetched` for local processing using function `f`, and `released` afterwards, only to be fetched within one and the same process in the next iteration step. Other control functions, like e.g. `whileControl`, need to gather data in-between iteration steps to decide termination and provide input for further iteration steps. Therefore, a *parallel iteration control* skeleton should be used to achieve locality and save communication without compromising abstraction by a manual decomposition of iteration data.

2.4 Parallel Iteration Control Skeletons

In many cases where the iteration body uses a skeleton to work on distributed data, a corresponding *control skeleton* with parallel processes can be used to

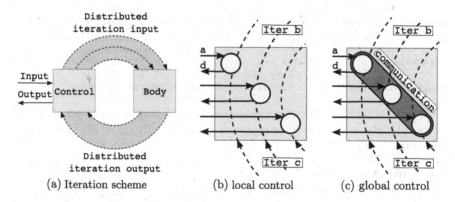

Fig. 4. Parallel iteration control

```
localControl :: (Trans a, Trans b, Trans c, Trans d)
  ⇒ (a → Iter c → (Iter b, d))   -- process-local control
  → [RD a]ᵏ                       -- initial Input
  → Iter [RD c]ᵏ                  -- output of loops
  → (Iter [RD b]ᵏ, [RD d]ᵏ)       -- input for loops, final result
```

Fig. 5. Local iteration control skeleton

inspect the distributed data, exchanging only the parts of it that are needed globally (see Fig. 4a). In addition, corresponding processes of control and body can be placed on the same processing element to avoid communication.[4] This concept can be used with arbitrary distributed data structures, in our implementation we focus on the special case of iterations over distributed lists (lists of remote data). Two different types of parallel iteration control can be distinguished: *local* and *global* iteration control, with respect to the data dependencies within the control processes.

Local Iteration Control means that no data exchange with other control processes is necessary – data dependency is *local*, as depicted in Fig. 4b. Otherwise, a *global* data exchange is necessary, as depicted in Fig. 4c. The type of a local iteration control skeleton for lists of remote data is given in Fig. 5. The implementation is similar to the implementation of parMapIterRD, but takes the two input values and the tuple output into account. The control processes will connect both to their predecessor processes that produce the distributed list beforehand and to the processes of the iteration body, fetching data on-demand, or else passing on the RD handles. Functionality in each process is described by the process-local control function which transforms the initial input and the output of a process in the iteration body (stream-wise) in the respective control process. This skeleton can implement several common iteration control variants simply by partially apply-

---

[4] Eden supports explicit placement of computations in a multi-node parallel system. We have omitted placement aspects from our code for simplicity throughout.

ing the control skeleton to a suitable control function. For example, a variant of whileControl where termination can be decided from local data would be:

```
localWhileCtrl :: (a → Either b d) →
                  [RD a]ᵏ → Iter [RD a]ᵏ → (Iter [RD b]ᵏ, [RD d]ᵏ)
localWhileCtrl checkNext = localControl (whileControl checkNext)
```

The control function checkNext works on the local part of a distributed list (of type [RD a]), and either produces input for the next iteration or the final output (again a distributed list).

Global Iteration Control. If the control function needs information from multiple processes to calculate the next input for the body or to determine termination, the processes of the control skeleton need to exchange these data. As an example of this kind of control skeleton, consider an *all-gather* pattern where all processes gather selected data from all other processes in a distributed manner (see Fig. 6). We only discuss the signature of the skeleton here:

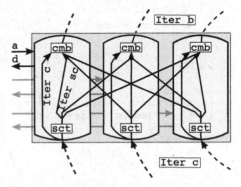

Fig. 6. all-gather control

```
allGatherControl ::(Trans a, Trans b, Trans c, Trans d, Trans sc)
  ⇒ (a → Iter c → Iter sc)                          --select
  → (Int → a → Iter c → Iter [sc]ᵏ → (Iter b, d))   --combine
  → [RD a]ᵏ → Iter [RD c]ᵏ → (Iter [RD b]ᵏ, [RD d]ᵏ)  --controlType
```

Aside from the iteration body output (distributed list of type [RD c], iterated), the input for the next iteration and the final result (distributed lists [RD b] and [RD d]) depend on additional synchronisation data (of type sc, iterated). Combine function cmb produces the local next input and result, but considers the entire list of synchronisation data (iterated) and the own position in the list of processes (Int). Select function sct yields the local synchronisation data which will be communicated to all other control processes.

A skeleton allGatherWhileCtrl can be defined as a specialisation of skeleton allGatherControl with simpler interface, where type a=c.

```
allGatherWhileCtrl :: (Trans a, Trans b, Trans d, Trans sc)
  ⇒ (a → sc)                              --select
  → (Int → a → [sc]ᵏ → Either b d)        --combine
  → [RD a]ᵏ → Iter [RD a]ᵏ → (Iter [RD b]ᵏ, [RD d]ᵏ)  --controlType

allGatherWhileCtrl sct cmb = allGatherControl sct' cmb' where
  sct' a (Iter as) = Iter $ map sct (a:as)
  cmb' self a (Iter as) (Iter scss) = (Iter $ lefts bs,d) where
    (bs,~((Right d):_)) = break isRight $
                          zipWith (cmb self) (a:as) scss
```

The select and combine function of this skeleton work on single elements of the iteration stream. The encoding of the termination condition in `cmb` is similar to the simple `whileControl` function presented in Sect. 2.2.

Running Example. The genetic algorithm described earlier needs to consider the entire population to decide about termination (`test`) and produce input for the next iteration step (`select`). Therefore, it uses a global control variant when implemented with parallel iteration control.

```
gaBodyRD :: Iter [RD[(Genome,Genome)]]^k → Iter [RD[Individual]]^k
gaBodyRD = parMapIterRD recomb_rate

gaControlRD :: [RD [Individual]]^k → Iter [RD [Individual]]^k
              → (Iter [RD [(Genome,Genome)]]^k, [RD Individual]^k)
gaControlRD = allGatherWhileCtrl id cmb where
  cmb self _ pop = case test_select pop of
                     Left  next → Left $ next !! self
                     Right res → Right res

gaIterRD :: [RD [Individual]]^k → Individual
gaIterRD = head ∘ fetchAll ∘ simpleIter gaControlRD gaBodyRD
```

Iteration control is constructed from `allGatherWhileCtrl`, broadcasting the *local* population (`sct=id`) to all sibling processes, such that every process can use the whole *global* population in function `cmb`. The latter calls `test_select` to either terminate (yielding `Right res`) or produce the next input (`Left next`) for *all* body processes. Each process then selects (by `!! self`) its own next input from the list.

2.5 Inlining the Iteration Streams

Up to now, we derived the type `Iter` and with `iterSimple` the signature of iterated skeletons. We introduced remote data to achieve direct communication among processes and used streams of parallel inputs (`Iter [RD x]`) to connect the processes of iteration control and body. This has two drawbacks: (1) In the skeleton definitions, we have to drag the iteration stream from the outside of the iterated list to its elements. (2) The channel connections between the processes of the body and the control skeleton have to be rebuilt in every iteration step. Instead of having a stream of parallel inputs, we will use parallel input streams, leading to type `[RD (Iter x)]`. The transpositions implied by `distribWith` and `combineWith` are now obsolete. Further, streams of data will be communicated over remote data connections established only once. The following `parMap` variant with modified interface implements these static remote data connections:

```
parMapIter :: (Trans b, Trans c)
              ⇒ (b → c) → [RD (Iter b)]^k → [RD (Iter c)]^k
parMapIter f = parMap (release ∘ fmap f ∘ fetch)
```

Notice that we can express the iterable skeleton simply by transforming the function parameter. We observed that the transformation of more complex topology skeletons, such as `allToAllRD` and `allReduceRD` (both developed in the context

of remote data [6]), are similarly easy, only involving the respective function parameters (all transformations done by the nodes are function parameters to these
skeletons).

The iteration streams to and from all processes have to be processed by a control
function or skeleton which exactly matches the particular distributed data shape.
This constraint can be fulfilled by adjusting the type signature of simpleIter to
reflect the change from a stream of parallel inputs to a parallel input stream:

```
iterD :: (a → [RD (Iter c)]ᵏ → ([RD (Iter b)]ᵐ,d))        --control
         → ([RD (Iter b)]ⁿ → [RD (Iter c)]ᵏ)              --body
         → a → d                                          --in/out
iterD = ...                              -- code from simpleIter
```

We need to define specialised versions of local and global iteration control cor-
respondingly, which again are simplifications of the existing implementations.

2.6 Unifying the Interface

The adjusted signature of iterD of the last section is not compatible with the
simpleIter function, even though their implementations are identical. It is easy
to specify a more general type for the iteration combinator,

```
type generalIter = (a → iterC → (iterB,d))
                    → (iterB → iterC)
                    → a → d
```

but we lose type safety when dropping the type of the Iter streams. This problem can be addressed using a type family which describes iteration types used to
interconnect iteration control and body. We want to have special instances for distributed data types. As an example we define a special type for distributed finite
lists.

```
type family Iterated a :: *

newtype DList a = DList [RD a]  --Distributed List
type instance Iterated (DList a) = DList (Iter a)
```

The distributed list type DList a is defined, containing a list of remote data
which represent the distributed elements of type a. Exchanging the iteration
stream and the distribution by [RD _] is now done automatically in the type
instance for DList of the Iterated type family, which yields DList (Iter a) − isomorphic to type [RD (Iter a)]. Other distributed data types and Iterated
instances can be defined in the same way, e.g. distributed trees or matrices.

We use the simple type mapping type instance Iterated a = Iter a to define
the types of iterations for ordinary types. It is not possible to allow overlapping
instances for type families, so we have to define these instances for every base-type

```
iter :: (b → c                          --b/c to typecheck Iterated b/c
          → a → Iterated c → (Iterated b,d))       --control
          → (Iterated b → Iterated c)              --body
          → a → d                                  --in/out
iter iterControl iterBody a = d where
  (iterB,d) = control undefined undefined a iterC
  iterC     = body iterB
```

Fig. 7. General iteration skeleton

separately. Quite advisedly, we have defined DList a as newtype, so an instance for lists can be defined without overlapping Iterated (DList a):

```
type instance Iterated [a] = Iter [a]
```

The type family approach enables us to finally define a generic but type-safe iteration skeleton iter (see Fig. 7) which subsumes all previously presented definitions. It works for both DLists and for any other reasonable type instance of Iterated. A small caveat is that two dummy parameters b and c need to be used in the control function, in order for the typechecker to check the types Iterated b and Iterated c. This is needed to determine the types, because the type family mapping might not be injective.

3 Evaluation

We measured the performance of our iteration framework on a 32 node Beowulf cluster at the Heriot-Watt University Edinburgh, each node with 2 x 4-core@2.00 GHz Intel Xeon E5504 processors, connected by gigabit Ethernet. Eden runtime system instances were co-located on the nodes to make use of all processor cores (which we further refer to as processors). The cluster provides a total of 256 processors. However, as it could not be used exclusively, measurements are limited to a maximum of 128 processors. All program versions where tested on 2^i processors with i ranging from 0 to 7. The reported runtimes are mean values of 5 program runs. They are presented in diagrams with logarithmically scaled axes, with runtimes corresponding to a linear speedup indicated by dotted lines. In the following we present measurement results for two non-trivial case studies: k-means and n-body.

K-means clustering is a heuristic method to partition a given data set of n d-dimensional vectors into k clusters. In an iterative approximation, the method identifies clusters such that the average distance (a metric such as the euclidian or Manhattan distance) between each vector and its nearest cluster centroid is minimal [12]. The algorithm proceeds as follows: (1) randomly choose k vectors from the data set as starting centroids, (2) define clusters by assigning each vector to the nearest centroid, (3) compute the centroids of these clusters, and (4) repeat the last two steps until the clusters do not change anymore. The iteration body takes a list of cluster centroids as input and computes the list of new centroids as output. The iteration continues until two subsequent iteration results are equal or their differences fall below a threshold. The cluster assignment and part of the centroid computation can be parallelised using parMap. Each parallel process receives a subset of the vectors, and the whole list of centroids. Every process then computes a list of weighted sub-centroids which are combined to the list of new centroids by the iteration control.

We measured the runtimes of this parallel k-means algorithm with a data set of 600000 vectors and $k = 25$ cluster centroids. The whole computation comprised 142 iterations. Three different implementations were compared:

- *recursive parMap* is a naïve implementation which creates new processes and re-distributes not only the centroids but also the (unchanged) list of vectors in each iteration step. As the parallel processes are newly created for each step, there is no way to share the vector list across iterations.
- *untilControl/simpleParMapIter* uses our iteration scheme with *stateful* versions of untilControl[5] and simpleParMapIter. Only the centroids are gathered and distributed for each iteration step, while the data vectors are once distributed and then kept in the worker states during the iteration.
- *monolithic iterUntil* uses a *special monolithic* iteration skeleton iterUntil presented in [13]. Like the composed version above, it uses a stable process system and holds the data set in local states. While a perfect match for the parallel k-means, other iterative algorithms would require a complete re-design and re-write of the skeleton.

Figure 8 shows the mean runtimes plotted against the number of processors. The modular skeleton *untilControl/ simpleParMapIter* performs as well as the specialised *monolithic iterUntil* version. Both scale well, showing an almost linear speedup up to 8 processors. On more than 32 processors, initialising and distributing the vectors increasingly influences runtime, leading to lower speedup.

The naïve *recursive parMap*

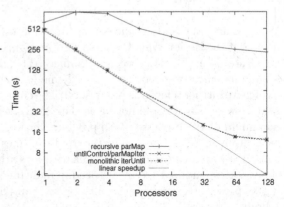

Fig. 8. Runtimes for k-means with 600000 vectors, 25 clusters, 142 iterations

version performs dramatically worse. The overhead of distributing the vectors for every iteration enormously slows down the computation.

N-body. The n-body problem is to simulate the movement of n particles in a 3-dimensional space, taking into account their mutual gravitational forces. In a

---

[5] Similar to whileControl, but forwards the initial input directly to the iteration body, thus doing at least one iteration before termination.

straightforward parallel N-body algorithm, particles are distributed to processes and each process computes the new velocity and position for its own particles. To update its particles' velocities, each process needs position and mass (but not velocity) of all other particles. This information needs to be exchanged in-between the iterations, leading to considerable communication between the parallel processes, in contrast to the parallel k-means algorithm described earlier.

We have used variants of the skeleton `allToAll` to parallelise the iteration body. Each process holds a subset of the particles and processes exchange particle information in every iteration step in a distributed manner using the all-to-all topology. We implemented the following versions:

- *recursive allToAllRD* recursively instantiates the skeleton `allToAllRD`. As the corresponding processes are allocated on the same processor in each iteration, all data transfers occur between processes on the same processors. The Eden runtime system optimises this processor-local communication by passing references to existing data instead of serialising and sending it. That is, processor-local communications do not incur any overhead. Thus, the only remaining overhead consists of the repeated process creations.
- *loopControl/allToAllIter* instantiates our iteration scheme with the skeletons `loopControl` for the iteration control and `allToAllIter` (`allToAllRD` lifted to the `Iter` type) for the body.

In the first setting, we ran the n-body simulation for 10 iterations with 15000 bodies. This constitutes a relatively high workload and large amounts of data have to be exchanged in every iteration. Runtimes against number of processes are plotted in Fig. 9.

Surprisingly, the *recursive allToAllRD* version performs slightly better on up to 32 processors, showing even a super-linear speedup on 2 and 4 processors. Only on 64 and 128 processors, the *loopControl/allToAllIter* version is faster than the recursive version. An analysis of runtime behaviors revealed that the *recursive allToAllRD* has no disadvantage in the communication steps due to the optimised local communications, but the computation phases

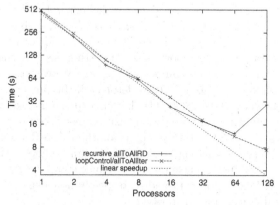

Fig. 9. Runtimes for n-body with 15000 bodies, 10 iterations

seem to be shorter, although sharing the same sequential code base with the iteration scheme version. Pending further investigation, we assume that the differences originate from the runtime system, maybe the garbage collection does not work as effectively for the data streams in our iteration scheme version. In any case, our measurements show that the *loopControl/allToAllIter* version scales better than the recursive version.

In the second setting (Fig. 10), we reduced the work-load and amount of data to be communicated for every iteration step, in order to measure the parallelism overhead. We used only 1500 bodies but increased the number of iteration steps to 100. This time, version *loopControl/allToAll-Iter* clearly outperforms the recursive version independent of the number of processors.

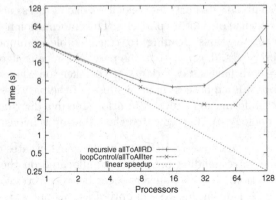

Fig. 10. Runtimes for n-body with 1500 bodies, 100 iterations (overhead measurement)

4 Related Work

The original skeleton work by Murray Cole [4] contains a chapter on an iterative completion, parallelised on a grid of processes, but does not generalise iteration as we do. Slightly more general is the iteration skeleton proposed in earlier Eden skeleton work [13], realising an iteration of a stateful parallel map. This work lays the grounds for our investigation, but does not generalise iteration bodies and types, nor does it consider parallel control skeletons.

Many skeleton libraries, especially those based on imperative programming languages, provide the constructs while for conditional iteration or for for fixed iteration and support skeleton nesting, see e.g. the Scandium library [11], which uses Java as computation language. However, no indications are made about whether iterated body skeletons will be optimised with respect to process creation overhead. A slightly larger corpus of related work can be found in the cloud computing community but usually restricted to map-reduce [1,5] computations, like e.g. [7,14]. HaLoop [2] is another Map-Reduce extension, which mainly capitalises on caching mechanisms for unmodified data and reduction results across several iterations of one map-reduce computation over the same dataset. A small API extension is provided to specify how existing map-reduce (Hadoop) computations should be iterated.

None of these publications addresses parallel iteration as a general concept or distills out algorithmic patterns as we do. This generalising conceptual angle is present in very recent work in the data-flow framework Stratosphere [8]. The authors propose the concept of "incremental" iteration and "microsteps" to exploit sparseness of data dependencies and optimise read-only data accesses, but thereby break up the iterative nature of the computation.

5   Conclusions and Future Work

Iteration is one of the main building blocks of programming. In this work, we developed a general approach to describing iteration that works not only in the common sequential setting but also in the case where the iterated computation is highly parallel and executed in a distributed setting. We allow for arbitrary parallel body skeletons and supply some parameterised control functions including step counting and termination conditions on local and global data. We have shown how body skeletons can be transformed in such a way that the body processes will be re-used for all iterations, how to handle streams of input and output data, and how to optimise communication between distributed processes in a parallel execution. Runtime measurements for two non-trivial example applications, k-means and n-body, clearly show that our framework performs similar to monolithic iteration skeletons and better than directly programmed iterations where the iterated skeletons are repeatedly instantiated.

We will further investigate the field of skeleton composition in the future. In particular, we plan to extend the work at hand by adding other distributed data structures, to augment programming comfort for such distributed data by suitable indexed types and type classes.

Acknowledgements. The authors thank the anonymous referees for their helpful comments on a previous version of this paper. Jost Berthold was partially supported by DSF under contract number 10-092299 (HIPERFIT).

References

1. Berthold, J., Dieterle, M., Loogen, R.: Implementing parallel google map-reduce in Eden. In: Sips, H., Epema, D., Lin, H.-X. (eds.) Euro-Par 2009. LNCS, vol. 5704, pp. 990–1002. Springer, Heidelberg (2009)
2. Bu, Y., Howe, B., Balazinska, M., Ernst, M.D.: The HaLoop approach to large-scale iterative data analysis. VLDB J. **21**(2), 169–190 (2012)
3. Bird, R.S.: Using circular programs to eliminate multiple traversals of data. Acta Inform. **21**, 239–250 (1984)
4. Cole, M.: Algorithmic Skeletons: Structured Management of Parallel Computation. MIT Press, Cambridge (1989)
5. Dean, J., Ghemawat, S.: Mapreduce: simplified data processing on large clusters. CACM **51**(1), 107–113 (2008)
6. Dieterle, M., Horstmeyer, T., Loogen, R.: Skeleton composition using remote data. In: Carro, M., Peña, R. (eds.) PADL 2010. LNCS, vol. 5937, pp. 73–87. Springer, Heidelberg (2010)
7. Ekanayake, J., Li, H., Zhang, B., Gunarathne, Th., Bae, S., Qiu, J., Fox, G.: Twister: a runtime for iterative mapreduce. In: HPDC '10. ACM (2010)
8. Ewen, St, Tzoumas, K., Kaufmann, M., Markl, V.: Spinning fast iterative data flows. PVLDB **5**(11), 1268–1279 (2012)
9. Loogen, R., Ortega-Mallén, Y., Peña-Marí, R.: Parallel functional programming in Eden. J. Funct. Program. **15**(3), 431–475 (2005)

10. Loogen, R.: Eden – parallel functional programming with Haskell. In: Zsók, V., Horváth, Z., Plasmeijer, R. (eds.) CEFP. LNCS, vol. 7241, pp. 142–206. Springer, Heidelberg (2012)
11. Leyton, M., Piquer, J.M.: Skandium: multi-core programming with algorithmic skeletons. In: PDP. IEEE Computer Society (2010)
12. MacKay, D.: Information Theory, Inference, and Learning Algorithms. Cambridge University Press, Cambridge (2003). See chapter 20, p. 284ff
13. Peña, R., Rubio, F.: Parallel functional programming at two levels of abstraction. In: PPDP'01, pp. 187–198. ACM (2001)
14. Zhang, Y., Gao, Q., Gao, L., Wang, C.: iMapReduce: a distributed computing framework for iterative computation. JOGC 10, 47–68 (2012)

Building JavaScript Applications with Haskell

Atze Dijkstra[✉], Jurriën Stutterheim, Alessandro Vermeulen,
and S. Doaitse Swierstra

Department of Information and Computing Sciences,
22 Universiteit Utrecht, 23 P.O.Box 80.089,
3508 TB Utrecht, The Netherlands
{atze, doaitse}@uu.nl, j.stutterheim@me.com, avermeulen@spockz.nl

Abstract. We introduce the Utrecht Haskell Compiler JavaScript back-end, which allows one to compile Haskell code to JavaScript, so it can be run in the browser. To interface with JavaScript and overcome part of the impedance mismatch between the two languages, we introduce the Foreign Expression Language; a small subset of JavaScript for use in Foreign Function Interface imports. Finally we discuss the implementation of a JavaScript application, completely written in Haskell, with which we show that it is now possible to write an entire JavaScript application completely in Haskell.

Keywords: Compilation · FFI · Web applications · Haskell · JavaScript

1 Introduction

When developing interactive web applications, JavaScript is often the language of choice due to native support in every major web browser. In contrast to other client-side programming languages, no plugins are needed to execute JavaScript. Unfortunately, JavaScript is currently the *only* client-side programming language that is supported by all major browsers. People wishing to use other programming languages or paradigms have to rely on using existing plugins such as Flash or Java Applets, writing custom browser plugins, or modifying the browsers themselves. None of these options is ideal, since they either require a lot of work, or force the use of strict, imperative programming languages. Instead of choosing between the aforementioned options, we use the Utrecht Haskell Compiler (UHC) [9,10] to compile Haskell code to JavaScript, effectively using JavaScript as a high-level byte-code, and allowing us to side-step the problems identified with the other approaches.

To overcome the impedance mismatch between Haskell and JavaScript, we have extended UHC's FFI with a small JavaScript-like expression language we call the Foreign Expression Language (FEL). With these enhancements to the FFI, we claim that it is now possible to write complete JavaScript applications using only Haskell. We back up this claim by porting a web-based Prolog "proof assistant" from JavaScript to Haskell. While this paper focusses on Haskell, the ideas should be relatively easy to implement in similar languages.

R. Hinze (Ed.): IFL 2012, LNCS 8241, pp. 37–52, 2013.
DOI: 10.1007/978-3-642-41582-1_3, © Springer-Verlag Berlin Heidelberg 2013

With this paper, we make the following contributions:

- We introduce the UHC JavaScript backend, a compiler backend that allows one to compile any Haskell code supported by UHC to JavaScript and execute it in the browser, maintaining Haskell's lazy semantics.
- We introduce the Foreign Expression Language (FEL), which allows for a more natural way of interfacing with object-oriented languages via the FFI.
- We provide evidence that it is now possible to write a web application completely in Haskell.
- We provide a basic library with bindings to common JavaScript APIs.

The rest of this paper is structured as follows: Section 2 introduces the UHC JavaScript runtime system (RTS). Section 3 covers the FFI with our additions, after which Sect. 4 shows how we have implemented a fully working JavaScript application completely in Haskell. Sects. 5 and 6 discuss future and related work respectively, after which Sect. 7 concludes.

We assume at least some familiarity with the Haskell Foreign Function Interface (FFI) and JavaScript.

2   Compiling Haskell to JavasScript

2.1   Runtime System

There exists an obvious mismatch between Haskell and Object-Oriented (OO) languages, such as JavaScript, which has been addressed in various ways over time (Sect. 6):

- Mapping the runtime machinery required for Haskell to an imperative language has to deal with the lazy evaluation strategy imposed by Haskell (rest of this section).
- Use of OO language mechanisms as available in JavaScript, in particular prototype based objects, in Haskell; we only mention this topic in passing.
- Use of available JavaScript libraries; we deal with this in the next section by exploiting the freedom offered by Haskell's Foreign Function Interface (FFI).

The design of any backend for a lazy functional language needs to deal with functions, their (lazy) application to arguments, and reducing such applications to Weak Head Normal Form (WHNF). The design should also cater for under- and over saturated function applications as well as tail recursion.

In UHC's JavaScript backend, functions and their applications are both represented straightforwardly by objects:

```
Fun.prototype = {
    applyN : function ( args ) . . .
    needsNrArgs : function ( ) . . .
}
function Fun ( fun ) { . . . }
```

We omit implementation details and only expose the programmatic interface as used by the runtime system. The actual implementation can be found in the UHC Git repository [1]. A *Fun* object wraps a JavaScript function so that it can be used as a Haskell function. The *applyN* field is only used when function applications are being evaluated (forced); only then it is necessary to know the *needsNrArgs* number of arguments which must be passed. For the time being it stays unevaluated as a *Fun* object wrapped inside an *App* or *AppLT* closure object, which will be explained below.

Similarly, closures stemming from partially applied (and thus undersaturated) functions need to store already passed arguments and how many arguments are still missing. An *AppLT* (*LT* stand for *less than*) object encodes this and again we provide its programmatic interface first:

```
AppLT.prototype = {
    applyN : function ( args) ...
    needsNrArgs : function ( ) ...
}
function AppLT ( fun, args) {...}
```

An *AppLT* only wraps other *AppLT* objects or *Fun* objects.

Finally, for all remaining saturation cases an *App* object is used. Knowledge about the degree of saturation is delegated to the encapsulated function object, which may be another *App*, *AppLT*, or *Fun*.

```
App.prototype = {
    applyN : function ( args) ...
}
function App ( fun, args) {...}
```

With this interface we now can embed Haskell functions; for example, assuming an elementary JavaScript representation of the Haskell function *id*, the function $\lambda x \to id(id\ x)$ is available, by:

```
new Fun ( function ( x) {
    return new App ( id, [ new App ( id, [ x])]);
})
```

Evaluation is forced by a separate function *eval* which assumes the presence of an *eOrV* (evaluator Or Value) field in all Haskell runtime values, which tells us whether the JavaScript object represents a Haskell non-WHNF value which needs further evaluation or not; in the former case it will be a JavaScript function of arity 0, which can be called. A Haskell function or application object does not evaluate itself since the tail recursion involved will cause the stack of the underlying JavaScript engine to flow over. The separate external function *eval* doing the evaluation allows non-WHNF values to be returned, thus implementing a trampoline mechanism:

```
function eval ( x ) {
    while ( x ∧ x.eOrV ) {
        if ( typeof x.eOrV == 'function' ) {
            x = x.eOrV ( );
        } else {
            x = x.eOrV;
        } }
    return x;
}
```

Even normal JavaScript values can be thrown at *eval*, provided they do not (accidentally) contain an *eOrV* field. The actual *eval* function is somewhat more involved as it provides some protection against null values and also updates the *eOrV* field for all intermediate non-WHNF objects computed in the evaluation loop.

As usual, the evaluation is driven by the need to pattern-match on a value, e.g. as the result of a case expression or by a built-in JavaScript primitive which is strict in the corresponding argument. As in the wrapper of the primitive multiplication function, which contains the actual multiplication ($*$): ·

```
new Fun ( function ( a, b ) {
    return eval ( a ) * eval ( b );
})
```

Depending on the number of arguments provided, either an undersatured closure is built, or the function is directly invoked using JavaScript's *apply*. In case too many arguments are provided, a JavaScript closure is constructed, which subsequently is evaluated in the evaluation loop of *eval*. The implementation of *AppLT* is similar to that of *Fun*. *App*'s implementation of *applyN* simply delegates to *applyN* of the function it applies to. Also omitted are the encodings of nullary applications, used for unevaluated constants (CAF, Constant Applicative Form) and indirection nodes required for mutual recursive definitions. Data types and tuples are straightforwardly mapped onto JavaScript objects with fields for the constructor tag and its fields. If available, record field names of the corresponding Haskell datatype are used. We map *Int, Double, Float, Integer*, and *PackedString* values to JavaScript objects, shown in Table 1. Despite the

Table 1. Mapping from Haskell Types to native JavaScript types

Haskell	JavaScript
Int, Double, Float	*Number*
Integer	*BigInt* (non-native, offered by a library)
PackedString	*String*
Otherwise	RTS representation

mapping to JavaScript objects, the expressions of these types are lazy. Currently, Haskell arrays are not yet translated to JavaScript arrays.

3 JavaScript Foreign Function Interface

We have extended the FFI with the Foreign Expression Language (FEL), a small JavaScript-like language that greatly simplifies interfacing with the JavaScript world from Haskell. The FEL allows one to number and reorder the function arguments, explicitly use them as arguments to JavaScript functions, or use them as objects. Other features include hard coding of literals, accessing array indices, and a built-in mechanism for converting datatypes to JavaScript objects. The new grammar for importing functions is shown in Fig. 1. In the current implementation, only string literals are supported, although there are no fundamental issues preventing implementation of numeric, boolean, undefined and null literals.

Common FFI features, such as the *dynamic* and *wrapper* [18] imports, work as expected, allowing one to use higher-order JavaScript functions in the same way as C function pointers.

As an example of how to use the FEL to import a JavaScript function, suppose we want to import the subString method from the JavaScript String class, where myStr is a concrete JavaScript string object:

```
myStr.subString(start, length);
```

This method is called on a JavaScript string object, and returns a substring, based on the integer value for a start offset and an integer value for the length of the substring, both of which are passed as arguments to the method. Importing this method shows the FEL's added value in several ways: the method is called on a JavaScript *object*, it takes multiple *arguments*, and it requires conversion

```
exp  ::= '{}'                  -- Haskell constructor to JavaScript object
       | (arg | i) post*       -- JavaScript expression
post ::= '.' i                 -- object field
       | '[' exp ']'           -- array indexing
       | '(' args ')'          -- function call
args ::= ε | arg (, arg)*      -- possible arguments
arg  ::= '%' ('*' | int)       -- all arguments, or a specific one
       | '"' str '"'           -- literal text
i    ::= a valid JavaScript identifier
int  ::= any integer
str  ::= any string
```

Fig. 1. Import entity notation for the JavaScript calling convention

from a Haskell *String* type to a native JavaScript string type[1]. The import is shown below:

foreign import js `"%1.subString(%2, %3)"`
   subString :: *JSString → Int → Int → JSString*

In addition to the **js** calling convention, the other noticeable difference with, for example, a C import, is the import definition in the string. Rather than having the FFI place all arguments in one position, we number the arguments and allow them to be placed in different positions in the imported method. Manually ordering arguments enables us to treat one of the arguments as an object, while treating the rest of the arguments as parameters to a method call on that object. In our example, the first argument, indicated by %1, before the dot, is treated as an object in the generated JavaScript code. The number of the argument corresponds to the position of the arguments in the type signature. The two remaining arguments are placed between parentheses, so that they become arguments in the method call in the generated JavaScript code. An alternative way of writing this import is shown below, where we replace the last two explicit argument positions with a wildcard. This says that all remaining arguments should be placed where the wildcard is, saving the programmer some work. Using a wildcard has as added advantage that it becomes easy to import variadic JavaScript methods; the function's arity is then only determined by the type signature, without the need to modify the foreign expression.

foreign import js `"%1.subString(%*)"`
   subString :: *JSString → Int → Int → JSString*

Exporting a function does not make use of the FEL, so it is not much different from exporting a function for the C FFI. The only concerns to keep in mind are using the **js** calling convention, and specifying a JavaScript-compatible type in the type signature.

3.1   The UHC-JavaScript Library

We provide a library [29], simply called the UHC-JavaScript library, to streamline the development of JavaScript applications with UHC. It contains bindings to standard ECMAScript [12], the formal standard behind JavaScript, as well as bindings to the jQuery library [26]. The library aims to provide a bare-metal interface that is consistent with the JavaScript functions. Eventually, this library should form a core upon which more (functional) abstractions are built. We shall make use of this library in the rest of this paper.

---

[1] Naively using a Haskell *String* would give us a JavaScript representation of a list of characters, rather than a JavaScript string. To obtain a native JavaScript string, we require the Haskell *String* to be converted to a *JSString*, which is a type synonym for *PackedString*.

3.2   Creating, Manipulating and Querying Objects

Being a purely functional programming language, Haskell has no notion of objects. JavaScript, however, does. Objects come in two flavours: anonymous and named objects. The former is denoted in JavaScript as { }, while the latter is created by defining a constructor function. Objects can then be instantiated with the **new** keyword, e.g. **new** *MyObj* ( ). Each constructor function also has a prototype object. New object instances will automatically have the same values and functions as the prototype.

UHC offers support for creating, manipulating and querying objects, using several new primitive functions in the runtime-system (RTS). Instead of showing the rather uninteresting function definitions in JavaScript, the code below shows the Haskell type signatures which need to be used when importing these primitives with the FFI:

$$
\begin{aligned}
&primMkCtor && :: JSString \rightarrow IO\ (\,) \\
&primMkObj && :: JSString \rightarrow IO\ (\,JSPtr\ c) \\
&primMkAnonObj && :: IO\ (\,JSPtr\ c) \\
&primGetAttr && :: JSString \rightarrow JSPtr\ c \rightarrow IO\ a \\
&primSetAttr && :: JSString \rightarrow a \rightarrow JSPtr\ c \rightarrow IO\ (\,JSPtr\ c) \\
&primModAttr && :: JSString \rightarrow (\,a \rightarrow b) \rightarrow JSPtr\ c \rightarrow IO\ (\,JSPtr\ c) \\
&primGetProtoAttr && :: JSString \rightarrow JSString \rightarrow IO\ a \\
&primSetProtoAttr && :: JSString \rightarrow a \rightarrow JSString \rightarrow IO\ (\,) \\
&primModProtoAttr && :: JSString \rightarrow (\,a \rightarrow b) \rightarrow JSString \rightarrow IO\ (\,)
\end{aligned}
$$

JSString is a type synonym for *PackedString*, the builtin type corresponding to JavaScript strings. The *primMkCtor* function creates a new constructor function if it does not yet exist in the *window* scope, where *window* is the variable containing everything pertaining the current window or tab. This function is usually only called from within the other functions listed above. The *primMkAnonObj* function creates an anonymous object { }, while *primMkObj* accepts a string with the class name of the object to be created. If the class does not exist yet, it is created using an empty constructor. The other functions manipulate objects and prototypes, using a mechanism inspired by lenses [16,19], an abstraction over accessors and mutators. The first argument is always the name of the object attribute of interest passed as a string. In case of the *set*-functions, the second argument is the value that needs to be set. Since JavaScript is a loosely typed language, this can be any type, even when interfacing with it from the Haskell world. The *mod*-functions take as second argument a function which modifies the attribute specified in the first argument. Modifying an attribute may change its type, hence the $a \rightarrow b$ type for the function. Finally, the last argument is either a reference to an object, or the name of a class as a string, in case of prototypes. These functions can be used by importing them as primitives:

```
foreign import prim "primGetAttr"
  _getAttr :: JSString → JSPtr p → IO a
```

Objects are represented in the UHC-JavaScript library by a *JSPtr* type, which has no constructors, so they can't be instantiated directly. The only way an object can be obtained is by getting it via the FFI. A *JSPtr* takes one phantom type as a parameter, which specifies the type of the JavaScript object. This should again be a type without constructor. Suppose we want a pointer to a JavaScript *Book* object, for which we have some definition in JavaScript. We define it in Haskell as follows:

```
data BookPtr
type Book = JSPtr BookPtr
```

We can now define functions on the *Book* type, giving us a type-safe way to deal with JavaScript objects. A similar approach is often taken in GHC's C FFI to deal with pointer types.

We offer the *Language.UHC.JS.Primitives* module in the UHC-JavaScript library, which defines primitive imports and abstracts away from *JSString*. Using these functions we can now create, manipulate and query an object:

```
main = do
    o ← mkObj "Book"
    setAttr "pages" 123 o
    modAttr "pages" (+1) o
    p ← getAttr "pages" o
    print p   -- Prints 124
```

While defining objects as shown in the previous example works fine, the process is rather verbose and tedious, especially when dealing with several object attributes. It would therefore be ideal if we could use Haskell datatypes to achieve the same results. In some ways, datatypes and JavaScript objects have a lot in common, especially when the datatype has record selectors. Suppose we have a simple *Book* type[2] in Haskell:

```
data Book = Book
            { author :: JSString
            , title  :: JSString
            , pages  :: Int }
```

A concrete *Book* value would look as follows:

```
myBook = Book
           { author = toJS "me"
           , title  = toJS "story"
           , pages  = 123 }
```

---

[2] We use *JSString* here so that the resulting Haskell record relates more closely to the JavaScript object.

The representation of *myBook* closely resembles an object with the same data in JavaScript:

```
myBook =
      { author  :  "me"
      , title   :  "story"
      , pages   :  123 }
```

In fact, a JavaScript object very similar to the one shown above is already being generated by the UHC. However, since it is generated as an application of a constructor to some values, the generated datatype values are not directly usable in other JavaScript libraries. We require a mechanism to convert the Haskell representation of the datatype into a JavaScript representation. This idea is similar to that of the FFI's wrapper import feature. Using a similar mechanism to the wrapper, we can make Haskell datatypes available as JavaScript objects. This mechanism is exposed via the FEL, simply as { }:

> **foreign import js "{}"**
> $mkObj :: a \rightarrow IO\ (\ JSPtr\ b)$

It takes a value of datatype a and converts it to a plain JavaScript object, resulting in a pointer to the new object. If the datatype contains record selectors, they will be used as the object's indices. When no record selectors are available, an integer is used instead.

Creating the object is achieved by recursively evaluating and cloning the data inside the datatype to a new, empty object, disposing of RTS-specific information in the process. Cloning is required, because modifications on the new object by plain JavaScript code must not be reflected in the original datatype value. Using the object wrapper, we can simplify our example above:

> $main = \textbf{do}$
> $\textbf{let}\ b' = myBook\ \{\ pages = pages\ myBook + 1\}$
> $b \leftarrow mkObj\ b'$
> $p \leftarrow getAttr\ \texttt{"pages"}\ b$
> $print\ p$ -- Prints 124

Note that even though this example is only one line shorter, we also have the two strings available in our JavaScript object, which would have taken two more lines in the original example. More importantly, Haskell's type system is in a much better position to catch programmer mistakes, since record selectors are used in the modification of the *pages* value instead of strings.

3.3   Pure Objects

Objects in JavaScript are mutable by nature. By modifying an object, you modify it for everything that has a pointer to that particular object. This forces any update operation to be defined in *IO*. In order to escape the *IO* monad, update operations need to become non-destructive, which is achieved by creating a copy of an object before modifying it. The RTS exports a primitive to do exactly this:

$$primClone :: JSPtr\ a \rightarrow JSPtr\ a$$

By cloning an object first, all pointers to the original object remain untouched when modifying the clone. This enables pure variants of the *primSetAttr* and *primModAttr* functions:

$$primPureSetAttr\ :: JSString \rightarrow a \rightarrow JSPtr\ c \rightarrow JSPtr\ c$$
$$primPureModAttr :: JSString \rightarrow (a \rightarrow b) \rightarrow JSPtr\ c \rightarrow JSPtr\ c$$

Since a potentially large graphs of objects will be cloned by these pure functions, they should be used with care. The cloning method used is a modification of the cloning method used by jQuery [26].

4   The JCU Application

To explore the limitations, and to demonstrate the features of the UHC JavaScript backend in a real-life scenario, we ported the 'JCU Prolog Proof Assistant' [31], a web application developed to aid in teaching [28] Prolog at the Junior College Utrecht, to Haskell. It is a tool developed for students to learn about important concepts in computer science, such as proofs, trees, unification, and backtracking, by means of proving Prolog queries manually. Students enter a Prolog query, after which they can build a proof of this query by dragging and dropping Prolog rules and facts on top of the query, and by applying substitutions manually throughout the proof tree.

The application was originally programmed in `coffeescript` [7], a layer of syntactic sugar for JavaScript, and used the `Brunch` [22] framework. In the original implementation, all Prolog logic was implemented server-side in Haskell, using the NanoProlog [30] library. We rewrote the application in Haskell using UHC and the UHC-JavaScript library. We also use jQuery for interacting with the Document Object Model (DOM) and the jQuery AjaxQueue [25] plugin for sequential non-blocking communication with the server. The resulting application has the same functionality as the original implementation and appears to be at least as stable, although this has only been manually tested. As is expected of applications that interact heavily with a graphical user interface, a large part of the application's code lives in the *IO* monad.

With the ability to compile Haskell to JavaScript comes the possibility of running any Haskell library that compiles on UHC in the browser, without modification. We use this feature in the JCU web application to run the NanoProlog library in the browser, allowing us to perform proof checking and unification at the client-side, eliminating the need for many AJAX requests. In a further step we eliminated the need for a server altogether by storing the set of rules and facts using HTML5 Local Storage, a browser-based database supported by most modern browsers, instead of in a database on the server. With this modification, the assistant can be run with only the requirement of a modern web browser; no Internet connection is required. A live demo is available online.[3]

4.1 Implementation Issues

Most of the problems we encountered in porting the JCU application to Haskell were due to the lack of advanced language features in UHC, such as functional dependencies and type families. Practically, this implies that only part of the libraries available on Hackage today can currently be compiled to JavaScript using the UHC JavaScript backend.

Another issue arises from JavaScript's scoping rules. In JavaScript, the keyword **this** is dynamically scoped while all other variables are lexically scoped. Since we emulate lazy evaluation by native JavaScript functions encapsulated by objects, the **this** keyword can in some cases point to the runtime system, rather than the expected scope, exposing the runtime system to the programmer. Simply importing **this** as a function using the FFI is not an option here. This might happen when an imported JavaScript library expects the programmer to make use of the **this** keyword in a callback function. The jQuery library, for example, expects event callbacks to get the active DOM-node using the **this** keyword. One way to still get a reference to the expected object when using **this** is to create a wrapper function that captures the expected scope and passes it to the wrapped function as explicit argument. We have implemented this solution in the *wrappedThis* function, which is part of our RTS.

Figure 2 shows how the *wrappedThis* function can be used to obtain the value of an HTML input field. The code above the definition of *bindInput* is copied from the JavaScript library; *valString* is a function that gets the value of a jQuery object as a *String*. We query the DOM using jQuery, retrieving all **input** elements, such as text fields, in the DOM. We define a function *alertHndlr* that takes the string value of a jQuery object and then shows it in an alert box. Note the explicit **this** parameter. We then wrap it so it becomes a JavaScript function, after which we partially apply it to an explicit **this** parameter using *wrappedThis*. Finally, we bind the event handler to all input fields retrieved by our jQuery selector.

A last example of implementation difficulties is found in the lack of threading support in our current implementation of the proof assistant, and in the current implementation of the UHC JavaScript backend. In addition to the web-based proof exerciser, we offer a web-based user interface to NanoProlog's interpreter. In some cases, the interpreter can get stuck in an infinite recursion when trying to unify a rule. For example, trying to prove the query *silly* (X), where *silly* is defined as *silly* (X) ⊢ *silly* (X)., will never terminate. Originally, we spawned a new thread on the server, which we would terminate after a given amount of time. Our current approach, however, does not yet offer threading, risking blocking the client-side process causing a tab or the whole browser to hang. JavaScript's WebWorkers might provide a solution to this problem, although we

---

[3] http://uu-computerscience.github.com/JCU/

```
data JQueryPtr
type JQuery = JSPtr JQueryPtr
type ThisEventHandler  = JQuery → JQuery → JEventResult
type JEventHandler     = JSFunPtr (JQuery → JEventResult)
type JThisEventHandler = JSFunPtr ThisEventHandler

foreign import js "%1.bind(%*)"
  bind :: JQuery → JSString → JEventHandler → IO ()

foreign import js "wrappedThis(%1)"
  wrappedThis :: JThisEventHandler → IO JEventHandler

valString :: JQuery → IO String
mkJThisEventHandler :: ThisEventHandler → IO JThisEventHandler

bindInput = do
  let alertHndlr :: ThisEventHandler
      alertHndlr this _ = valString this ≫= alert
  inputField ← jQuery "input"
  eh ← mkJThisEventHandler alertHndlr ≫= wrappedThis
  bind inputField (toJS "blur") eh
```

Fig. 2. Code for adding an event handler to an input field

have yet to investigate this option. Another solution would be to change the implementation to limit its recursion depth.

4.2 Performance

In general, the performance of the web application is on par with the original implementation in JavaScript, but only when using a state of the art JavaScript engine, as is found in Google Chrome or Safari. The largest bottleneck seems to be memory management. Building up lazy Haskell expressions leads to a large number of JavaScript objects. The quick creation and then successive destruction of these large expressions places a strain on the memory manager and garbage collector. Other popular browsers, such as Firefox, Opera, and Internet Explorer, perform significantly worse than the aforementioned browsers, although this has only been tested informally.

5 Future Work

While we have shown that it already is possible to implement an entire JavaScript application in Haskell, there is still a lot of room for improvement. As mentioned before, UHC itself lacks support for the more advanced Haskell features, such as type families and functional dependencies. This prevents us from compiling many packages from Hackage directly to JavaScript.

Our current UHC-JavaScript library relies on the programmer to use imported functions correctly. The object-wrapper import, for example, will try to wrap anything, possibly failing at runtime. Extra constraints could be added, although the RTS cannot currently deal with them. Eventually, one could imagine a higher-level library being built on top of the low-level imports to provide improved type-safety. Such libraries may be based on generic programming to eliminate repetition, functional reactive programming [6,14,32] to interact with the DOM, or they may be an entire user-interface toolkit, such as wxHaskell [20].

Working with WebWorkers as a JavaScript counterpart to Haskell threads is not investigated yet. Our JCU application would become significantly more usable with a threading alternative.

Communication with the server is currently encoded manually. One could imagine an approach inspired by Cloud Haskell's [15] typed channels, where communication proceeds over type-safe communication channels, abstracting away from the actual AJAX call.

Currently the only way of converting a datatype to a JavaScript object is to do so at runtime. This, however, is a process with time complexity linear in the number of datatype records. Future work could focus on generating (parts of) JavaScript objects at compile-time, so that only dynamic values will need to be copied to the object at runtime.

Targeting Haskell to a different platform means that some assumptions following from using a single platform only are no longer valid. First, a different platform means a different runtime environment. Almost all of the UNIX functionality is available for the usual Haskell UNIX runtime, but is naturally not available inside a web browser and, vice versa, specific JavaScript libraries like jQuery are not available on a UNIX platform. Some library modules of a package (partially) cannot be built on some platforms, while others (partially) can. To cater for this, UHC rather ad-hoc marks modules to be unavailable for a backend by a pragma `{-# EXCLUDE_IF_TARGET js #-}`. Of course *CPP* can still be used to select functionality inside a module. However, in general, awareness of platform permeates all aspects of a language system, from the compiler itself to the library build system like Cabal. In particular, Cabal needs a specification mechanism for such variation in target and platform to allow for selective compilation of a collection of variants. Currently this means that UHC compilation for the JavaScript backend cannot be done through Cabal.

Currently, we generate JavaScript from the compiler's core language. It might be possible to generate faster code which uses native JavaScript language features when generating JavaScript at a later stage in the compiler pipeline, where the intermediate code is more imperative in nature.

6   Related Work

The idea of running Haskell in a browser is not new. To our knowledge, the first attempts to do so using JavaScript were made in the context of the York Haskell Compiler (YHC) [3]. The DOM inside a browser was accessed via wrapper code generated from HTML standard definitions [2]. However, YHC is no longer maintained, and direct interfacing to the DOM nowadays is replaced by libraries built on top of the multiple DOM variations.

GHCJS [21, 23] is an attempt to use the GHC API to create a dedicated Haskell to JavaScript compiler. It uses the C calling convention, rather than a dedicated js calling convention. A major advantage of using the GHC API is that a mature, production-ready compiler, with support for advanced type-system features is at the programmer's disposal, solving some of the issues we are currently experiencing due to lack of these features in UHC. Currently, GHCJS does not support an import system like the one described in this paper, so its ability to use external APIs is limited. GHCJS' authors remarked on the glasgow-haskell-users mailing list (13 November 2012) that adding an FEL-like import mechanism to GHCJS should be relatively straight- forward.

A very recent, and very promising looking attempt at compiling Haskell to JavaScript is the Fay language [11] by Chris Done, which aims to support a subset of Haskell and compile to JavaScript. It, too, makes extensive use of GHC, giving it a production-ready Haskell compiler and type-checker to build on. In designing Fay's FFI, Done drew some inspiration from the work we present here, namely the FEL.

We ran a benchmark between UHCJS, GHCJS, Fay and Native JavaScript and noticed that the code generated by UHCJS performs the worst by far. This is largely due to excessive memory allocation of objects and subsequent garbage collection. The full details of this benchmark can be found in our git repository.[4]

Another recent attempt is Haste[13] by Anton Ekblad. It, too, builds on top of GHC, and it attempts to be easy to use and generate "relatively lean code". It comes with a small reactive library for interacting with the DOM.

Rather than focusing on source-to-source compiling, "Functional JavaScript" [27] offers a library for a more functional style of programming in JavaScript. "Haskell in JavaScript" [4] offers an interpreter for Haskell, written in JavaScript.

The workflow framework *iTasks*, built on top of the Clean system [5], uses a minimal platform-independent functional language, SAPL, which is interpreted in the browser by code written in Java. The latest interpreter incarnations are written in JavaScript [8, 17, 24]. Although currently a Haskell front-end exists for Clean, the use of it in a browser appears to be limited to the iTasks system. The intermediate language SAPL also does not provide the facilities as provided by our Haskell FFI.

7   Conclusion

We have shown that UHC is capable of supporting the development of complete client-side web applications, opening the door to Haskell-only web development. In the process we added the FEL to UHC and provided a library that exposes the JavaScript world to Haskell. Considering the increasing maturity of the GHC-based solutions, we can conclude that the two biggest contributions of this paper are the FEL, and our evidence that writing a complete, non-trivial web application, optionally using external JavaScript libraries is now possible in

---

[4] https://github.com/UU-ComputerScience/uhc-js/tree/benchmark

Haskell. Since UHC does not support advanced Haskell language features, and GHC's development is faster and more consistent, it remains to be seen whether our implementation in UHC can grow to become a mature tool for developing JavaScript applications. While still keeping this option open, we also call on authors of GHC-based solutions to consider using the contributions of this paper in their work.

When it comes to libraries for writing JavaScript applications in Haskell, better abstractions are still required to reduce the amount of code that lives in the *IO* monad directly, and to give programming with the UHC JavaScript backend a more functional feel. While performance, in most cases, is acceptable, it needs to be improved if computationally heavy functions are to be run on the client. In order for most of the frequently used Hackage libraries to be run on the client, additional work on UHC and Cabal will have to be performed.

References

1. UHC Git repository. https://github.com/UU-ComputerScience/uhc/
2. Haskell in web browser. http://www.haskell.org/haskellwiki/Haskell_in_web_browser (2007)
3. Yhc/Javascript. http://www.haskell.org/haskellwiki/Yhc/Javascript (2007)
4. A Haskell interpreter in JavaScript. https://github.com/johang88/haskellinjavascript (2010)
5. Clean. http://wiki.clean.cs.ru.nl/Clean (2011)
6. Apfelmus, H.: Reactive banana. http://www.haskell.org/haskellwiki/Reactive-banana
7. Ashkenas, J.: CoffeeScript. http://coffeescript.org/
8. Bruël, E., Jansen, J.M.: Implementing a non-strict purely Functional Language in JavaScript. In: Implementation of Functional Languages (2010)
9. Dijkstra, A., Fokker, J., Swierstra, S.D.: The Architecture of the Utrecht Haskell Compiler. In: Haskell Symposium (2009)
10. Dijkstra, A., Fokker, J., Swierstra, S.D.: UHC Utrecht Haskell Compiler. http://www.cs.uu.nl/wiki/UHC (2009)
11. Done, C.: Fay programming language. http://fay-lang.org/
12. ECMA International, Geneva, Switzerland. ECMAScript Language Specification. http://www.ecma-international.org/publications/standards/Ecma-262.htm (2011)
13. Ekblad, A.: Towards a declarative web. Master's thesis, University of Gothenburg, Chalmers University of Technology, Department of Computer Science and Engineering, Göteborg, Sweden (2012) (To appear) http://ekblad.cc/hastereport.pdf
14. Elliott, C.M.: Push-pull functional reactive programming. In: Proceedings of the 2nd ACM SIGPLAN Symposium on Haskell, Haskell '09, pp. 25–36. ACM, New York (2009)
15. Epstein, J., Black, A.P., PeytonJones, S.: Towards Haskell in the Cloud (2011)
16. Hofmann, M., Pierce, B., Wagner, D.: Symmetric lenses. SIGPLAN Not. 46(1), 371–384 (2011)
17. Jansen, J.M.: Functional web applications, implementation and use of client-side interpreters. Ph.D. thesis, Radboud University Nijmegen (2010)

18. Jones, S.P. (ed.): Haskell 98 Language and Libraries: The Revised Report. http://haskell.org/, September 2002
19. Kagawa, K.: Compositional references for stateful functional programming. SIGPLAN Not. **32**(8), 217–226 (1997)
20. Leijen, D.: wxHaskell: A portable and concise GUI library for Haskell. In: Proceedings of the 2004 ACM SIGPLAN Workshop on Haskell, Haskell '04, pages 57–68. ACM, New York (2004)
21. Mackenzie, H., Nazarov, V., Stegeman, L.: GHCJS: Haskell to JavaScript translator. https://github.com/ghcjs/ghcjs/tree/gen2 (2012)
22. Miller, P., Graf, N., Schranz, T., Gerstmayr, A.: Brunch. IO. http://brunch.io/
23. Nazarov, V.: GHCJS: Haskell to Javascript compiler (via GHC). https://github.com/ghcjs/ghcjs (2011)
24. Plasmeijer, R., Jansen, J.M., Koopman, P.: Declarative Ajax and Client Side Evaluation of Workflows using iTasks. In: Principles and Practice of Declarative Programming (2008)
25. Podolsky, O.: jquery-ajaxq. http://code.google.com/p/jquery-ajaxq/
26. Resig, J.: jQuery. http://jquery.com
27. Steele, O.: Functional JavaScript. http://osteele.com/sources/javascript/functional/ (2007)
28. Stutterheim, J., Swierstra, W., Swierstra, D.: Forty hours of declarative programming - Teaching Prolog at the Junior College Utrecht (2012)
29. Stutterheim, J., Vermeulen, A., Dijkstra, A.: UHC-JavaScript libraries. https://github.com/UU-ComputerScience/uhc-js
30. Swierstra, D., Stutterheim, J.: NanoProlog package. http://hackage.haskell.org/package/NanoProlog
31. Swierstra, W., Doaitse Swierstra, S., Stutterheim, J.: Logisch en Functioneel Programmeren voor Wiskunde D. Technical Report UU-CS-2011-033, Universiteit Utrecht (2011)
32. Wan, Z., Hudak, P.: Functional reactive programming from first principles. In: Proceedings of the ACM SIGPLAN 2000 Conference on Programming Language Design and Implementation, PLDI '00, pp. 242–252. ACM, New York (2000)

Advances in Lazy SmallCheck

Jason S. Reich[1](✉), Matthew Naylor[2], and Colin Runciman[1]

[1] Department of Computer Science, University of York, York, UK
{jason, colin}@cs.york.ac.uk
[2] Computer Laboratory, University of Cambridge, Cambridge, UK
matthew.naylor@cl.cam.ac.uk

Abstract. A property-based testing library enables users to perform lightweight verification of software. This paper presents improvements to the *Lazy SmallCheck* property-based testing library. Users can now test properties that quantify over *first-order functional values* and *nest universal and existential* quantifiers in properties. When a property fails, Lazy SmallCheck now accurately *expresses the partiality of the counter-example*. These improvements are demonstrated through several practical examples.

Keywords: Automated testing · Lazy SmallCheck · Functional values · Existential quantification · Search-based software engineering

1 Introduction

Property-based testing is a lightweight approach to verification where expected or conjectured program properties are defined in the source programming language. For example, consider the following conjectured property[1] that in Haskell every function with a list of Boolean values as an argument, and a single Boolean value as result, can be expressed as a *foldr* application.

```
prop_ ReduceFold :: ([ Bool] ↝ Bool) → Property
prop_ ReduceFold r = exists $ λf z → forAll $ λxs → r xs ≡ foldr f z xs
```

When this property is tested using our advanced version of *Lazy SmallCheck*, a small counterexample is found for *r*.

```
>>> test prop_ReduceFold
... Depth 2: Var 0: { [] -> False
      ; _:[] -> False
      ; _:_:_ -> True }
```

---

[1] Like all other properties used as examples in this paper, this property does not hold; our goal is to find a counterexample.

R. Hinze (Ed.): IFL 2012, LNCS 8241, pp. 53–70, 2013.
DOI: 10.1007/978-3-642-41582-1_4, © Springer-Verlag Berlin Heidelberg 2013

The counterexample is a function that tests for a multi-item list. It is expressed in the style of Haskell's case-expression syntax. Several new features of Lazy SmallCheck are demonstrated by this example. (1) Two of the quantified variables, r and f, are *functional values*. (2) An *existential quantifier* is used in the property definition. (3) The counterexample found for r is *concise* and understandable.

Previous property-based testing libraries struggle with such a property. The QuickCheck [2] library does not support existentials as random testing '*would rarely give useful information about an existential property: often there is a unique witness and it is most unlikely to be selected at random* [14]'. QuickCheck also requires that functional values be wrapped in a *modifier* [1] for shrinking and showing purposes.

The original Lazy SmallCheck [14] supports neither existentials nor functional values. SmallCheck [14] supports all the necessary features of the property. However, it takes longer to produce a more complicated looking counterexample. This is because SmallCheck enumerates only fully defined test data and shows functions only in part, by systematically enumerating small arguments and corresponding results.

1.1 Contributions

This paper discusses the design, implementation[2] and use of new features in Lazy SmallCheck. We present several contributions:

- An algorithm for checking properties that may contain universal and existential quantifiers in a Lazy SmallCheck-style testing library.
- A method of lazily generating and displaying *functional values*, enabling the testing of higher-order properties.
- An evaluation of these additions with respect to *functionality and run-time performance*.

1.2 Roadmap

Section 2 is a brief reminder of the Lazy SmallCheck approach to property-based testing. Section 3 demonstrates the new features of the Lazy SmallCheck through several examples. Section 4 describes architectural changes that enable these new features. Section 5 presents the formulation of functional values. Section 6 evaluates the new Lazy SmallCheck in comparison to other Haskell property-based testing libraries. Section 7 offers conclusions and suggestions for further work.

2 The Lazy SmallCheck Search Strategy

A property-based testing library uses a *strategy* to search the test data space for counterexamples to a given property. For example, QuickCheck [2] randomly

---

[2] Source code available at http://github.com/UoYCS-plasma/LazySmallCheck2012.

Table 1. Values of *xs* used by Lazy SmallCheck when testing *prop_ListSizes xs*.

	Test-data	Result		Test-data	Result
(1)	$\perp$	*Refine test-data*	*(5)*	$\perp : \perp : \perp$	*Refine test-data*
(2)	[]	*Property satisfied*	*(6)*	$\perp : \perp : []$	*Property satisfied*
(3)	$\perp : \perp$	*Refine test-data*	*(7)*	$\perp : \perp : \perp : \perp$	*Refine test-data*
(4)	$\perp : []$	*Property satisfied*	*(8)*	$\perp : \perp : \perp : []$	*Counterexample*

selects a fixed number of test-data values. SmallCheck [14], on the other hand, exhaustively constructs all possible values of a particular type, bounded by the depth of construction (or some appropriate metric for non-algebraic types).

Lazy SmallCheck instead begins by testing *undefined* — $\perp$ — as the value and *refines it by need*. The demands of the test property guide the exploration of the test-data space. When evaluation of a property depends on an *undefined* component of the test-data, *exactly* that component is refined. For algebraic datatypes, *undefined* is refined to all possible constructions, each with *undefined* arguments. To ensure termination, when Lazy SmallCheck is run, a bound is set on the depth of possible refinements.

Consider the illustrative property *prop_ ListSize*. It asserts that all lists with *Bool*-typed elements have lengths less than three.

prop_ ListSize :: [*Bool*] → *Bool*
prop_ ListSize xs = *length xs* < 3

Clearly this property is false. Lazy SmallCheck finds the following counterexample where each occurrence of _ means *any value*.

```
>>> test prop_ListSize
... Depth 3: Var 0: _:_:_:[]
```

As Lazy SmallCheck searches for this counterexample, it refines the test values bound to *xs* as shown in Table 1. Notice that the elements of the list *xs* are *never refined* as their values are *never needed* by the property. This pruning effect is the key benefit of Lazy SmallCheck over eager SmallCheck.

3   New Features in Action

The following examples further illustrate the new features in Lazy SmallCheck. The first generates *functional values* and displays *partial counterexamples*. The second shows the benefits of generating *small, partial functional values*. The final example demonstrates *existential quantification*.

3.1   Left and Right Folds

Let us look for a counterexample of another conjectured property. This property states that *foldl1 f* gives the same result as *foldr1 f* for non-empty list arguments with natural numbers as the element type.

$$prop\_ \ foldlr1 :: (Peano \rightarrow Peano \rightarrow Peano) \rightarrow [Peano] \rightarrow Property$$
$$prop\_ \ foldlr1 \ f \ xs = (\neg \circ null) \ xs \implies foldl1 \ f \ xs \equiv foldr1 \ f \ xs$$

As in the original Lazy SmallCheck [14], testing this property requires a *Serial* instance for the *Peano* datatype. Additionally, an *Argument* instance must be defined so that Lazy SmallCheck can produce functional values with *Peano* arguments. We have defined a *Template Haskell* function [15] — *deriveArgument* — that automatically derives a suitable *Argument* instance. Section 5.2 discusses this in more detail.

data *Peano* = *Zero* | *Succ Peano* **deriving** (*Eq, Ord, Show, Data, Typeable*)

instance *Serial Peano* **where** *series* = *cons0 Zero* <|> *cons1 Succ*
deriveArgument "*Peano*

Lazy SmallCheck finds a counterexample at depth 3. The function *f* returns *Succ Zero* if its input is *Zero* and returns *Zero* in all other cases. The list *xs* is of length three where the last element is *Zero*.

```
>>> test prop_foldlr1
Depth 3: ... Var 0: { _ -> { Zero -> Succ _
             ; Succ _ -> Zero } }
Var 1: _:_:Zero:[]
```

3.2   Generating Predicates

Our next example is based on *prop_ PredicateStrings* from Claessen [1].

$$prop\_ \ PredStrings :: (String \rightarrow Bool) \rightarrow Property$$
$$prop\_ \ PredStrings \ p = p \ "Lazy \ SmallCheck" \implies p \ "SmallCheck"$$

Lazy SmallCheck finds as a counterexample the function *p* that returns *True* when the second character in its argument is 'a' and *False* when any other character occurs in the second position. The function is *undefined* for strings of length less than two.

```
>>> test prop_PredStrings
...
Depth 4:
Var 0: { _:'a':_ -> True
       ; _:_:_ -> False }
```

Why is this the first counterexample found? We might expect a function that distinguishes an initial 'L' from an initial 'S'. As the depth-bound for testing increases, the extent to which the spines of list arguments can be refined increases. But also the range of character values used in refinements increases and the smallest non-empty range contains just 'a'.

QuickCheck also finds counterexamples for this property but the functions are stricter. They test equality with one of whole strings "Lazy SmallCheck" or "SmallCheck".

3.3 Prefix of a List

This example is taken from Runciman et al. [14]. We assert that a (flawed) definition of *isPrefix* satisfies a soundness specification of the function.

$$
\begin{array}{l}
isPrefix :: Eq\ a \Rightarrow [a] \rightarrow [a] \rightarrow Bool \\
isPrefix\ [\,]\quad\quad\ \_\quad\quad = True \\
isPrefix\ (x:xs)\ (y:ys) = x \equiv y \lor isPrefix\ xs\ ys \\
isPrefix\ \_\quad\quad\quad \_\quad\quad = False \\
prop\_isPrefixSound\ xs\ ys = isPrefix\ (xs :: [Peano])\ ys \implies \\
\quad (exists\ \$\ \lambda xs' \rightarrow xs \mathbin{+\!\!+} xs' \equiv ys)
\end{array}
$$

In Runciman et al. [14], this property could only be checked by SmallCheck as Lazy SmallCheck did not support existential properties. Running it through the new Lazy SmallCheck gives another concise counterexample: if the first argument of *isPrefix* is a multi-item list with first element Zero, and the second argument is [Zero]; then *isPrefix* incorrectly returns True.

```
>>> test prop_isPrefixSound
... Depth 2: Var 0: Zero:_:_ Var 1: Zero:[]
```

A smallest counterexample with both *xs* and *ys* non-empty suggests an error in the second equation defining *isPrefix*. Indeed, a disjunction has been used in place of a conjunction.

4   Implementation of New Lazy SmallCheck

This section describes in detail how *new Lazy SmallCheck* achieves the process outlined in Sect. 2. We shall return to the *prop_ ListSize* example discussed in Sect. 2 to illustrate the data-types used in the implementation.

```
class Functor f where
    fmap :: (a → b) → f a → f b
infixl 3 <|>
infixl 4 <*>, <$>
(<$>) = fmap
class Functor f ⇒ Applicative f where
    pure  :: a → f a
    (<*>) :: f (a → b) → f a → f b
class Applicative f ⇒ Alternative f where
    empty :: f a
    (<|>) :: f a → f a → f a
```

Fig. 1. Definition of *Functor*, *Applicative* and *Alternative* type-classes.

In places, instead of the actual definitions used in the implementation, we give simpler versions that are less efficient but easier to read. These differences will be summarised in Sect. 4.5.

Abstractions We will make extensive use of the *Functor*, *Applicative* and *Alternative* type-classes. All are defined in Fig. 1. Functors are *containers* with an associated *fmap* operation that applies functions to each contained element. Lists, for example, are functors under the *map* function.

Applicative functors [12] extend this by viewing containers as *contexts* from which values may be obtained. Any ordinary value can be wrapped up in a context using *pure*. A function-in-context can be applied to a value-in-context using the (<*>) operator. Returning to the lists example, *pure* places the value into a singleton list and *fs* <*> *xs* applies every function in the collection *fs* to every argument in collection *xs* to obtain a collection of results.

Alternative functors are an extension of applicative functors by the addition of an *empty* container and an operation, (<|>), to merge containers. For lists, *empty* is the empty list and (<|>) is list concatenation.

4.1   Partial Values

Refinement exceptions As highlighted in Sect. 2, the test-data space includes partial values that are refined by need during the search for a counterexample. When the value of an *undefined* is needed, an exception tagged with the location of the *undefined* is raised and caught by the testing algorithm. The implementation uses GHC's *user-defined exceptions*. [11] The definition of Lazy SmallCheck's *refinement exceptions* can be found in Fig. 2.

The *Location* information uniquely identifies the component of a partial test-data value that is needed by a property under test. The *Path* in a *Location* gives directions from the root of a binary-tree representation to some specific

```
type Location = (Nesting, Path)
type Nesting = Int
type Path = [Bool]
data Refine = RefineAt Location deriving (Show, Typeable)
instance Exception Refine
```

Fig. 2. Definition of *Location* carrying exceptions.

subtree. The *Nesting* in a *Location* is akin to a *de Bruijn* [4] *level*: it identifies the quantifier for the test-data variable that needs refining.

Partial values functor A functor of *Partial* values is defined in Fig. 3. The only method of accessing the value inside the *Partial* functor is through *runPartial*. It forces the result of a computation using partial values and catches any refinement exception that may be raised.

A *Show* instance is defined so that *Partial* values can be printed. The definition is omitted here but it follows the *'Chasing Bottoms'* [3] technique. This is what allows the display of *wildcard patterns* in counterexamples.

Running example Consider the third value, $\bot : \bot$, tested in Table 1 from Sect. 2. Here is its simplified representation and the results of two small computations using it.

```
newtype Partial a = Partial { unsafePartial :: a }
instance Functor Partial where
    fmap f (Partial x) = Partial (f x)
instance Applicative Partial where
    pure = Partial
    Partial f <*> Partial x = Partial $ f x
runPartial :: (NFData a) ⇒ Partial a → Either Refine a
runPartial value = unsafePerformIO $
    (Right <$> evaluate (force (unsafePartial value)))
        `catch` (return ∘ Left)
refineAt :: Location → Partial a
refineAt = Partial ∘ throw ∘ RefineAt
```

Fig. 3. Definition of the *Partial* values functor.

```
>>> let step3 = (:) <$> refineAt (0, [False, True])
                 <*> refineAt (0, [True])  :: Partial [a]

>>> runPartial (prop_ListSize <$> step3)
Left (RefineAt (0,[True]))

>>> print (step3 :: Partial [Bool])
_:_
```

The *undefined* arguments of the list-*cons* are uniquely tagged by locations. The result of applying *prop_ ListSize* shows that the second argument is needed. Pretty-printing this partial value hides the complexity underneath.

4.2   Test-Value Terms

The representation of a test-value term contains *tValue*, the information needed to obtain a partial test-data value, and *tRefine*, its possible refinements. The *Term* datatype is defined in Fig. 4.

The *Applicative* instance for terms shows how: (1) the *Path* component of a location is extended through the argument of *tValue* and (2) the *tRefine* uses this information to pass the rest of the path to the relevant subterm.

The *mergeTerms* function demonstrates how a collection of terms can be turned into a single *undefined* value paired with the ability to obtain the collection when required. This is key to the strategy illustrated in Sect. 2.

Test-value environments After test data is generated but before a property is applied to it, a pretty-printed representation of the partial value is recorded. The benefit of this technique is that we need not record a pretty-printing that

```
data Term a = Term { tValue  :: (Location → TVE (Partial a))
                   , tRefine :: (Path      → [Term a])}

instance Functor Term where
    fmap f (Term v es) = Term ((fmap ∘ fmap ∘ fmap $ f) v)
                              ((fmap ∘ fmap ∘ fmap $ f) es)

instance Applicative Term where
    pure x = Term (pure ∘ pure ∘ pure $ x) (pure [])
    fs <*> xs = Term
        (λ(n, ps) → (<*>) <$> tValue fs  (n, ps ++ [False])
                           <*> tValue xs  (n, ps ++ [True]))
        (λ(p : ps) → if p then fmap (fs <*>) (tRefine xs ps)
                          else fmap (<*> xs) (tRefine fs ps))

mergeTerms :: [Term a] → Term a
mergeTerms xs = Term (TVE [string "_"] ∘ refineAt) (const xs)
```

Fig. 4. Definition of test-value terms and a merging operation.

```
data TVE a = TVE { tveEnv :: TVInfo, tveVal :: a}
type TVInfo = [AlignedString]
instance Functor TVE where
   fmap f (TVE ctx val) = TVE ctx (f val)
instance Applicative TVE where
   pure = TVE []
   TVE ctx0 f <*> TVE ctx1 x = TVE (ctx0 ++ ctx1) (f x)
```

Fig. 5. Definition of test-value environments.

could be obtained from the *final test-value* derived from the term. This will be especially useful for the display of functional values in Sect. 5.

The *test-value environments* type is shown in Fig. 5. We omit *AlignedString* in this paper but it follows established pretty-printing techniques, such as that used by Hughes [7].

4.3   Test-Value Series Generators

Series functor Properties are tested against a series of depth-bounded test-data terms. The Lazy SmallCheck library defines instances for the test-data *Series* functor that implicitly enforces depth-bounding and the introduction of partial test-data values. These definitions are in Fig. 6.

As with the original Lazy SmallCheck, a depth-cost is only introduced on the right-hand side of binary applications so that each child of a constructor is bounded by the same depth.

```
type Depth = Int
newtype Series a = Series { runSeries :: Depth → [Term a]}
instance Functor Series where
   fmap f xs = pure f <*> xs
instance Applicative Series where
   pure = Series ∘ pure ∘ pure ∘ pure
   Series fs <*> Series xs = Series $ λd →
      [f <*> mergeTerms x | d > 0, f ← fs d
                        , let x = xs (d − 1), (¬ ∘ null) x]
instance Alternative Series where
   empty = Series $ pure []
   Series xs <|> Series ys = Series $ (++) <$> xs <*> ys
```

Fig. 6. Definition of *Series* generators.

```
class (Data a, Typeable a) ⇒ Serial a where
  series :: Series a

  seriesWithEnv :: Series a
  seriesWithEnv = Series $ fmap storeShow <$> runSeries series

  storeShow :: (Data a, Typeable a) ⇒ Term a → Term a
  storeShow (Term v es) = Term
    ((fmap $ λ(TVE _ x) → TVE [string $ show x] x) v)
    (fmap storeShow <$> es)
```

Fig. 7. Definition of the *Serial* type-class.

Running example The following are definitions for depth-bounded values of Booleans, polymorphic lists and Boolean lists.

```
>>> let boolSeries = pure False <|> pure True
>>> let listSeries elem = pure []
                     <|> (:) <$> elem  <*> listSeries elem
>>> let listBoolSeries = listSeries boolSeries
```

Serial class A class of *Serial* types is defined in Fig. 7. Lazy SmallCheck uses *Serial* instances to automatically generate test values for argument variables in properties. Using the generic *Series* operators of Fig. 6, a family of $cons_n$ combinators can be defined exactly as described by Runciman et al. [14].

Running example again The library defines the series generators for many datatypes. The *Serial* instances for *Bool* and lists are as below. Notice that we no longer explicitly define how the arguments of list-*cons* are instantiated. It is automatically handled by the type system.

```
instance Serial Bool where
  series = cons0 False <|> cons0 True
instance Serial a ⇒ Serial [a] where
  series = cons0 [] <|> cons2 (:)
```

4.4 Properties and Their Refutation

Properties The *Property* data-type in Fig. 8 defines the abstract syntax of a domain-specific language. It includes standard Boolean operators. Crucially, it also provides a representation of universal and existential quantifiers that supports searches for counterexamples and witnesses.

Though not defined here, smart wrappers are provided for all six *Property* constructions. These automatically lift *Bool*-typed expressions to *Property* and

```
data Property = Lift Bool | Not Property
            | And Property Property  | Implies Property Property
            | ForAll (Series Property) | Exists (Series Property)
```

Fig. 8. The underlying representation of the *Property* DSL.

instantiate free variables in properties with appropriate series from *Serial* instances.

Refutation of properties The *depthCheck* function takes as arguments an integer depth-bound and a *Testable* property that may contain free variables of types of any *Serial* type. The *counterexample* and *refute* functions given in Fig. 9 search for a failing example.

A key point to observe is that *refute* recurses when it encounters a nested quantification. All refinement requests must therefore be tagged with the *Nesting level* for the associated quantifier. The *RefineAt* information can then be passed onto the relevant *tRefine* function. Those refined terms are then prepended onto the list of terms left to test.

```
counterexample :: Depth → Series Property → Maybe TVInfo
counterexample d xs = either ⊥ id $ refute 0 d xs

refute :: Nesting → Depth → Series Property → Either Refine (Maybe TVInfo)
refute n d xs = terms (runSeries xs d)
  where
      terms :: [Term Property] → Either Refine (Maybe TVInfo)
      terms []                 = Right Nothing
      terms (Term v es : ts) = case (join ∘ runPartial ∘ fmap prop) <$> v (n, []) of
          TVE _    (Left (RefineAt (m, ps))) | m ≡ n    → terms $ es ps ++ ts
                                             | otherwise → Left  $ RefineAt (m, ps)
          TVE info (Right False)                        → Right $ Just info
          TVE _    (Right True)                         → terms $ ts

      prop :: Property → Either Refine Bool
      prop (Lift    v)   = pure v
      prop (Not     p)   = ¬        <$> prop p
      prop (And     p q) = (∧)      <$> prop p <*> prop q
      prop (Implies p q) = ( ⟹ )    <$> prop p <*> prop q
      prop (ForAll  xs)  = isNothing <$> refute (succ n) d xs
      prop (Exists  xs)  = isJust    <$> refute (succ n) (succ d) (fmap Not xs)
```

Fig. 9. Definition of the refutation algorithm.

4.5 Differences Between Versions of Lazy SmallCheck

The main differences between the new Lazy SmallCheck and the original Lazy SmallCheck described in [14] are as follows. In the new implementation:

- Terms are always represented in a type-specific way. Previously they were generated from a generic description.
- Terms can carry a *test-value environment* enabling the display of test-data types (such as functions) that cannot be directly pretty-printed.
- The testing algorithm calls itself recursively, refining information about enclosing quantifiers.

The main differences between real implementation of the new Lazy Small-Check and the slightly simplified variant described in this paper are as follows. In the real implementation:

- The *Path* datatype is a *difference list* to optimise the list-*snoc* operation.
- Terms representing total and partial values are distinguished to optimise performance and to allow the use of existing *Show* instances for total terms.
- Terms representing partial values record the total number of potential refined values they represent up to the depth bound. The refutation algorithm counts the actual number of refinements performed. *(This is useful for performance measurements and comparison with other approaches.)*

5 Implementing Functional Values

The key to generating functional values is the ability to represent them as tries, also known as prefix trees. New Lazy SmallCheck supports the derivation of appropriate tries for given argument types, and the conversion of tries into functions to be used as test values.

The use of test-value environments allows a trie to be pretty-printed *before* it is converted into a Haskell function. This removes the need for the kind of modifier used by Claessen [1].

5.1 Trie Representations of Functions

We define a generic trie datatype in Fig. 10. It is expressed as a two-level, mutually recursive GADT. Level one describes functions that either ignore their argument — *Wild*, or perform a case inspection of it — *Case*.

Level two represents details of a case inspection. The *Valu* construction occurs when the argument is of unit type and therefore returns the single result. The *Sum* construction represents functions with a tagged union as argument type, performing further inspection on their constituent types. The *Prod* construction represents functions with arguments of a product type, producing a trie that first inspects the left component of the product, then the right to return a value.

A construction *Natu vs v* represents a function with a natural number argument. If an argument n is less than the length of *vs*, the value of *vs* !! n is

```
type (:→:) = Level1
data Level1 k v where
   Wild :: v → Level1 k v
   Case :: Level2 k v → Level1 k v
data Level2 k v where
   Valu :: v                              → Level2 () v
   Sum :: Level2 j v → Level2 k v         → Level2 (Either j k) v
   Prod :: Level2 j (Level2 k v)          → Level2 (j, k) v
   Natu :: [v] → v                        → Level2 Nat v
   Cast :: Argument k ⇒ Level1 (Base k) v → Level2 (BaseCast k) v
applyT :: (k :→: v) → k → v
applyT (Wild v) = const v
applyT (Case t) = applyL2 t

applyL2 :: Level2 k v → k → v
applyL2 (Valu v)     _          = v
applyL2 (Sum t _)   (Left k)    = t 'applyL2' k
applyL2 (Sum _ t)   (Right k)   = t 'applyL2' k
applyL2 (Prod t)    (j, k)      = t 'applyL2' j 'applyL2' k
applyL2 (Natu m d) (Nat k)      = foldr const d $ drop k m
applyL2 (Cast t)    (BaseCast k) = t 'applyT' k
```

Fig. 10. Definition of the two-level trie data structure.

returned. Otherwise *v* is returned as default. The *Cast* construction is used in all other cases. We shall say more about it in Sect. 5.2. The function *applyT* converts a trie into a Haskell function.

5.2 Custom Data-Types for Functional Value Arguments

The *Argument* class is defined in Fig. 11. Users supply an instance *Argument t* to enable generated functional test values with an argument of type *t*. Each instance defines a *base type representation* and an *isomorphism* between the argument type and the base type. This is a variation of the generic trie technique used by Hinze [6]. The *Cast* construction of the trie datatype performs the necessary type conversions using the *Argument* instances.

The *BaseCast* functor is used at recursive points to prevent infinite representations of recursive datatypes. It is a type-level thunk indicating that an arbitrary type can be translated into a *Base* type. For example, Fig. 12 shows the *Argument Peano* instance. The Template Haskell function *deriveArgument* automatically produces *Argument* instances for any Haskell 98 type.

5.3 Serial Instances of Functional Values

Functional values have been reified through the trie datatype, so we first need to define series of types. The *Serial* instances are defined in Fig. 13. A special

```
class (SerialL2 (Base k), Typeable k, Data k) ⇒ Argument k where
  type Base k
  toBase   :: k → Base k
  fromBase :: Base k → k

data BaseCast a = BaseCast { forceBase :: Base a }

toBaseCast :: Argument k ⇒ k → BaseCast k
toBaseCast = BaseCast ∘ toBase

fromBaseCast :: Argument k ⇒ BaseCast k → k
fromBaseCast = fromBase ∘ forceBase
```

Fig. 11. Definition of the *Argument* type-class.

```
instance Argument Peano where
  type Base Peano = Either () (BaseCast Peano)
  toBase Zero       = Left ()
  toBase (Succ n)   = Right $ toBaseCast n
  fromBase (Left _) = Zero
  fromBase (Right n) = Succ $ fromBaseCast n
```

Fig. 12. The *Argument* instance for *Peano*.

```
seriesT :: (SerialL2 k) ⇒ Series v → Series (k :→: v)
seriesT srs = (Wild <$>^ srs) <|> (Case <$> seriesL2 srs)

class SerialL2 k where
  seriesL2 :: Series v → Series (Level2 k v)

instance SerialL2 () where
  seriesL2 srs = Valu <$>^ srs

instance (SerialL2 j, SerialL2 k) ⇒ SerialL2 (Either j k) where
  seriesL2 srs = Sum <$>^ seriesL2 srs <*>^ seriesL2 srs

instance (SerialL2 j, SerialL2 k) ⇒ SerialL2 (j, k) where
  seriesL2 srs = Prod <$>^ seriesL2 (seriesL2 srs)

instance SerialL2 Nat where
  seriesL2 srs = Natu <$>^ fullSizeList srs <*>^ srs

instance Argument k ⇒ SerialL2 (BaseCast k) where
  seriesL2 srs = Cast <$>^ seriesT srs
```

Fig. 13. Definition of *Series* generators for tries and functions.

Table 2. Comparision of property-based testing library features.

Feature	QuickCheck	SmallCheck	Original LSC	New LSC
Test strategy	Random	Bounded exhaustive	Bounded exhaustive	Bounded exhaustive
Test-space pruning	N/A	N/A	Lazy generation	Lazy generation
Minimal result	Shrinking	Natural	Natural	Natural
Functional values	Yes[a]	Yes	No	Yes
Existentials	No	Yes	No	Yes
Nested quantification	Yes	Yes	No	Yes
Displays partial counterexamples	N/A	N/A	No	Yes
Haskell 98/2010	Partial[b]	Compatible	Compatible	No[c]

[a] Functional value is wrapped in a modifier at its quantification binding if showing or shrinking is required.
[b] Originally Haskell 98 compatible but functional values modifier requires GADTs.
[c] Requires Haskell extensions: GADTs, type families and flexible contexts.

type-class *SerialL2* is defined. It represents types that can be represented as trie constructions. The applicative operators with a *carret suffix* introduce *no depth cost*, as opposed to those defined in Sect. 4.3. These specialist operators have been carefully placed to give a natural depth metric for functions while keeping the series finite.

Using these definitions, a *Serial* instance for functional values is defined. The default definition of *seriesWithEnv* is overridden to store the pretty-printed form of the trie before it is converted into a Haskell function. This instance definition is omitted here due to lack of space.

6 Discussion and Related Work

A feature comparison of several Haskell property-based testing libraries can be found in Table 2. The test-space exploration strategy is the main distinction between the QuickCheck library and SmallCheck family of libraries. QuickCheck assumes that test data detecting a failure is likely within some probability distribution. SmallCheck, on the other hand, appeals to the *Small Scope hypothesis* [8] — programming errors are likely to appear for small test data.

6.1 Runtime Performance

The repository includes performance benchmarks to compare this implementation with the previously published Lazy SmallCheck. Experiments performed using GHC 7.6.1 with -O2 optimisation on a 2GHz quad-core PC with 16GB of RAM show very little difference in execution times between the two encodings.

6.2 Functional Values

The original QuickCheck paper [2] explains how functional test values can be generated through the *Arbitrary* instance of functions with a *Coarbitrary* instance of argument types. At this stage, QuickCheck could not display the failing example without bespoke use of the *whenFail* property combinator.

QuickCheck has since gained the ability not only to display functional counterexamples but also to reduce their complexity through *shrinking*. Claessen [1] achieves this by transforming functions generated using the existing *Coarbitrary* technique into tries.

Claessen's formulation of tries slightly differs from ours. Existential types are used in place of type families and there is no provision for non-strict functions. Partiality of functions is explicitly expressed instead of being a result of partially defined tries. Claessen also requires that functions are wrapped in a *'modifier'* at quantification binding. This *Fun* modifier retains information for showing and shrinking at the expense of a slightly more complex interface presented to users.

In Lazy SmallCheck, on the other hand, we directly generate a trie and then convert it into a Haskell function. A pretty-printed representation of the trie is stored at the time of generation and retrieved for counterexample output.

The SmallCheck representation of functional values uses a *coseries* approach, analogous to QuickCheck's *Coarbitrary*. However, functional values are displayed by systematically enumerating arguments.

6.3 Existential and Nested Quantification

As previously discussed in Sect. 1, it does not make sense to use QuickCheck for existential quantification. The previous design of Lazy SmallCheck made it difficult to conceive of a refutation algorithm that could handle the nested quantification required to make existential properties useful.

The use of the *Partial* values functor in this implementation gives statically typed guarantees that term refinements are performed at the correct quantifier nesting.

6.4 Benefits of Laziness

Runciman et al. [14] discussed the benefits and fragility of exploiting the laziness of the host language to prune the test-data search space. When applied to functional values, we see further benefits. The partiality of a trie representation corresponds directly with the partiality of the function it represents. Whereas Claessen [1] needs to shrink total function to partial functions, the latest Lazy SmallCheck has partial functions as a natural result of its construction.

7 Conclusions and Further Work

This paper has described the extension of Lazy SmallCheck with several new features; (1) quantification over functional values, (2) existential and nested quantification in properties and (3) the display of partial counterexamples.

Properties that quantify over functional values occur often in higher-order functional programming. Similarly, many properties may involve existential quantification and even nesting of quantification within property definitions. The examples in this paper have demonstrated the power of a tool that can find counterexamples for such properties.

This paper takes an *extensional* view of functional values, characterising them as mappings from input to output. An alternative would be to characterise functions *intensionally* as lambda abstractions or other defining expressions, perhaps allowing recursion [9,10]. We would expect the generic machinery for typed functional series to be more complex. Also, when functions are needed as test values, alternative definitions of the same extensional function are not interesting [13].

Parallelisation of the refutation algorithm is a current area of investigation. A prototype implementation shows near-linear speedups, in multicore shared-memory environments, for benchmarks in which no counterexample is found. This benefit is derived from the tree structure of the Lazy SmallCheck test-value search space. However, in some benchmarks where a counterexample is found the overheads of continued searches in other threads can cause slowdowns rather than speedups.

Acknowledgements. We would like to acknowledge an e-mail suggestion from Max Bolingbroke pointing to Elliott's [5] *MemoTrie* library as a possible starting point for the generation of functional values. We thank Andy Gill, IFL reviewers and Michael Banks for helpful comments and suggestions.

This research was supported, in part, by the EPSRC through the Large-Scale Complex IT Systems project, EP/F001096/1.

References

1. Claessen, K.: Shrinking and showing functions: (functional pearl). In: Proceedings of the 2012 Symposium on Haskell, pp. 73–80. Haskell '12, ACM (2012)
2. Claessen, K., Hughes, J.: QuickCheck: a lightweight tool for random testing of Haskell programs. In: Proceedings of the Fifth ACM SIGPLAN International Conference on Functional Programming, pp. 268–279. ICFP '00. ACM (2000)
3. Danielsson, N.A., Jansson, P.: Chasing bottoms. In: Kozen, D. (ed.) MPC 2004. LNCS, vol. 3125, pp. 85–109. Springer, Heidelberg (2004)
4. de Bruijn, N.G.: Lambda calculus notation with nameless dummies: a tool for automatic formula manipulation, with application to the Church-Rosser theorem. Indagationes Math. **34**, 381–392 (1972)
5. Elliott, C.: Elegant memoization with functional memo tries. http://conal.net/blog/posts/elegant-memoization-with-functional-memo-tries (October 2008). Accessed 26 July 2012
6. Hinze, R.: Generalizing generalized tries. J. Funct. Program. **10**(04), 327–351 (2000)
7. Hughes, J.: The design of a pretty-printing library. In: Jeuring, J., Meijer, E. (eds.) AFP 1995. LNCS, vol. 925, pp. 53–96. Springer, Heidelberg (1995)

8. Jackson, D.: Software Abstractions: Logic, Language and Analysis. MIT Press, Cambridge (2012). Revised edn
9. Katayama, S.: Systematic search for lambda expressions. In: Trends in Functional Programming, TFP2005, vol. 6, pp. 111–126. Intellect Books (2007)
10. Koopman, P., Plasmeijer, R.: Synthesis of functions using generic programming. In: Schmid, U., Kitzelmann, E., Plasmeijer, R. (eds.) AAIP 2009. LNCS, vol. 5812, pp. 25–49. Springer, Heidelberg (2010)
11. Marlow, S.: An extensible dynamically-typed hierarchy of exceptions. In: Proceedings of the 2006 ACM SIGPLAN Workshop on Haskell, pp. 96–106. Haskell '06. ACM (2006)
12. McBride, C., Paterson, R.: Applicative programming with effects. J. Funct. Program. **18**(1), 1–13 (2008)
13. Reich, J.S., Naylor, M., Runciman, C.: Lazy generation of canonical test programs. In: Gill, A., Hage, J. (eds.) IFL 2011. LNCS, vol. 7257, pp. 69–84. Springer, Heidelberg (2012)
14. Runciman, C., Naylor, M., Lindblad, F.: SmallCheck and Lazy SmallCheck: automatic exhaustive testing for small values. In: Proceedings of the First ACM SIGPLAN Symposium on Haskell, pp. 37–48. Haskell '08, ACM (2008)
15. Sheard, T., Peyton Jones, S.: Template metaprogramming for Haskell. In: Proceedings of the 2002 ACM SIGPLAN Workshop on Haskell, pp. 1–16. Haskell '02. ACM (2002)

OCaml-Java:
From OCaml Sources to Java Bytecodes

Xavier Clerc[✉]

France
ocamljava@x9c.fr
http://www.ocamljava.org/

Abstract. This article presents the code generation scheme of the
OCaml-Java compiler. The goal of the OCaml-Java project is to allow
execution of OCaml programs on a Java Virtual Machine. In order to
achieve decent performance, it is necessary to build a compiler producing optimized bytecode that will rely on an efficient support library at
runtime.

The OCaml-Java project thus provides (*i*) an efficient runtime written in pure Java, and (*ii*) an optimizing compiler based on the original
OCaml compilers for the front-end and on the Barista library for the
back-end.

Keywords: OCaml · Java · Bytecode · Compiler · Code generation

1 Introduction

The OCaml-Java project has been presented at large in previous work [1]; in the
present article, we will focus on the code generation process as implemented in
the OCaml-Java compiler. In the remainder of this section, we will nevertheless
summarize the goals and state of the OCaml-Java project. Then, Sect. 2 will expose the architecture of the various OCaml compilers. Section 3 will present the
runtime representation of values in the different compilers, and Sect. 4 will give
an overview of the Barista library that is used as the compiler back-end. Section 5 shows examples of actual bytecode generation, and Sect. 6 shows how the
compiler performs on some benchmarks. Finally, Sect. 7 will discuss future work.

Why the JVM is an Interesting Target

The official OCaml distribution features both bytecode (for a dedicated virtual
machine), and native compilers (for common architectures and OSes). It may
seem at first sight that nothing more is needed, the former meeting portability
needs and the latter meeting performance needs. However, being able to run
OCaml code on a Java Virtual Machine is appealing for mainly two reasons:

- access to a larger choice of libraries;
- access to multicore programming.

R. Hinze (Ed.): IFL 2012, LNCS 8241, pp. 71–85, 2013.
DOI: 10.1007/978-3-642-41582-1_5, © Springer-Verlag Berlin Heidelberg 2013

The number of available libraries is still a known weakness of the OCaml ecosystem in spite of a vibrant community. Having the ability to run on a Java Virtual Machine gives access to all the libraries of the Java ecosystem. The Java community is huge, and has developed frameworks and tools for almost any purpose. There are obvious benefits for OCaml developers to use these libraries.

To be able to use the Java libraries, it is not sufficient to produce Java byte-code. It is also necessary to give to the OCaml developer means to manipulate Java objects from an OCaml program. For this reason, the OCaml-Java compiler features an extension of the type system to allow the construction and manipulation of Java instances from a pure OCaml program. More details regarding the extensions to the type system can be found in our introductory article [1].

Multicore programming can be done in OCaml without resorting to compilation to Java bytecodes. However, the original implementation of OCaml is based on a global runtime lock allowing only one OCaml thread to run at a time. For this reason, leveraging multiple cores is often done through libraries using indeed multiple processes (most notably, map/reduce implementations [2,3]).

Another option is to modify the OCaml runtime to get rid of the global runtime lock. Such a modification implies of course to develop a parallel garbage collector [4] and needs a lot of manpower, as well as some modifications to core OCaml libraries that are not reentrant. At the opposite, by targeting a Java Virtual Machine, we get a parallel garbage collector for free, and in addition can take advantage of Java standard libraries such as the fork/join framework to develop multicore OCaml programs based upon shared-memory.

Java 1.7 Features for Functional Programming

The latest major release of the Java platform has brought a lot of exciting new features. Among them, two are particularly interesting when implementing functional languages:

- the `invokedynamic` framework;
- the *G1* garbage collector.[1]

The `invokedynamic` framework is a very powerful addition to the Java platform as it allows a language implementor to define new semantics for method dispatch. In the OCaml-Java project, we in fact only use the method handles (which are akin to function pointers in C) provided by the framework in order to easily and efficiently implement closures.

The *G1* garbage collector is actually pretty important for functional language implementors because it is known to better suit the allocation/collection pattern found in functional programs. Such programs are typically allocating a lot of small and short-lived values while classical Java programs tend to put less pressure on the allocator.

---

[1] Already present in previous version, but not production-ready.

Past and Present of OCaml-Java

The 1.x versions of the OCaml-Java project should be regarded as mere proofs of concept, whose goal was to reach compatibility with the original implementation. The compatibility is almost total: all language constructs are supported and most OCaml libraries exhibit the same behavior (some minor differences are due to the fact that the Java Virtual Machine does not implement all POSIX primitives).

The 2.0 version described in this paper keeps the same compatibility level, and features great improvements in both memory usage and performance. The goal is to be able to execute typical OCaml code on a Java Virtual Machine while remaining at worst two times slower than native code. The current prototype fulfills this objective on the majority of tested benchmarks.

2   Compiler Architecture

Original Compilers

The original OCaml distribution ships with two compilers: one producing byte-code for a dedicated virtual machine, and the other one producing native code. The bytecode compiler is available on every architecture while the native one is only available on the following:

- tier 1 (i.e. officially maintained): amd64, ia32, powerpc, and arm under Linux, MacOS X or Windows;
- tier 2 (i.e. unofficially maintained): sparc, and tier 1 architectures under BSD or Solaris flavors.

Both compilers naturally share a large codebase: parsing and typing are identical, thus relying on the very same code. Figure 1 shows the successive passes of both compilers from an implementation source file (i.e. a .ml file) to an implementation compiled file (i.e. a .cmo file for the bytecode compiler, and a .cmx file for the native compiler). We do not detail the compilation of an interface source file because it (i) does not produce code, and (ii) it is identical in both compilers.

Figure 1 presents the various passes from a source file to a binary file, as well as the different data structures used during the process. We only skip the passes that are just intended to optionally pretty-print the intermediate data structures on standard output to ease debugging. As previously stated, both compilers share the passes related to parsing (Pparse.file) and typing (Typemod.type_implementation). They also share the very first passes related to code generation: Translmod.transl_implementation and Simplif.simplify _lambda. These passes produces so-called *lambda code*, which is the most abstract representation of code to be compiled.

From this point, the two compilers diverge. The bytecode compiler only needs two more passes to produce its result; these passes are straightforward because the instruction set of the OCaml virtual machine was designed to provide the pieces allowing to almost execute *lambda code*. Of course, the native compiler

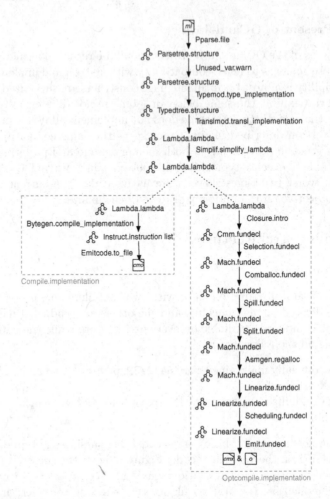

Fig. 1. Passes of OCaml compilers.

has far more work to do because it has to accommodate an instruction set that was not specifically designed for functional programming, and has to target a register-based machine rather than a stack-based machine.

The first step, `Closure.intro`, handles the transformations associated with closures, uncurrification, and related optimizations. From this point, the code is represented by *machine code* which is an abstract representation that is still largely independent from the target platform, based on pseudo-instructions. The `Selection.fundecl` and `Comballoc.fundecl` are designed to perform the selection of pseudo-instructions for the code, and the optimization of allocations linked to a given block. Then, `Spill.fundecl`, `Split.fundecl`, and `Asmgen.regalloc` are responsible for actual register allocation, using information from the target platform. Finally, `Linearize.fundecl` reifies pseudo-instructions into actual lists of instructions, and `Scheduling.fundecl` optimizes the resulting order. The very last step is to output the assembly source code that will be used by an external assembler to produce object code.

OCaml-Java Compiler

The OCaml-Java compiler can be seen as a third branch of the tree depicted by Fig. 1. This means that passes up to `Simplif.simplify_lambda` are shared with the original compilers. Figure 2 shows which transformations are then made on *lambda code*. First, very similarly to the native compiler, `Jclosure.jlambda_of_lambda` is responsible for the handling of closures, producing a slightly different and optimized *lambda code*. Then, `Macrogen.translate` decomposes operations from the *lambda code* into *macro instructions* that are not Java bytecode instructions but can be easily mapped to. This pass is also responsible for variable allocation which entails the choice of their actual representation, thus opening the possibility of value unboxing. Finally, `Bytecodegen.compile_function` produces actual Java bytecode using the Barista library (detailed at Sect. 4).

The point where native and OCaml-Java compilers diverge (namely `Jclosure.jlambda_of_lambda`) has been chosen because the latter has to be more aggressive regarding constants handling and propagation. Indeed, the native compiler does not need to optimize long values, as they are always unboxed. Another construct is treated in a different way in OCaml-Java: switches because the Java instruction set features both table and lookup instruction while the native code generator only emits code corresponding to table switches.

The next pass of the OCaml-Java compiler (that is `Macrogen.translate`) determines how values are locally stored by compiled functions. Most notably, this implies to choose between boxed and unboxed representations for integer and float types. This is a crucial operation as we observed a gain in the 25 %–33 % interval between programs without any unboxing and the current strategy (based on the initialization value of a variable to determine its type). This compilation pass is also responsible for the handling of exceptions, as there is a mismatch between the OCaml and Java semantics on the subject. The difference is that, in Java, when an exception is thrown the stack is immediately emptied and the instance of the

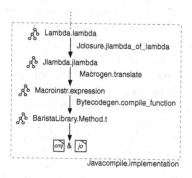

Fig. 2. Architecture of OCaml-Java compiler.

thrown exception is then pushed onto the stack. In OCaml, the raise of an exception will only pop stack values until it finds the enclosing `try`/`with` construct. As a consequence, we have to do some code motion such that an exception can only be raised at a point where the stack is empty: by enforcing this rule we guarantee that both semantics are actually aligned.

Finally, the last compiler pass, `Bytecodegen.compile_function`, uses the Barista library to build an in-memory representation of the class file to emit. This pass is quite straightforward as boilerplate operations such that the computation of stack maps are handled by the Barista library. Indeed, the only important optimization handled by this pass is the tail call optimization. Whenever a call to a function is to be generated, it is checked whether it is a call to the current function. If so, function parameters are placed into locals, and a jump to the method start is emitted. Otherwise, function parameters are placed onto the stack, and a bare static method call is emitted.

Once compilation is done, two files are produced: a `.cmj` file corresponding to the `.cmx` file of the native compiler, and a `.jo` file corresponding to its `.o` file. The `.jo` file is actually a Java archive containing two entries:

- `Module.class` is the class file containing the implementation of all module functions as Java static methods;
- `Module.consts` is a binary file respecting the OCaml marshal format containing the (structured) constants used by the module.

A module is later linked to produce an executable jar file. At runtime, the initialization code for a module (located in its `entry` method) is responsible for the loading of the constants from the `Module.consts` resource. The constants[2] are then accessed through thread-local storage. This indirection is indeed necessary in order to allow several OCaml programs to run on the very same Java Virtual Machine.

3   Value Representation

The compilation scheme of OCaml performs type erasure, meaning that *almost* all typing information is lost during the compilation process. This is of course not a problem as OCaml is statically and strongly typed, meaning that no type test has to be performed at runtime. This is not a problem either for Java interoperability: a Java instance will be wrapped in an OCaml value, but its actual class can still be retrieved at runtime if needed through the mechanism of reflection.

Basically, all values share a common type, namely `value` (in the original runtime, written in C). Having a common type for all values at runtime greatly simplifies the compilation process because such a common representation makes polymorphism compilation trivial.

More precisely, use of the `value` type is mandatory at function boundaries (i.e. to call an OCaml function, or a C primitive), but a function is free to use whatever

---

[2] Despite their name, some constants may in fact be modified, hence the impossibility to share them between programs running in the very same Java Virtual Machine.

representation it prefers for local values. This freedom is indeed crucial in order to reach good performance because it allows unboxing of values. Values still need to be boxed at function's call site, but this penalty can also be partially avoided through function inlining.

In the remainder of this section, we first present the *de facto* specification of runtime values set by the original OCaml implementation, and then present how such a specification is implemented in OCaml-Java.

Original Runtime

The various values manipulated at runtime by OCaml program can be specified by the following grammar.

$$
\begin{array}{rl}
\textbf{value} ::= & \text{long unboxed value} \\
| & \text{pointer to managed block} \\
| & \text{pointer to unmanaged block}
\end{array}
$$

A long value is differentiated from a pointer value using tagging: the lowest bit is set to one for long values, while it is set to zero for pointer values. The encoding of an integer value i as a long unboxed value l is thus done according to the following equation: $l = (i \times 2) + 1$. A managed pointer (i.e. inside the OCaml heap) is discriminated from an unmanaged one (i.e. allocated by C code) by keeping the list of memory block allocated as parts of the OCaml heap.

$$
\begin{array}{rl}
\textbf{managedblock} ::= & \text{tag} \oplus \text{size} \oplus \text{list of } size \text{ blocks} \\
| & \text{closure-tag} \oplus \text{size} \oplus \text{code pointer} \oplus \text{list of } size \text{ - 1 blocks} \\
| & \text{string-tag} \oplus \text{size} \oplus \text{array of } size \text{ bytes} \\
| & \text{double-tag} \oplus \text{64-bit float value} \\
| & \text{double-array-tag} \oplus \text{size} \oplus \text{array of } size \text{ 64-bit float value} \\
| & \text{custom-tag} \oplus \text{identifier} \oplus \text{size} \oplus \text{array of } size \text{ bytes}
\end{array}
$$

As seen by the possible contents of a managed block, some typing information seems to be retained at runtime. However, this is not enough to recover the typing information present in the source, because several different types in the source can be mapped to the same runtime representation. Again, strong typing has been enforced at compile time, so no confusion could be made at runtime between values of different types.

OCaml-Java Runtime

The representation of values is based on multiple classes for the various kinds of values. All classes inherit from a parent `Value` abstract class. This class implements the operations for all the kinds of values, possibly proposing a dummy or failing implementation. It is then the responsibility of children classes to override that base implementation with a correct one. The guarantee that a dummy or failing implementation will never be called is based on the static and strong typing occurring at compile time.

Derived classes are defined for long values, string values, double values, double array values, and block values. Contrary to the original runtime, all values even long ones are allocated because the Java Virtual Machine does not support tagged values. However, every creation of a value has to be done through a factory method, which allows us to share values through a cache. As an example, long values are immutable and a cache allows to share values between -128 and 255. These values are allocated once at program startup, and also allow to use reference comparisons for values between the bounds.

The compilation scheme of OCaml will turn a type such as a record or a tuple of values into a mere block at runtime. Again, strong and static typing ensures that the program will not try to access an element that does not exist (e.g. trying to access the third component of a pair). For this reason the original OCaml compilers will not generate code for testing such bounds. However, in Java it is not possible to remove bounds checks when accessing the elements of an array.[3] As a consequence, if the elements of a block were stored into an array, we would have to pay the price of a bound check at every access. Moreover, due to the covariant nature of arrays, each array store operation incurs a check that the actual class of the object to be stored is correct with respect to the array type.

For this very reason, we resorted to what could be called *data inlining*. Rather than having only one class named `BasicBlockValue` storing its elements as one `Value[]` field, we define a bunch of classes named `BasicBlockValue`n that store n elements as n `Value` fields. This allows to defines methods such as `get0()` that will return the first element of a value with no bound check. The same is done for double arrays and allows "small" tuples, records and all types sharing the same runtime representation to avoid bound checks when accessing the element at a given index.

Experimentation showed measurable speedups when growing the n value up to 8. The current version of the runtime hence contains classes with n ranging from 0 to 8. The source code for these classes is, of course, generated to avoid maintenance issues. Of course, besides those classes, a `BasicBlockValue` (respectively a `DoubleArrayBlockValue`) is defined to be able to store an unbounded number of elements in an array. Then, array bound checks cannot be avoided but experience indicates that this representation is indeed used for OCaml types that turn out to be arrays, and should test bounds at runtime for every access.

Alternative Encoding of Values

At first, one may question why the encoding of values in OCaml-Java is a direct translation of the encoding set by the original compilers. The use of tags, in particular, seems superfluous as different Java classes can be used to discriminate

---

[3] The Hotspot compiler can remove such tests if it can *prove* that no illegal access will happen, but the developer can not request to remove such tests.

between the various kinds of blocks. Unfortunately, we have to closely follow the encoding of the original compilers because some core libraries of the OCaml distribution have implementations based on the low-level memory layout of values. As an example, the `Printf` and `Scanf` modules directly manipulate closures, thus enforcing to use the very same memory layout in OCaml-Java as in the original compilers.

Even under those constraints, other encoding schemes could be devised, and previous versions explored some alternatives. We experimented with an encoding based on the classes from `java.lang` with `Object` rather than `Value` as the parent class of all values, but performance was inferior due to the number of casts to perform. Another scheme was used in versions 1.x of the project: rather than having multiple subclasses, only one `Value` class was used for every kinds of values. In order to avoid casts, we used multiple fields to store the multiple kinds of values. This encoding led not only to a waste of memory, but also to a great performance penalty as the garbage collector had far more references to iterate over.

When comparing the encoding scheme to the ones of other JVM languages, it is important to only compare to languages sharing the same constraints: whether there is an existing reference implementation. Indeed, languages such as Clojure [5] or Scala [6] are completely free to design their encoding scheme because they do not have to abide to an existing specification. At the opposite, projects such as JRuby [7] or OCaml-Java have a more constrained design space. For example, the idea of *data inlining* in order to avoid array bounds checks is also used in JRuby.

4 The Barista Library

Overview

Barista [8], by the same author, is initially an OCaml library designed to load, construct, manipulate, and save Java class files. The library supports the whole class file format as defined by Oracle (formerly Sun) up to version 1.7. On top of the library, a command-line utility (also named "barista") has been developed: both an assembler and a disassembler for the Java platform.

The assembler will turn an assembly source file into a class file to be run on a Java Virtual Machine. The disassembler does the same work in the opposite direction: it takes the fully qualified name of a Java bytecode class file present in the classpath, and transforms it into an assembler source. Two other utilities allow to inspect the contents of a bytecode file: it is possible to just print the list of methods of a given class, and also to print the control flow of a given method as a graph.

While other libraries for bytecode manipulation already existed at the time we started the development of Barista, they were not satisfactory alternatives in our case. The most important thing is that we wanted to generate code through a proper library, and not by invoking an external assembler. The underlying motivation is that we want to use the type system to reject obviously wrong bytecode (e.g. pushing an integer value instead of a float one). When using an external assembler, one generates bare text and even type errors only show up at runtime.

Moreover, Barista is also used in the opposite direction: to load class definitions rather than to produce them. This feature is of utmost importance for the extension of the type system: as we deal with manipulation of Java entities, we need to be able to inspect a class contents at compilation time.

Finally, Barista provides some features that are not available in other bytecode libraries, such as the ability to visualize the bytecode of a given method as an hypergraph, or the ability to create/inspect serialized values.

Hypergraph

Besides the representation of methods as lists of instructions, the code of a method can also be represented as a graph. Precisely, a method code can be represented as a rooted hypergraph. The rooted property stems from the fact that there is only one entry point for a given method. The hypergraph nature of the structure is indeed a design choice that allows to represent the conditionals by edges with one source and as many destinations as there are possible outcomes.

The nodes of the hypergraph are labelled with instruction lists that contain no jump, jumps being represented by edges. Edges hence represent the control flow of the method and can be:

- classical edges with one source and one destination, in order to encode sequential execution (the edge is then with no label);
- three-legged edges with one source and two destinations, in order to encode a test and its two possible consequences (the edge is then labelled with the condition associated with the test);
- n-legged edges with one source and $n - 1$ destinations, in order to encode switch instructions (the edge is then labelled with the definition of the switch, that is either a list of values or lower and upper bounds);
- *special* edges with one source and one destination, in order to indicate that the source is protected by a `try`/`catch` construct, the destination being the exception handler (the edge is then labelled with the class name of the exceptions that can be caught).

Given the hypergraph structure, there are two kinds of optimizations that can be performed by the Barista library:

- structural optimizations, modifying the hypergraph structure;
- non-structural optimizations, modifying only the labels of nodes.

In the first category, Barista currently features two optimizations: dead code elimination, and jump optimization. Dead code elimination removes all nodes that cannot possibly be reached from the root. Jump optimization short-circuits consecutive jumps with no bytecode between them.

In the second category, Barista features several peephole optimizations that are performed independently on the hypergraph nodes. These include, among others:

- code size optimizations (e.g. replacing a *generic* instruction such as aload by a more compact aload$n$);
- removal of unnecessary load and/or store operations (e.g. if a loaded value is discarded or if a stored value is overwritten with no use);
- expression simplifications related to neutral or absorbing elements (e.g. addition to zero);
- basic strength reduction (e.g. shifting rather than multiplying when the multiplier is a power of 2).

Example

As an example, we consider the following Java static method, doing some computation over integer values:

```
public static int meth(final int x, final int y) {
  if (x > y) {
    try {
      return compute1(x);
    } catch (final Exception e) {
      return 0;
    }
  } else {
    return compute2(y);
  }
}
```

After compiling it with the javac compiler, we can dump its bytecode by invoking the javap utility, leading to the following output:

```
public static int meth(int, int);
  Code:
    0: iload_0
    1: iload_1
    2: if_icmple    13
    5: iload_0
    6: invokestatic #2            // Method compute1:(I)I
    9: ireturn
    10: astore_2
    11: iconst_0
    12: ireturn
    13: iload_1
    14: invokestatic #4           // Method compute2:(I)I
    17: ireturn
  Exception table:
    from   to target type
       5    9    10   Class java/lang/Exception
```

Barista can be used to transform a method bytecode into an hypergraph by executing the barista flow 'C.meth(int,int):int' command where C is the class defining the method. The result is a graph representation in dot[4] format and is represented in Fig. 3.

Figure 3 features seven graph elements:

- four nodes (represented by rectangular boxes), containing the bytecode for the various code blocks (condition evaluation, if block, else block, and exception handler);

---

[4] See http://www.graphviz.org/.

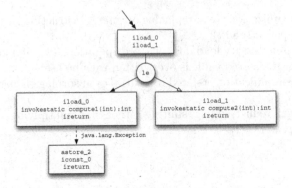

Fig. 3. Hypergraph for method `meth(int,int):int`.

- a double arrow, indicating which node is the root;
- a dotted edge, from the protected node to the handler node and also labelled with the class of exceptions to be caught;
- an hyperedge, linking three nodes: (*i*) the block evaluating the condition, (*ii*) the block to execute next if condition is true, (*iii*) the block to execute next if condition is false; the hyperedge is also labelled with the kind of condition to perform.

5   Example of Bytecode Generation

Our example has been designed to show how the unboxing of values allows to reach good performance in the case of numerical code. The left column shows the OCaml code of the complete function, while the right one shows the generated bytecode for the loop body:

```
let float () =                  (...)
  let x = ref 1. in             33: dload 5
  let y = ref 2. in             35: dload_1
  let acc = ref 0. in           36: dload_3
  for i = 1 to 1_000_000_000 do 37: dmul
    acc := acc +. (!x *. !y);   38: dadd
    x := !x +. 1.;              39: dstore 5
    y := !y *. 2.               41: dload_1
  done;                         42: dconst_1
  !acc                          43: dadd
                                44: dstore_1
                                45: dload_3
                                46: ldc2_w 2.0d
                                49: dmul
                                50: dstore_3
                                (...)
```

Variables `x`, `y`, and `acc` are respectively stored at local indexes 1, 3, and 5. The compiler has determined from their initial values that they are double values. Instructions at offsets $33-39$ compute the expression `!acc +. (!x *. !y)` and store its value back. Then, instructions at offsets $41-44$ update the value of the x variable, and instructions at offsets $45 - 50$ update the value of the y variable. It is obvious from the instructions that all operations are done using the Java `double` primitive type, no boxing is done at all. This ensures that we get the best possible performance, and also avoid to put any pressure on the memory allocator and garbage collector.

When comparing the performance of the original OCaml compiler to the OCaml-Java compiler, we measured the code generated by the former to take 3.8 s and the code generated by the latter to take 5.6 s. Then, we changed the upper bound of the loop by multiplying it by ten, and then measured times to be respectively 38.6 s and 48.0 s. This means that in the second setting, OCaml-Java is less than 25 % slower than original OCaml. Of course, the ratios are better when measuring longer runs because virtual machine startup and just-in-time compiling are amortized.

6 Benchmarks

Procedure

Rather than developing benchmark programs from scratch, we decided to reuse established ones: those from the "Benchmarks Game" (that was previously known as the "Language Shootout"[5]). In order to compare performance between `ocamlopt`- and `ocamljava`-compiled code, we resorted to the following procedure:

- each program is executed 7 times;
- the best and worse times for each program are dropped;
- the remaining times for each program are averaged.

Running the programs several times is of course mandatory to mitigate possible interference from other processes on the testing computer. In the case of performance evaluation for programs running on a JVM, it is also very important to ensure that the virtual machine has been warmed up. This explains why we have to drop the worst execution time (that is, in practice, the first execution time). Finally, it is important to state which options are passed to the JVM: `-server`, `-XX:+TieredCompilation`, and `-XX:+AggressiveOpts`.

Numbers

Table 1 shows the results as ratios (execution time of `ocamljava`-compiled code over execution time of `ocamlopt`-compiled code). The *meteor** program is just the repetition of *meteor* 64 times: the running time for *meteor* is so short that virtual machine startup is significant.

Those results show that the OCaml-Java compiler is on par with the original one on some benchmarks (thread-based and numerical ones), and most of the time between two and three times slower than original OCaml. Given that the

---

[5] See http://benchmarksgame.alioth.debian.org.

Table 1. Some benchmarks from the Benchmarks Game.

Benchmark	ocamljava/ocamlopt	Benchmark	ocamljava/ocamlopt
binarytrees	1.75	*nbody*	1.00
fannkuch	3.11	*revcomp*	2.01
mandelbrot	1.58	*spectralnorm*	2.66
meteor	6.81	*threadring*	1.12
meteor*	4.50		

OCaml-Java compiler is still at prototype stage, and the ability to leverage multiple cores from an `ocamljava`-compiled code, we regard the results as encouraging. Our goal of making OCaml-Java competitive with original OCaml from a performance standpoint seems reachable. However, we clearly need to add new benchmarks to our suite in order to gain more confidence on the preliminary results presented here.

7   Future Work

Most of our short-term effort will be focused on the unboxing of values. It proved to produce large speedups in the past, and a lot of things can be done to make it more aggressive. First, currently, the kind of storage is chosen according to the initial value of a variable; we could design an heuristic also based on the uses of the variable. Second, as previously said, boxing is mandatory at function boundaries; there are two ways to lift this restriction: (i) avoid such a boundary (e.g. by using inlining) or (ii) allow the compilation to functions taking unboxed parameters when typing information allows to do so. Also, unboxing is currently done only for the following OCaml types: `int`, `int32`, `int64`, `nativeint`, and `float`. It could also be done on others types, particularly ones constructed (e.g. records with mutable fields) over those that can already be unboxed.

Inlining itself can also be greatly improved. For example, the current version of the compiler is unable to inline recursive functions. This seems like a reasonable limitation at first, but some recursive functions can be tail-call optimized and thus be compiled as mere loops. In this case, it would be possible to inline such functions.

Another area we should definitely investigate is the possible influence of garbage collection parameters over performance. It would have had little sense for the example presented in this paper, but we expect performance to be sensitive to garbage collector parameters in real-world applications. Indeed, the default parameters are chosen to allow good performance for typical Java applications, not OCaml ones. The former ones tend to use big and long-lived instances, while the latter ones tend to use small and short-lived instances.

Finally, we could also optimize compile-time performance by generating the Barista hypergraph directly during code generation. Currently, the compiler produces plain bytecode that is then passed to Barista for low-level optimizations. This incurs the price of hypergraph construction from a list of bytecode instructions, which can be avoided.

To conclude, some words about optimization opportunities that are linked to the future development of the Java platform. Among those considered for inclusion in the next revision of Java, two would be particularly useful to functional languages targeting the Java Virtual Machine. The first feature is tagged values, and would allow us to avoid boxing of `int` values: it would not only allow faster operations but would also relieve the pressure over garbage collection by avoiding allocation. The second feature is support for tail calls, and would allow us to mark a method call as terminal to indicate to the *just-in-time* compiler that a call can be optimized. It would allow, of course, faster execution, but would also make the life of users easier because the absence of tail call optimization interacts with semantics when calls come to blow up the stack.

References

1. Clerc, X.: OCaml-Java: OCaml on the JVM. In: Loidl, H.-W., Peña, R. (eds.) TFP 2012. LNCS, vol. 7829, pp. 167–181. Springer, Heidelberg (2013)
2. Danelutto, M., Di Cosmo, R.: Parmap: minimalistic library for multicore programming. https://gitorious.org/parmap
3. Stolpmann, G.: Plama: Map/Reduce and distributed filesystem. http://plasma.camlcity.org/
4. Chailloux, E., Canou, B., Wang, P.: OCaml for Multicore Architectures. http://www.algo-prog.info/ocmc/web/
5. Hickey, R.: The clojure programming language. In: Proceedings of the 2008 Symposium on Dynamic Languages. DLS '08, pp. 1:1–1:1. ACM, New York (2008)
6. Odersky, M., et al.: The Scala Language. http://www.scala-lang.org/
7. Nutter, C.O., et al.: JRuby. http://jruby.org
8. Clerc, X.: The Barista library. http://barista.x9c.fr

The HERMIT in the Tree
Mechanizing Program Transformations in the GHC Core Language

Neil Sculthorpe[✉] , Andrew Farmer, and Andy Gill

Information and Telecommunication Technology Center,
The University of Kansas, Lawrence, KS, USA
{neil, afarmer, andygill}@ittc.ku.edu

Abstract. This paper describes our experience using the HERMIT tool-kit to apply well-known transformations to the internal core language of the Glasgow Haskell Compiler. HERMIT provides several mechanisms to support writing general-purpose transformations: a domain-specific language for strategic programming specialized to GHC's core language, a library of primitive rewrites, and a shell-style–based scripting language for interactive and batch usage.

There are many program transformation techniques that have been described in the literature but have not been mechanized and made available inside GHC — either because they are too specialized to include in a general-purpose compiler, or because the developers' interest is in theory rather than implementation. The mechanization process can often reveal pragmatic obstacles that are glossed over in pen-and-paper proofs; understanding and removing these obstacles is our concern. Using HERMIT, we implement eleven examples of three program transformations, report on our experience, and describe improvements made in the process.

Keywords: GHC · Mechanization · Transformation · Worker/wrapper

1 Introduction

HERMIT (Haskell Equational Reasoning Model-to-Implementation Tunnel) [4] is a recently implemented plugin for the Glasgow Haskell Compiler (GHC) [5] that provides an interactive interface for applying transformations directly to GHC's internal intermediate language. This plugin is part of a larger HERMIT toolkit, a Haskell framework that is being developed with the aims of supporting equational reasoning and allowing custom optimizations to be applied without modifying either GHC or the Haskell users' source code.

There are a wide variety of transformation techniques for optimizing functional programs. Many such transformations have been implemented, and many are used by modern compilers. However, there are also techniques that have been described on paper but not mechanized, either because the transformation is too specialized to include as an optimization in a general-purpose compiler, or because the developers' interest is in theory rather than implementation. We

R. Hinze (Ed.): IFL 2012, LNCS 8241, pp. 86–103, 2013.
DOI: 10.1007/978-3-642-41582-1_6, © Springer-Verlag Berlin Heidelberg 2013

want to implement these more specialized transformations using the custom optimization capabilities of HERMIT.

We believe there is a lot to be learned from mechanizing program transformations. The mechanization process can often reveal obstacles that do not appear in pen-and-paper proofs, either because of implementation-specific details, or because the pen-and-paper proofs gloss over details that may seem obvious to a human, but are less obvious to a machine.

This paper reports on our experience using HERMIT to mechanize optimization techniques, using the worker/wrapper [7,25], concatenate vanishes [28] and tupling [1,9] transformations as case studies. We first introduce these transformations (Sect. 2), then we overview HERMIT and what it offers to the mechanization process (Sect. 3). We then give an extended example of using HERMIT to specifically apply tupling (Sect. 4), then discuss our general experience using HERMIT on our 11 examples (Sect. 5). Finally we discuss related work (Sect. 6), and draw conclusions from our mechanization efforts (Sect. 7).

Whereas the previous HERMIT publication [4] described HERMIT itself, this paper describes HERMIT in use, on a suite of examples. The main contribution of this work is pragmatic — showing by example that the HERMIT system is sufficiently mature to be able to encode and apply well-understood transformation techniques, in the context of the full power of GHC. We report on our experience, the obstacles that arose during mechanization, and our approaches to overcoming them, including a new combinator for tree traversal: any-call. Additionally, we demonstrate that it is straightforward to augment HERMIT with new specialized transformations as needed.

At this stage of our investigations we are explicitly concerned with mechanization rather formal proof; for example, a number of the transformations we use have pre-conditions that HERMIT does not verify. We return to this shortcoming in Sect. 5.1, and for now observe that correctness and mechanization are both important, but independently challenging.

2 Transformations for Mechanization

This section overviews the program-transformation techniques that we chose as case studies. While mechanizing these techniques we observed that the concatenate vanishes transformation, and our main tupling transformation, are instances of the worker/wrapper transformation. A proof of the former, and an informal sketch of the latter, are given in the extended version of this paper, which is available on the first author's webpage.

2.1 Concatenate Vanishes

The concatenate vanishes transformation (CV) [28] is a technique for increasing the efficiency of programs that make repeated use of list concatenation. Consider the following standard definition:

$$(+\!\!+) \qquad :: [a] \to [a] \to [a]$$
$$[] \quad +\!\!+ \ bs = bs$$
$$(a : as) +\!\!+ \ bs = a : (as +\!\!+ bs)$$

The time complexity of this definition is linear in the length of its first argument, but constant in the length of its second argument. Thus, while $+\!\!+$ is associative, $(as +\!\!+ bs) +\!\!+ cs$ will evaluate less efficiently than $as +\!\!+ (bs +\!\!+ cs)$. The essence of CV is to exploit this observation to restructure programs using repeated concatenation into a more efficient form.

CV can be summarized as follows. Given a function that returns a list,[1]

$$f \quad :: a \to [b]$$
$$f \ a = expr$$

where $expr$ is an expression that may contain f and a, define a new function that returns a list-to-list function (known as a *difference list* [10]):

$$f' \qquad :: a \to [b] \to [b]$$
$$f' \ a \ bs = expr +\!\!+ bs$$

Then redefine the original function f as:

$$f \quad :: a \to [b]$$
$$f \ a = f' \ a \ []$$

The efficiency gains (if any are possible) are then achieved through refactoring the definition of f': first by applying the associativity and unit laws of $+\!\!+$, and then by folding [2] the definition of f' to eliminate any recursive calls to f.

2.2 Tupling Transformations

Tupling transformations come in several forms. The main one we consider in this paper involves transforming a recursive function that repeatedly solves subproblems into one that uses tabulation, a form of dynamic programming optimization where each subproblem is only solved once, and the solutions to subproblems are only stored as long as needed [1,15,16]. We will refer to this particular tupling transformation as TT.

As an example, consider the call tree for the Fibonacci function, in Fig. 1a. Computing $fib \ n$ requires computing $fib(n-1)$ and $fib(n-2)$, but computing $fib(n-1)$ also requires computing $fib(n-2)$. We would like to avoid this duplication by exploiting sharing, such that our transformation results in the call *graph* in Fig. 1b.

In general, to perform TT on a function f, we define a function t whose body is an n-ary tuple of the n calls to f that share a common recursive call. By case-splitting on the arguments to t, we establish base cases for well-founded recursion. The recursive case of t is then calculated by selectively unfolding calls

---

[1] For clarity of presentation we assume the function is in uncurried form, but CV is valid for functions that take any number of arguments; see [28].

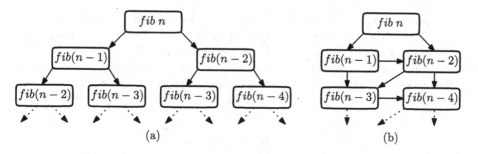

Fig. 1. Call graphs for *fib*, illustrating duplicated computation.

to f to expose the common recursive call. All distinct calls to f are let-bound, introducing sharing, which is the goal of the transformation. These let-bound calls are themselves grouped into an n-ary tuple, which can be folded into a call to t, leaving t recursively defined. Finally, f is redefined non-recursively in terms of t. This is demonstrated in detail for the Fibonacci function in Sect. 4.

2.3   Worker/Wrapper Transformation

The worker/wrapper transformation (WW) [7, 25] is a technique for improving the efficiency of a recursive program by changing the data type being operated on. The idea is to factorize a program $prog :: a$ into a more efficient *worker* program $work :: b$, and a *wrapper* function $wrap :: b \rightarrow a$ that converts the result into a value of the original type.

The first step is to ensure that the program is expressed as the least fixed point of a non-recursive function f, which may involve rewriting as follows (where *expr* is an expression that may contain *prog*):

$$prog = expr \qquad \Rightarrow \qquad prog = \textbf{let } f = \lambda prog \rightarrow expr$$
$$\textbf{in } fix \; f$$

Next comes the key step: choosing a more efficient data type. Once chosen, we define conversion functions between the two types:

$$unwrap :: a \rightarrow b$$
$$wrap \quad :: b \rightarrow a$$

These conversion functions are required to satisfy the property that

$$fix \; (wrap \circ unwrap \circ f) \equiv fix \; f$$

and often satisfy the stronger property $wrap \circ unwrap \equiv id$. It is then valid to redefine the original program as follows (this is called *WW factorization*):

$$prog = wrap \; work$$

The definition of *work* can be derived in a number of ways [25]. Typically, we start from either $work = fix \; (unwrap \circ f \circ wrap)$ or $work = unwrap \; prog$, and then simplify the definition using any laws specific to the types a and b.

In practice, Haskell programs are typically defined using general recursion, rather than a fixed-point operator. Consequently, using the WW transformation often involves the following sequence of steps: introduce *fix*; perform WW factorization; eliminate *fix*. To factor out this repetition, we define an additional transformation that comprises the three steps, converting a generally recursive function into a non-recursive function that calls a recursive worker (we call this the *WW split*):

$$prog = expr \quad \Rightarrow \quad \begin{array}{l} prog = \textbf{let } f = \lambda prog \rightarrow expr \\ \quad \textbf{in let } work = unwrap \; (f \; (wrap \; work)) \\ \quad \textbf{in } wrap \; work \end{array}$$

3   HERMIT

This section briefly overviews the HERMIT toolkit; for more details consult [4].

3.1   GHC Core

GHC recently added support for custom compiler plugins that can be inserted amid GHC's optimization passes [5]. HERMIT uses this mechanism to provide a transformation system for GHC Core, GHC's internal intermediate language.

GHC Core is an implementation of System $F_C^\uparrow$ [26,29], which is System F [21] extended with let-bindings, constructors, type coercions and algebraic and polymorphic kinds. Figure 2 shows HERMIT's representation of GHC Core, omitting a few constructors that aren't used in this paper.

3.2   User Interface

HERMIT provides several interfaces at different levels of abstraction. In this paper we will use just one of those interfaces: a read-eval-print loop (REPL).

The REPL allows navigation over a GHC Core abstract syntax tree (AST), displaying the current sub-tree via a choice of pretty printers. The REPL provides a statically typed monomorphic functional language with overloading. Most commands construct a *rewrite* from AST to AST, and the result of executing such a command is the newly transformed AST. Historic versions of the AST are maintained, and it is possible to step back and forth through the history of ASTs, or create branches to explore alternative transformation sequences. That is, HERMIT provides a version-control tree, where each node of the tree is an AST. When the user has finished applying transformations, she selects one of the ASTs for GHC to compile, and the rest are discarded. We give an extended example using the REPL in Sect. 4.

3.3   Extendability

HERMIT is designed to facilitate the addition of new transformations. There are three methods of doing this: writing a script to combine existing transformations,

```
data ModGuts  = ModGuts { _ :: [CoreBind], ... }
data CoreBind = NonRec Var CoreExpr | Rec [CoreDef]
data CoreDef  = Def Var CoreExpr
data CoreExpr = Var Var | Lit Literal | Type Type
              | App CoreExpr CoreExpr | Lam Var CoreExpr
              | Let CoreBind CoreExpr  | Case CoreExpr Var Type [CoreAlt]
type CoreAlt  = (AltCon, [Var], CoreExpr)
```

Fig. 2. GHC Core.

leveraging the GHC RULES mechanism [20], or adding an internal primitive. We used all three methods extensively while mechanizing our examples.

Scripting is the least powerful method, as it can only construct transformations by sequencing HERMIT-shell commands. However, it does allow transformations to be named and abstracted, as scripts can be called by other scripts.

RULES allow Haskell source files to be annotated with directed rewrite rules. HERMIT exposes any such rules as rewrite commands, allowing the user to selectively apply them as desired. This provides a lightweight mechanism for adding transformations that cannot be expressed in terms of existing commands, albeit limited to those that can be expressed by RULES.

Adding an internal primitive is the most powerful method, and our experience has been that typically new transformations can be constructed fairly easily out of the large suite of low-level congruence combinators and strategic traversals provided by HERMIT and its underlying strategic-programming library, KURE (see [4,24]). The main drawback of this approach is that it requires additions to the HERMIT source code, and consequently recompilation of the package.

4   Example: Fibonacci Tupling

In this section we demonstrate the mechanization process in detail by performing TT on the Fibonacci function using the HERMIT REPL. Starting with the clear but inefficient (exponential time) definition over Peano naturals,

```
data Nat = Z | S Nat
fib            :: Nat → Nat
fib Z          = Z
fib (S Z)      = S Z
fib (S (S n))  = fib (S n) + fib n
```

we transform it into the following efficient (linear time) definition:

```
fib'  :: Nat → Nat
fib' n = fst (work n)
      where work :: Nat → (Nat, Nat)
            work Z     = (Z, S Z)
            work (S m) = let (x, y) = work m in (y, x + y)
```

As TT is an instance of WW, we will make use of our existing WW infrastructure. Following [25], we choose the more efficient data type to be a function that returns a tuple of consecutive Fibonacci numbers, and define *wrap* and *unwrap* as follows:

$$wrap \quad :: (Nat \rightarrow (Nat, Nat)) \rightarrow Nat \rightarrow Nat$$
$$wrap\ h = fst \circ h$$
$$unwrap :: (Nat \rightarrow Nat) \rightarrow Nat \rightarrow (Nat, Nat)$$
$$unwrap\ h\ n = (h\ n, h\ (\textsf{S}\ n))$$

Trivially, the *wrap* ∘ *unwrap* ≡ *id* precondition holds.

Placing the definitions of *fib*, *wrap* and *unwrap* into a file Fib.hs, we load the file into HERMIT, give some initialization commands (see Sect. 5.1), and zoom to the definition of *fib* using the `consider` command:

```
hermit "Fib.hs"
```
```
hermit> set-pp-expr-type Show ; flatten-module ; consider 'fib
```
```
fib = λ ds → case ds of wild
                 Z    → Z
                 S ds → case ds of wild
                          Z   → S Z
                          S n → (+) (fib (S n)) (fib n)
```

We can now see the GHC Core that has been generated.

The next step is to apply the WW split. We have written a script for this transformation (see Sect. 5.1), which we load and apply with the `load` command:

```
hermit> load "WWSplitTactic.hss"
```
```
fib = let f = λ fib ds → case ds of wild
                 Z    → Z
                 S ds → case ds of wild
                          Z   → S Z
                          S n → (+) (fib (S n)) (fib n)
          rec work = unwrap (f (wrap work))
      in wrap work
```

As we will need this definition of *work* later, we save it under the name *origwork* using the `remember` command:

```
hermit> consider 'work ; remember origwork
```
```
work = unwrap (f (wrap work))
```

We now need to η-expand the body of *work* so that we can unfold *unwrap*:

```
hermit> 0 ; eta-expand 'n
hermit> any-call (unfold 'unwrap)
```
```
λ n → (,) Nat Nat (f (wrap work) n) (f (wrap work) (S n))
```

There are several things to note here. Numbers designate a child node to descend into, with 0 designating the right-hand-side of the definition in this case (the sole child, as variables and literals are not considered to be children). `any-call` is a higher-order command that applies its argument everywhere it can succeed in the current sub-tree (we discuss this further in Sect. 5.4). Finally, the tuple constructor is polymorphic, and thus takes two type arguments (both *Nat* in this case).

Next we case-split on n to establish a base case for *work*:

```
hermit> 0 ; case-split-inline 'n

case n of n
  Z   → (,) Nat Nat (f (wrap work) Z) (f (wrap work) (S Z))
  S a → (,) Nat Nat (f (wrap work) (S a)) (f (wrap work) (S (S a)))
```

Now we selectively unfold f in three of the four places it is called[2]:

```
hermit> { 1 ; any-call (unfold 'f) }
hermit> { 2 ; 0 ; 1 ; any-call (unfold 'f) }
hermit> simplify

case n of n
  Z   → (,) Nat Nat Z (S Z)
  S a → (,) Nat Nat (f (wrap work) (S a))
                    ((+) (wrap work (S a)) (wrap work a))
```

We move into the second case alternative for the remainder of the derivation. In the second tuple component, we unfold the saved definition of *work*:

```
hermit> 2 ; 0 ; { 1 ; any-call (unfold origwork) }

(,) Nat Nat (f (wrap work) (S a))
            ((+) (wrap (unwrap (f (wrap work)))) (S a))
            (wrap (unwrap (f (wrap work))) a))
```

This creates an opportunity for fusing *wrap* and *unwrap* via the worker/wrapper precondition, which we encoded in the source file as a GHC RULES pragma:

```
{-# RULES  "precondition"  ∀ x.  wrap (unwrap x) = x #-}

hermit> any-call (unfold-rule precondition)

(,) Nat Nat (f (wrap work) (S a))
            ((+) (f (wrap work) (S a)) (f (wrap work) a))
```

Now the duplicated computation of f (*wrap work*) (S *a*) is evident. We name each *distinct* call to f by introducing let bindings, float the lets outside of the tuple, and then fold the duplicated computation of y:

---

[2] Curly braces denote scoping: within a scope it is impossible to navigate above the node at which the scope starts, and when the scope ends the cursor returns to the starting node.

```
hermit> { 1 ; 1 ; let-intro 'x }
hermit> { 0 ; 1 ; let-intro 'y }
hermit> innermost let-float
hermit> any-call (fold 'y)

let x = f (wrap work) a
    y = f (wrap work) (S a)
in (,) Nat Nat y ((+) y x)
```

These steps caused us to wish for better navigation capabilities for moving into case alternatives and tuples, as the use of numbers is unclear and brittle. We think that this will be especially problematic as examples grow in size.

We now combine x and y into a case-analyzed tuple,

```
hermit> let-tuple 'xy

case (,) Nat Nat (f (wrap work) a) (f (wrap work) (S a)) of xy
  (,) x y → (,) Nat Nat y ((+) y x)
```

thereby exposing the opportunity to fold *unwrap*:

```
hermit> any-call (fold 'unwrap)

case unwrap (f (wrap work)) a of xy
  (,) x y → (,) Nat Nat y ((+) y x)
```

All that remains is to fold our saved definition of *work*. This results in a definition with no calls to f, and no conversions via *wrap* and *unwrap*:

```
hermit> any-call (fold origwork)

case work a of xy
  (,) x y → (,) Nat Nat y ((+) y x)
```

Zooming out to see all of *fib*, we notice that f is now dead code. This would be removed by GHC's optimizer, but for presentation purposes we do so here. We also unfold the remaining call of *wrap*:

```
hermit> top ; consider 'fib
hermit> innermost dead-let-elimination
hermit> any-call (unfold 'wrap) ; simplify

fib = let rec work = λ n → case n of n
                              Z   → (,) Nat Nat Z (S Z)
                              S a → case work a of xy
                                      (,) x y → (,) Nat Nat y ((+) y x)
      in λ x → fst Nat Nat (work x)
```

We now have the efficient version of *fib*, and so tell GHC to resume compilation:

```
hermit> resume
```

5   User Experiences

In this section we discuss our experience using HERMIT to mechanize our suite of transformations. After selecting the three transformation techniques, we chose the following representative examples from the literature as our suite, and mechanized them using HERMIT:

- WW: CPS [7], Last [25], Reverse [4,7], Memoization [7], Unboxing [7,18]
- CV: Flatten [11,28], Quicksort [28], Reverse [11,28]
- Tupling: Fibonacci [1,2,25], Mean [9], Towers of Hanoi [3,16]

Our resulting scripts are bundled with the HERMIT package, and are summarized in Table 1. The Fibonacci script presented in Sect. 4 should provide the reader with a point of comparison.

5.1   Worker/Wrapper

WW was the first transformation that we mechanized. Introducing *fix*, the first step of WW, was not a transformation originally provided by HERMIT, nor was it definable in terms of other HERMIT commands. However, using the existing HERMIT infrastructure, it was straightforward to add a new rewrite for this task. Adding a rewrite to eliminate *fix* was unnecessary, as that can be achieved by using HERMIT's existing `unfold` command.

We chose to encode WW factorization using GHC RULES. Thus no modification to HERMIT was required, we just included the following pragma in the source code of each example, along with appropriate *wrap* and *unwrap* functions:

$$\{\text{-\# RULES \quad "ww" \quad} \forall f. \quad \textit{fix } f = \textit{wrap } (\textit{fix } (\textit{unwrap} \circ f \circ \textit{wrap})) \text{ \#-}\}$$

Table 1. HERMIT script sizes.

Script name	Number of HERMIT commands[a]				Scripts called
	Rewrites	Strategy combinators	Navigation	Total	
WWSplit	12	0	8	20	–
CPS	13	4	10	27	WWSplit
Last	10	1	8	19	WWSplit
Reverse	21	16	7	44	WWSplit
Memoisation	6	2	6	14	WWSplit
Unboxing	15	7	10	32	WWSplit
ConcatVanishes	23	8	5	36	–
Flatten	1	0	2	3	ConcatVanishes
Quicksort	3	1	2	6	ConcatVanishes
Reverse	1	0	2	3	ConcatVanishes
Fibonacci	21	12	21	54	WWSplit
Hanoi	34	21	36	91	WWSplit
Mean	19	5	27	51	–

[a] Rewriting commands are those that modify the syntax tree, navigation commands focus the cursor onto specific nodes, and strategy combinators modify rewrites to apply them in some systematic manner.

This use of GHC RULES works, but is clunky to use, being specific to each *wrap* and *unwrap*. We are currently working on creating a HERMIT command that takes *wrap* and *unwrap* functions as parameters, thereby avoiding the need to repeat this rule for every specific *wrap* and *unwrap*.

We encoded the WW split as a HERMIT script that calls WW factorization. That is, it assumes the existence of an appropriate ww rule in the source file. This is even more clunky, and we likewise intend to replace this script with a paramaterized HERMIT command.

HERMIT does not yet have a mechanism for checking preconditions, so it is up to the user to ensure that factorization is used only when the WW precondition holds. This is not ideal, and providing some mechanism within HERMIT for verifying pre-conditions, or at least for recording which pre-conditions have been assumed during the transformation, is an obvious next step in its development. Furthermore, as well as the danger of the HERMIT user incorrectly using a rule, it is also possible that the GHC optimizer may apply a rule (which is the intended purpose of GHC RULES after all). We addressed this using GHC's phase annotations, which allow the user to specify which optimization phases the rule is eligible to be applied in. Inconveniently, these annotations required at least one phase to be specified, but patching the GHC parser to accept zero phases was trivial. This patch will be included in the GHC 7.8 release.

Another issue is that, unlike in a Haskell source file, the top-level bindings are not treated as a mutually recursive group. During type checking (before generating GHC Core), a dependency analysis separates the bindings into minimal recursive groups and orders these groups by their dependencies [17, Sect. 6.2.8]. This can be problematic when applying GHC RULES, as some of the variables in the rule may not be in scope. To address this, we added a `flatten-module` rewrite that combines the top-level binding groups into a single recursive group, thereby ensuring that all variables that can appear in a rule will be in scope.

Other than these issues, we found mechanizing the WW examples to be straightforward uses of HERMIT's basic transformations and GHC RULES. A detailed walk-through of the Reverse example, in the spirit of Sect. 4, can be found in our earlier description of HERMIT [4].

We also encountered some unexpected behavior involving type-level universal quantification. GHC Core passes around type arguments explicitly; thus when a call is made to a polymorphic function, the type argument has to be provided. For example, the Core generated from *last* has the following type and structure:

$$last :: \forall \tau . [\tau] \rightarrow \tau$$
$$last = \Lambda \tau \rightarrow \lambda \ as \rightarrow ...last \ \tau ...$$

However, we discovered that if the type signature of a top-level polymorphic function is omitted in the source code, GHC generates different Core. Specifically, it performs the static-argument transformation [22], producing an outer non-recursive polymorphic function, and an inner recursive monomorphic function. That is, the type is fixed outside the recursion, avoiding the need to provide the type as an argument to each recursive call.

$$last :: \forall \tau . [\tau] \rightarrow \tau$$
$$last = \Lambda \tau \rightarrow \textbf{let } last :: [\tau] \rightarrow \tau$$
$$last = \lambda \ as \rightarrow ...last ...$$
$$\textbf{in } last$$

This difference, which is not noticeable at the level of Haskell source code, is significant enough to allow a GHC rule to fire in one case and not another. For example, WW factorization only fires for monomorphic functions, not polymorphic ones. In our opinion, HERMIT's ability to interactively display information on selected fragments of GHC Core was most helpful in understanding why the rule was not firing. Indeed, we believe that experimenting with and debugging GHC RULES is a potential application of the HERMIT system.

5.2 Concatenate Vanishes

Mechanizing CV proved straightforward. The main step can be expressed as WW factorization, so most of the transformation proceeded in the same manner as in Sect. 5.1. Mechanizing Flatten and Quicksort proved very similar to Reverse, with only a few differences in the basic rewrites required to simplify the resultant worker function. It was not necessary to add any new functionality to HERMIT.

Encouraged by the similarity of the three HERMIT scripts, we wrote a single generic script that works for all three examples, using HERMIT's higher-level commands. For this we did need to add a new command to HERMIT. The issue was that case-floating (taking a function applied to a case expression and applying it to each case alternative instead) is only valid if the function is strict:

f (**case** x **of**		**case** x **of**
$a_1 \rightarrow e_1$		$a_1 \rightarrow f \ e_1$
$a_2 \rightarrow e_2$	$\Rightarrow$	$a_2 \rightarrow f \ e_2$
...		...
$a_n \rightarrow e_n)$		$a_n \rightarrow f \ e_n$

As HERMIT lacks a mechanism for verifying preconditions (Sect. 5.1), it is the user's responsibility to ensure that case-floating is only applied to strict functions. This was fine when considering each example in isolation, as we explicitly stated when and where to float a case. But as this differed between examples, the usage in the generic script was potentially unsafe. To address this, we added a command that floats case (and let) expressions, but only past a specific function that it takes as a parameter. Again, adding this was straightforward.

Our generic CV script makes heavy use of GHC RULES, which encode the monoid laws for $((+\!\!+), [\,])$ and $((\circ), id)$, and a monoid homomorphism between them. We also used a rule to encode the fusion law relating the conversion functions between lists and difference lists [7]. This rule also has a precondition, and currently its usage in the generic script is unsafe in general (although in each specific example it is used safely). We are working on adding a rewrite to HERMIT that will allow us to restrict this rule to situations where the precondition is met, in a similar manner to the case-floating previously discussed.

Note that we do not claim that our generic script would work for any CV example; indeed we are quite confident it would not. Its purpose was just to test how well HERMIT copes with abstracting from multiple similar examples. HERMIT is designed as an interactive system where transformations are user-guided; we do not aim nor expect to be able to fully automate transformations in general. What we do aim for is to make HERMIT commands as robust as possible, in an effort to minimize the changes required if the source code changes, and more abstract commands help in this regard.

5.3   Tupling Transformations

The tupling examples motivated several new capabilities in HERMIT. Recall that in the Fibonacci example (Sect. 4) we established a base case for *work* by case-splitting on a variable. This functionality required us to create a new rewrite, `case-split-inline`,[3] that performs the following transformation (where $C_1..C_n$ are the constructor patterns of type T):

$$expr\,[\,x :: T\,] \quad \Rightarrow \quad
\begin{array}{l}
\textbf{case } x \textbf{ of} \\
\quad C_1 \;\rightarrow\; expr\,[\,C_1\,/\,x\,] \\
\quad C_2 \;\rightarrow\; expr\,[\,C_2\,/\,x\,] \\
\quad \ldots \\
\quad C_n \;\rightarrow\; expr\,[\,C_n\,/\,x\,]
\end{array}$$

This rewrite was straightforward to implement using capabilities provided by the HERMIT API. It exposes an issue, however, when dealing with primitive types. For example, the only constructor for the *Int* type is *I#*, which wraps a primitive unboxed integer, rendering case-splitting rather unproductive. One could imagine an alternative rewrite that accepts a literal value as the case to introduce, rather than enumerating the constructors. However, implementing this rewrite would require modifying the HERMIT REPL parser to parse Haskell values (or at the very least, Haskell literals), and so remains future work.

The tupling examples use the fold/unfold equational-reasoning technique [2]. When using fold/unfold, it is common to need access to *past* definitions of functions; a non-issue when working on paper (one simply looks up the page), but one that we needed to address. While the HERMIT kernel maintains a record of every version of the AST, we found it preferable to provide a command `remember` that explicitly saves a definition, rather than dig through the kernel's history. This also allows fold/unfold to be a lower-level notion that does not assume the existence of a version-control history, and means a definition can be saved and then applied within a single composite rewrite.

Our implementation of `fold` performs a straightforward structural comparison of two expressions, attempting to instantiate one in terms of the other, and thus is currently limited to folding syntactically α-equivalent expressions. This was the most challenging new rewrite to add because it traverses two ASTs in lockstep, and therefore cannot use much of the automation provided by KURE.

---

[3] There is also a `case-split` command, which does not inline x in the alternatives.

Exposing fold opportunities required a new rewrite `let-tuple` that combines the right-hand sides of multiple non-recursive let-bindings into a tuple, which is then scrutinized by a case statement to project out the original bindings:

$$
\begin{array}{l}
\textbf{let } v_1 = e_1 \\
\quad v_2 = e_2 \\
\quad ... \\
\quad v_n = e_n \\
\textbf{in } expr
\end{array}
\qquad \Rightarrow \qquad
\begin{array}{l}
\textbf{case } (e_1, e_2, ..., e_n) \textbf{ of} \\
\quad (v_1, v_2, ..., v_n) \rightarrow expr
\end{array}
$$

The only complication in encoding this rewrite was locating GHC's tuple constructor, as the name (,) is used at both the type and value level, and in GHC Core they share the same name space. There is also a more general need to improve name lookup, as currently the source code has to explicitly import constructors for them to be visible to HERMIT.

We found the Towers of Hanoi example to be substantially similar to the Fibonacci example, and it did not require any new capabilities beyond those we had already added. The Mean example on the other hand did require a handful of new transformations. However, these were simple local rewrites (such as let-floating) that had been omitted from HERMIT's suite of local transformations, and were straightforward to encode using KURE.

5.4 Observations on Inlining

Initially, it was unclear how best to provide function inlining. We found that the `inline` rewrite was in practice often followed by the general-purpose cleanup command `bash` [4]. Among other things, `bash` performs beta-reduction and inlining repeatedly, and thus was serving as a crude way of unfolding a definition. However, in some cases this was undesirably reducing the content of the inlined function or its arguments. Consider the following bindings:

$$
\begin{array}{l}
f = \lambda x \rightarrow (+) \; x \; 4 \\
e = f \; (g \; x)
\end{array}
$$

What should the result of inlining f in the right-hand-side of e be? After consideration, we settled on three distinct rewrites, summarized in Table 2.

Table 2. Inlining terminology and usage examples.

Terminology	Description	Example
To *inline*	To replace a value with its definition	$(\lambda x \rightarrow (+) \; x \; 4) \; (g \; x)$
To *apply*	To inline in the context of (zero or more) arguments, and perform beta-reduction (to let-binding) on *all* the arguments	**let** $x_n = g \; x$ **in** $(+) \; x_n \; 4$ (where n is unique)
To *unfold*	To apply, then *attempt* safe/cheap substitution on all the new let-bindings introduced by the application	$(+) \; (g \; x) \; 4$

Building on this decision, we found KURE's traversal combinators [4,24] insufficient for our needs: specifically, it was difficult to include as many arguments as possible when unfolding curried functions, while at the same time ensuring termination of unfolding. This is not an issue with `inline`, only `apply` and `unfold`. To address this, we invented a traversal strategy to support `apply` and `unfold` called `any-call`, which visits nodes in an order that maximizes the number of arguments provided to an inlined function, as well as traversing any arguments before performing the apply/unfold. We have used `any-call` in our examples, as it is now our standard traversal combinator for working with apply and unfold.

When inlining case wildcard binders, there is a choice between using either the case scrutinee, or the pattern matched by the current case alternative. For example, consider the following situation:

> **case** *expr* **of** *wild*
>   *pat* → ... *wild* ...

If we inline *wild* on the right-hand-side of the case alternative, should we replace it with *expr* or *pat*? HERMIT initially did the former, but in practice we found that we usually wanted the latter. We thus modified the `inline` rewrite accordingly, and added a rewrite `inline-scrutinee` to provide the old behavior.

6   Related Work

There are several refactoring tools for Haskell programs, including the Haskell Refactorer (HaRe) [14], the Programming Assistant for Transforming Haskell (PATH) [27], the Ulm Transformation System (Ultra) [8], and the Haskell Equational Reasoning Assistant (HERA) [6]. The key distinction of HERMIT from these systems is that they operate on Haskell source code, or some variant thereof, whereas HERMIT operates on GHC Core, midway through the compilation process. The principal advantage of this approach is that GHC Core is a small language, having stripped away all of Haskell's syntactic sugar. This makes HERMIT simpler to use, implement and maintain, as there are far fewer cases to consider. Other advantages are that this automatically supports GHC language extensions, as GHC compiles them to GHC Core, and that inserting HERMIT inside the GHC optimization pipeline allows transformations to be intermixed with GHC's optimization passes. However, a disadvantage is that HERMIT cannot output Haskell source code.

More generally, there are a wide variety of refactoring tools for other languages. However, unlike HERMIT, most do not support higher-order commands and the scripting of composite refactorings [12]. One exception is Wrangler [13], a refactoring tool for Erlang, which has recently added such support [12].

One can also use proof assistants such as Coq or Agda to mechanize program transformations interactively. However, this requires modeling the syntax and semantics of the object language, encoding the program in that model, and then, after transformation, transliterating the result back into the object language before it can be compiled and executed. Even were we to ignore GHC language extensions, or consider only a limited subset of Haskell 98, the presence of partial values and lazy semantics mean we cannot simply define our programs directly in the total languages provided by such proof assistants, but instead have to model Haskell's domain-theoretic setting of continuous functions over pointed ω-complete partial orders [23]. We emphasize that one of the aims of the HERMIT project is to make transforming Haskell programs easy for the user: we do not want familiarity with domain theory and proof assistants to be prerequisites.

7   Conclusions and Future Work

Our experience thus far has been that it is viable to mechanize basic program transformations, and that performing the transformations in HERMIT is no more complicated than on paper. However, while encoding our examples we repeatedly found it necessary to add additional transformations, and higher-level transformation strategies. This is unsurprising, as the HERMIT system is still in an early stage of development. What remains to be seen is whether, as we try more complex examples, we continue to need to add new transformations, or whether those we have now will scale. In general, we found adding new transformations to HERMIT to be a fairly simple procedure, whether by building them from HERMIT's existing low-level transformations, or by using GHC RULES. More challenging has been verifying the correctness of these transformations, and debugging our HERMIT programs when they fail to do as we expect.

Working within GHC has proved convenient. GHC Core has already been type checked before HERMIT acts on it, making all type information available. Much implementation effort was saved by using existing GHC functions such as substitution and variable de-shadowing, and safety checks such as the Core Lint pass [19], which ensures that the resultant code is type-correct and well-scoped.

More work is now needed. We have mechanized a collection of small examples as a proof of concept, but we need to try transforming larger real-world programs.

Acknowledgements. We thank Ed Komp for his work on implementing the HERMIT system, Jason Reich for suggesting the Mean example, and the anonymous reviewers for their constructive comments and feedback. This material is based upon work supported by the National Science Foundation under Grant No. 1117569.

References

1. Bird, R.S.: Tabulation techniques for recursive programs. ACM Comput.Surv. **12**(4), 403–417 (1980)
2. Burstall, R.M., Darlington, J.: A transformation system for developing recursive programs. J. ACM **24**(1), 44–67 (1977)
3. Chin, W.N., Khoo, S.C., Jones, N.: Redundant call elimination via tupling. Fundam. Informaticae **69**(1–2), 1–37 (2006)
4. Farmer, A., Gill, A., Komp, E., Sculthorpe, N.: The HERMIT in the machine: a plugin for the interactive transformation of GHC core language programs. In: 2012 ACM SIGPLAN Haskell Symposium, pp. 1–12. ACM, New York (2012)

5. GHC Team: The Glorious Glasgow Haskell Compilation System User's Guide, Version 7.6.2. http://www.haskell.org/ghc (2013)
6. Gill, A.: Introducing the Haskell equational reasoning assistant. In: 2006 ACM SIGPLAN Haskell Workshop, pp. 108–109. ACM, New York (2006)
7. Gill, A., Hutton, G.: The worker/wrapper transformation. J. Funct. Program. **19**(2), 227–251 (2009)
8. Guttmann, W., Partsch, H., Schulte, W., Vullinghs, T.: Tool support for the interactive derivation of formally correct functional programs. J. Univ. Comput. Sci. **9**(2), 173–188 (2003)
9. Hu, Z., Iwasaki, H., Takeichi, M., Takano, A.: Tupling calculation eliminates multiple data traversals. In: 2nd ACM SIGPLAN International Conference on Functional Programming, pp. 164–175. ACM, New York (1997)
10. Hughes, R.J.M.: A novel representation of lists and its application to the function "reverse". Inf. Process. Lett. **22**(3), 141–144 (1986)
11. Hutton, G.: Programming in Haskell. Cambridge University Press, Cambridge (2007)
12. Li, H., Thompson, S.: A domain-specific language for scripting refactoring in Erlang. In: de Lara, J., Zisman, A. (eds.) FASE 2012. LNCS, vol. 7212, pp. 501–515. Springer, Heidelberg (2012)
13. Li, H., Thompson, S., Orosz, G., Tóth, M.: Refactoring with wrangler, updated: data and process refactorings, and integration with eclipse. In: 7th ACM SIGPLAN Erlang Workshop, pp. 61–72. ACM, New York (2008)
14. Li, H., Thompson, S., Reinke, C.: The Haskell refactorer, HaRe, and its API. Electron. Notes Theor. Comput. Sci. **141**(4), 29–34 (2005)
15. Liu, Y.A., Stoller, S.D.: Dynamic programming via static incrementalization. Higher-Order Symbolic Comput. **16**(1–2), 37–62 (2003)
16. Pettorossi, A.: A powerful strategy for deriving efficient programs by transformation. In: 1984 ACM Symposium on LISP and Functional Programming, pp. 273–281. ACM, New York (1984)
17. Peyton Jones, S.: The Implementation of Functional Programming Languages. Prentice Hall, New York (1987)
18. Peyton Jones, S.L., Launchbury, J.: Unboxed values as first class citizens in a non-strict functional language. In: 5th ACM Conference on Functional Programming Languages and Computer Architecture, pp. 636–666. Springer, Heidelberg (1991)
19. Jones Peyton, S., Santos, A.L.M.: A transformation-based optimiser or Haskell. Sci. Comput. Program. **32**(1–3), 3–47 (1998)
20. Peyton Jones, S., Tolmach, A., Hoare, T.: Playing by the rules: rewriting as a practical optimisation technique in GHC. In: 2001 ACM SIGPLAN Haskell Workshop, pp. 203–233. ACM, New York (2001)
21. Pierce, B.C.: Types and Programming Languages. MIT Press, Cambridge (2002)
22. Santos, A.: Compilation by transformation in non-strict functional languages. Ph.D. thesis, University of Glasgow (1995)
23. Schmidt, D.A.: Denotational Semantics: A Methodology for Language Development. Allyn and Bacon, Newton (1986)
24. Sculthorpe, N., Frisby, N., Gill, A.: KURE: A Haskell-embedded strategic programming language with custom closed universes (in preparation)
25. Sculthorpe, N., Hutton, G.: Work it, wrap it, fix it, fold it (in preparation)
26. Sulzmann, M., Chakravarty, M.M.T., Peyton Jones, S., Donnelly, K.: System F with type equality coercions. In: 3rd ACM SIGPLAN Workshop on Types in Language Design and Implementaion, pp. 53–66. ACM, New York (2007)

27. Tullsen, M.: PATH, a program transformation system for Haskell. Ph.D. thesis, Yale University (2002)
28. Wadler, P.: The concatenate vanishes. University of Glasgow, Tech. rep. (1989)
29. Yorgey, B.A., Weirich, S., Cretin, J., Peyton Jones, S., Vytiniotis, D., Magalhães, J.P.: Giving Haskell a promotion. In: 7th ACM SIGPLAN Workshop on Types in Language Design and Implementation, pp. 53–66. ACM, New York (2012)

Optimisation of Generic Programs Through Inlining

José Pedro Magalhães[(✉)]

Department of Computer Science, University of Oxford, Oxford, UK
jpm@cs.ox.ac.uk

Abstract. It is known that datatype-generic programs often run slower than type-specific variants, and this factor can prevent adoption of generic programming altogether. There can be multiple reasons for the performance penalty, but often it is caused by conversions to and from representation types that do not get eliminated during compilation. However, it is also known that generic functions can be specialised to specific datatypes, removing any overhead from the use of generic programming. In this paper, we investigate compilation techniques to specialise generic functions and remove the performance overhead of generic programs in Haskell. We pick a representative generic programming library and look at the generated code for a number of example generic functions. After understanding the necessary compiler optimisations for producing efficient generic code, we benchmark the runtime of our generic functions against handwritten variants, and conclude that the overhead can indeed be removed automatically by the compiler.

1 Introduction

Datatype-generic programming is a form of abstraction that allows defining functions that operate on every suitable datatype. Generic programs operate on the general structure of datatypes, therefore remaining agnostic of the individual detail of each datatype. Examples of behaviour that can be defined generically are (de)serialisation, equality testing, and traversing data. It is convenient to define such functions generically because less code has to be written, and this code has to be adapted less often. However, generic programs operate on the underlying structure of datatypes, and not on datatypes themselves directly. This indirection often causes a runtime penalty, as conversions to and from the generic representation are not always optimised away.

The performance of generic programs has been analysed before. Rodriguez Yakushev et al. [14] present a detailed comparison of nine libraries for generic programming in Haskell, with a brief performance analysis. This analysis indicates that the use of a generic approach could result in an increase of the running time by a factor of as much as 80. Van Noort et al. [10] also report

This work has been funded by EPSRC grant number EP/J010995/1. We thank the anonymous reviewers for the helpful feedback.

R. Hinze (Ed.): IFL 2012, LNCS 8241, pp. 104–121, 2013.
DOI: 10.1007/978-3-642-41582-1_7, © Springer-Verlag Berlin Heidelberg 2013

severe performance degradation when comparing a generic approach to a similar but type-specific variant. While this is typically not a problem for smaller examples, it can severely impair adoption of generic programming in larger contexts. This problem is particularly relevant because generic programming techniques are especially applicable to large applications where performance is crucial, such as structure editors or compilers.

To understand the source of performance degradation when using a generic function from a particular generic programming library, we have to analyse the implementation of the library. The fundamental idea behind generic programming is to represent all datatypes by a small set of representation types. Equipped with conversion functions between user datatypes and their representation, we can define functions on the representation types, which are then applicable to all user types via the conversion functions. While these conversion functions are typically trivial and can be automatically generated, the overhead they impose is not automatically removed. In general, conversions to and from the generic representations are not eliminated by compilation, and are performed at run-time. These conversions are the main source of inefficiency for generic programming libraries. In the earlier implementations of generic programming as code generators or preprocessors [4], optimisations (such as automatic generation of type-specialised variants of generic functions) could be implemented externally. Modern implementations of generic programming are libraries, removing the need for cumbersome work on parsing and type checking, for instance. With the switch to library approaches, however, all optimisations have to be performed by the compiler.

The Glasgow Haskell Compiler (GHC, the main Haskell compiler) compiles a program by first converting the input into a core language and then transforming the core code into more optimised versions, in a series of sequential passes. While it performs a wide range of optimisations, with the default settings it seems to be unable to remove the overhead incurred by using generic representations. Therefore generic libraries perform worse than handwritten type-specific counterparts. Alimarine and Smetsers [1,2] show that in many cases it is possible to remove all overhead by performing a specific form of symbolic evaluation in the Clean compiler. In fact, their approach is not restricted to optimising generics, and GHC performs symbolic evaluation as part of its optimisations. Our goal is to convince GHC to optimise generic functions so as to achieve the same performance as handwritten code, without requiring any additional manipulation of the compiler internals.

We have investigated this problem before [8], and concluded that tweaking GHC optimisation flags can achieve significant speedups. The problem with using compiler flags is that these apply to the entire program being compiled, and while certain flags might have a good effect on generic functions, they might adversely affect performance (or code size) of other parts of the program. In this paper we take a more fine-grained approach to the problem, looking at how to localise our performance annotations to the generic code only, by means of rewrite rules and function pragmas.[1] In this way we can improve the performance of generic functions with minimal impact on the rest of the program.

We continue this paper by defining two representative generic functions which we focus our optimisation efforts on (Sect. 2). We then see how these functions can be optimised manually (Sect. 3), and transfer the necessary optimisation techniques to the compiler (Sect. 4). We confirm that our optimisations result in better runtime performance of generic programs in a benchmark in Sect. 5, and conclude in Sect. 6.

2   Example Generic Functions

For analysing the performance of generic programs we choose the `generic-deriving` library, now integrated in GHC. Due to space considerations we can only provide the (simplified) interface of this library:

data U_1 $\rho = U_1$	**class** $Generic\ \alpha$ **where**
data $K_1\ \alpha$ $\rho = K_1\ \alpha$	**type** $Rep\ \alpha :: \star \to \star$
data $(\alpha :+: \beta)\ \rho = L_1\ (\alpha\ \rho)\ \|\ R_1\ (\beta\ \rho)$	to :: $Rep\ \alpha\ \rho \to \alpha$
data $(\alpha :\times: \beta)\ \rho = \alpha\ \rho :\times: \beta\ \rho$	$from$ :: $\alpha \to Rep\ \alpha\ \rho$

U_1 encodes constructors without arguments. $K_1\ \alpha\ \rho$ encodes recursion into some datatype α. Finally, $(:+:)$ encodes choice between constructors, and $(:\times:)$ is used for constructors with multiple arguments. The parameter ρ, present in all the representation types, is not used by our example generic functions and can be safely ignored. The type class $Generic$ encodes the conversion between a datatype α and its representation $Rep\ \alpha$, witnessed by the conversion functions to and $from$. The reader is referred to Magalhães [7] for a full description of `generic-deriving`.

We present two generic functions that will be the focus of our attention: equality and enumeration. These are chosen as representative examples; equality is a generic consumer, taking generic values as input, and enumeration is a generic producer, since it generates generic values. Equality is a relatively simple, standard example, while enumeration requires the use of auxiliary (non-generic) functions.

2.1   Generic Equality

A notion of structural equality can easily be defined as a generic function. We first define a class for equality on the representation types:

class $GEqRep\ \phi$ **where**
$geqRep :: \phi\ \alpha \to \phi\ \alpha \to Bool$

---

[1] http://www.haskell.org/ghc/docs/7.4.1/html/users_guide/pragmas.html

We can now give instances for each of the representation types:

> **instance** *GEqRep* U_1 **where**
>   *geqRep* _ _ = *True*
> **instance** (*GEqRep* α, *GEqRep* β) $\Rightarrow$ *GEqRep* (α :+: β) **where**
>   *geqRep* (L_1 x) (L_1 y) = *geqRep* x y
>   *geqRep* (R_1 x) (R_1 y) = *geqRep* x y
>   *geqRep* _   _   = *False*
> **instance** (*GEqRep* α, *GEqRep* β) $\Rightarrow$ *GEqRep* (α :×: β) **where**
>   *geqRep* (x_1 :×: y_1) (x_2 :×: y_2) = *geqRep* x_1 x_2 $\wedge$ *geqRep* y_1 y_2

Units are trivially equal. For sums we continue the comparison recursively if both values are either on the left or on the right, and return *False* otherwise. Products are equal if both components are equal.

For recursive occurrences we fall back to a user-facing *GEq* class:

> **instance** (*GEq* γ) $\Rightarrow$ *GEqRep* (K_1 γ) **where**
>   *geqRep* (K_1 a) (K_1 b) = *geq* a b

This user-facing class is similar to *GEqRep*, but is used for user datatypes, and comes with a generic default method:

> **class** *GEq* α **where**
>   *geq* :: $\alpha \rightarrow \alpha \rightarrow$ *Bool*
>   **default** *geq* :: (*Generic* α, *GEqRep* (*Rep* α)) $\Rightarrow \alpha \rightarrow \alpha \rightarrow$ *Bool*
>   *geq* x y = *geqRep* (*from* x) (*from* y)

This class is similar to the Prelude *Eq* class, but we have left out inequality for simplicity. The generic default simply calls *from* on the arguments, and then proceeds using the generic equality function *geqRep*.

Adhoc instances for base types can reuse the Prelude implementation:

> **instance** *GEq* *Int* **where**
>   *geq* = ($\equiv$)

User datatypes, such as lists, can use the generic default:

> **instance** (*GEq* α) $\Rightarrow$ *GEq* [α]

2.2 Generic Enumeration

We now define a function that enumerates all possible values of a datatype. For infinite datatypes we have to make sure that every possible value will eventually be produced. For instance, if we are enumerating integers, we should not first enumerate all positive numbers, and then the negatives. Instead, we should interleave positive and negative numbers.

We enumerate values by listing them with the standard list type. There is only one unit to enumerate, and for datatype occurrences we refer to a user-facing $GEnum$ class:

```
class GEnumRep φ where
  genumRep :: [ φ α ]
```

```
instance GEnumRep U₁ where
  genumRep = [ U₁ ]
instance (GEnum α) ⇒ GEnumRep (K₁ α) where
  genumRep = map K₁ genum
```

The more interesting cases are those for sums and products. For sums we enumerate both alternatives, but interleave them with a ($|||$) operator:

```
instance (GEnumRep α, GEnumRep β) ⇒ GEnumRep (α :+: β) where
  genumRep = map L₁ genumRep ||| map R₁ genumRep
```

```
infixr 5 |||
(|||) :: [ α ] → [ α ] → [ α ]
```

For products we generate all possible combinations of the two arguments, and diagonalise the result matrix, ensuring that all elements from each sublist will eventually be included, even if the lists are infinite:

```
instance (GEnumRep α, GEnumRep β) ⇒ GEnumRep (α :×: β) where
  genumRep = diag(map (λx → map (λy → x :×: y) genumRep) genumRep)
```

```
diag :: [ [ α ] ] → [ α ]
```

We omit the implementation details of ($|||$) and $diag$ as they are not important; it only matters that we have some form of fair interleaving and diagonalisation operations. The presence of ($|||$) and $diag$ throughout the generic function definition makes enumeration more complicated than equality, since equality does not make use of any auxiliary functions. We will see in Sect. 4.3 how this complicates the specialisation process. Note also that we do not use the more natural list comprehension syntax for defining the product instance, again to simplify the analysis of the optimisation process.

Finally, we define the user-facing class, with a default implementation:

```
class GEnum α where
  genum :: [α]
  default genum :: (Generic α, GEnumRep (Rep α)) ⇒ [α]
  genum = map to genumRep
```

3   Specialisation, by Hand

We now focus on the problem of specialisation of generic functions. By specialisation we mean removing the use of generic conversion functions and representation types, replacing them by constructors of the original datatype. To convince
ourselves that this task is possible, we first develop a hand-written derivation of
specialisation by equational reasoning. For simplicity we ignore implementation
mechanisms such as the use of type classes and type families, and focus first on
a very simple datatype encoding natural numbers:

```
data Nat = Ze | Su Nat
```

We give the representation of naturals with standard Haskell datatypes using a
type synonym:

```
type RepNat = Either () Nat
```

We use a shallow representation (with *Nat* at the leaves, and not *RepNat*), remaining faithful with `generic-deriving`. We also need a way to convert between
RepNat and *Nat*:

```
toNat :: RepNat → Nat
toNat    n = case n of { Left () → Ze; Right n → Su n; }
fromNat :: Nat → RepNat
fromNat n = case n of { Ze → Left (); Su n → Right n; }
```

We now analyse the specialisation of generic equality and enumeration on this
datatype.

3.1   Generic Equality

We consider two versions of an equality function. The first is a handwritten,
type-specific definition of equality for *Nat*:

```
eqNat :: Nat → Nat → Bool
eqNat m n = case (m , n) of
              (Ze  , Ze ) → True
              (Su m , Su n) → eqNat m n
              ( _  , _ ) → False
```

The second is generic equality on *Nat* through *RepNat*, for which we need equality on units and sums:

$eqU :: () \to () \to Bool$
$eqU\ x\ y = \textbf{case}\ (x\ ,\ y)\ \textbf{of}\ \{((),\ ()) \to True;\ \}$
$eqPlus :: (\alpha \to \alpha \to Bool) \to (\beta \to \beta \to Bool) \to Either\ \alpha\ \beta \to Either\ \alpha\ \beta \to Bool$
$eqPlus\ ea\ eb\ a\ b = \textbf{case}\ (a\ ,\ b)\ \textbf{of}$
$\qquad\qquad\qquad\qquad (Left\quad x\ ,\ Left\quad y) \to ea\ x\ y$
$\qquad\qquad\qquad\qquad (Right\ x\ ,\ Right\ y) \to eb\ x\ y$
$\qquad\qquad\qquad\qquad (\quad\_\quad\ ,\quad\_\quad\ ) \to False$

Now we can define equality for *RepNat*, and generic equality for *Nat* through conversion to *RepNat*:

$eqRepNat :: RepNat \to RepNat \to Bool$
$eqRepNat = eqPlus\ eqU\ eqNatFromRep$

$eqNatFromRep :: Nat \to Nat \to Bool$
$eqNatFromRep\ m\ n = eqRepNat\ (fromNat\ m)\ (fromNat\ n)$

Our goal now is to show that *eqNatFromRep* is equivalent to *eqNat*. In the following derivation, we start with the definition of *eqNatFromRep*, and end with the definition of *eqNat*:

$\quad eqRepNat\ (fromNat\ m)\ (fromNat\ n)$

$\equiv\langle$ inline *eqRepNat* and *eqPlus* $\rangle$

$\quad \textbf{case}\ (fromNat\ m\ ,\ fromNat\ n)\ \textbf{of}$
$\quad\quad (Left\quad x\ ,\ Left\quad y) \to eqU\ x\ y$
$\quad\quad (Right\ x\ ,\ Right\ y) \to eqNatFromRep\ x\ y$
$\quad\quad \_\qquad\qquad\qquad\quad \to False$

$\equiv\langle$ inline *fromNat* $\rangle$

$\quad \textbf{case}\ (\ \ \textbf{case}\ m\ \textbf{of}\ \{\ Ze \to Left\ ();\ Su\ x_1 \to Right\ x_1\ \}$
$\quad\quad\quad\ ,\ \textbf{case}\ n\ \ \textbf{of}\ \{\ Ze \to Left\ ();\ Su\ x_2 \to Right\ x_2\ \})\ \textbf{of}$
$\quad\quad (Left\quad x\ ,\ Left\quad y) \to eqU\ x\ y$
$\quad\quad (Right\ x\ ,\ Right\ y) \to eqNatFromRep\ x\ y$
$\quad\quad \_\qquad\qquad\qquad\quad \to False$

$\equiv\langle$ case-of-case transform $\rangle$

$\quad \textbf{case}\ (m\ ,\ n)\ \textbf{of}$
$\quad\quad (Ze\quad\ ,\ Ze\quad\ ) \to eqU\ ()\ ()$
$\quad\quad (Su\ x_1\ ,\ Su\ x_2) \to eqNatFromRep\ x_1\ x_2$
$\quad\quad \_\qquad\qquad\qquad \to False$

$\equiv\langle$ inline eqU and case-of-constant $\rangle$

case $(m \; , \; n)$ **of**
$\quad (Ze \quad , \; Ze \quad) \rightarrow True$
$\quad (Su \; x_1 \; , \; Su \; x_2) \rightarrow eqNatFromRep \; x_1 \; x_2$
$\quad \quad \_ \quad \quad \quad \quad \quad \rightarrow False$

This shows that the generic implementation is equivalent to the type-specific variant, and that it can be optimised to remove all conversions. We discuss the techniques used in this derivation in more detail in Sect. 4.1, after showing the optimisation of generic enumeration.

3.2 Generic Enumeration

A type-specific enumeration function for Nat follows:

$enumNat :: [\, Nat \,]$
$enumNat = [\, Ze \,] \; ||| \; map \; Su \; enumNat$

To get an enumeration for $RepNat$ we first need to know how to enumerate units and sums:

$enumU :: [\, () \,]$
$enumU = [\, () \,]$
$enumPlus :: [\, \alpha \,] \rightarrow [\, \beta \,] \rightarrow [\, Either \; \alpha \; \beta \,]$
$enumPlus \; ea \; eb = map \; Left \; ea \; ||| \; map \; Right \; eb$

Now we can define an enumeration for $RepNat$:

$enumRepNat :: [\, RepNat \,]$
$enumRepNat = enumPlus \; enumU \; enumNatFromRep$

With the conversion function $toNat$, we can use $enumRepNat$ to get a generic enumeration function for Nat:

$enumNatFromRep :: [\, Nat \,]$
$enumNatFromRep = map \; toNat \; enumRepNat$

We now show that $enumNatFromRep$ and $enumNat$ are equivalent[2]:

---

[2] Given that these are recursive structures, we have to be careful to preserve correctness over the whole proof, even if each step is clearly correct [15]. None of the steps in the proof changes the productivity of the entire expression, so we are confident of its overall correctness.

$map\ toNat\ enumRepNat$

$\equiv\langle$ inline $enumRepNat$ and $enumPlus$ $\rangle$

$map\ toNat\ (map\ Left\ enumU\ |||\ map\ Right\ enumNatFromRep)$

$\equiv\langle$ inline $enumU$ and map $\rangle$

$map\ toNat\ ([\,Left\ ()\,]\ |||\ map\ Right\ enumNatFromRep)$

$\equiv\langle$ free theorem $(|||) : \forall f\ a\ b.map\ f\ (a\ |||\ b) = map\ f\ a\ |||\ map\ f\ b$ $\rangle$

$map\ toNat\ [\,Left\ ()\,]\ |||\ map\ toNat\ (map\ Right\ enumNatFromRep)$

$\equiv\langle$ inline map and $toNat$, case-of-constant $\rangle$

$[\,Ze\,]\ |||\ map\ toNat\ (map\ Right\ enumNatFromRep)$

$\equiv\langle$ functor composition law: $\forall f\ g\ l.map\ f\ (map\ g\ l) = map\ (f \circ g)\ l$ $\rangle$

$[\,Ze\,]\ |||\ map\ (toNat \circ Right)\ enumNatFromRep$

$\equiv\langle$ inline $toNat$ and case-of-constant $\rangle$

$[\,Ze\,]\ |||\ map\ Su\ enumNatFromRep$

Like equality, generic enumeration can also be specialised to a type-specific variant without any overhead.

4   Specialisation, by the Compiler

After the manual specialisation of generic functions, let us now analyse how to convince the compiler to automatically perform the specialisation.

4.1   Optimisation Techniques

Our calculations in Sect. 3 rely on a number of lemmas and techniques that the compiler will have to use. We review them here:

Inlining. Inlining replaces a function call with its definition. It is a crucial optimisation technique because it can expose other optimisations. However, inlining causes code duplication, and care has to be taken to avoid non-termination through infinite inlining.

GHC uses a number of heuristics to decide when to inline a function or not, and loop breakers for preventing infinite inlining [11]. The programmer can provide explicit inlining annotations with the *INLINE* and *NOINLINE* pragmas, of the form:

$\{-\#\ INLINE\ [n]\ f\ \#-\}$

In this pragma, f is the function to be inlined, and n is a phase number. GHC performs a number of optimisation phases on a program, numbered in decreasing order until zero. Setting n to 1, for instance, means "be keen to inline f in phase 1 and after". For a *NOINLINE* pragma, this means "do not inline f in phase 1 or after". The phase can be left out, in which case the pragma applies to all phases.[3]

Application of free theorems and functor laws. Free theorems [16] are theorems that arise from the type of a polymorphic function, regardless of the function's definition. Each polymorphic function is associated with a free theorem, and functions with the same type share the same theorem. The functor laws arise from the categorical nature of functors. Every *Functor* instance in Haskell should obey the functor laws.

GHC does not compute and use the free theorem of each polymorphic function, in particular because it may not be clear which direction of the theorem is useful for optimisation purposes. However, we can add special optimisation rules to GHC via a *RULES* pragma [13]. For instance, the rewrite rule corresponding to the free theorem of (|||) follows:

$$\{-\# \; RULES \; \texttt{"ft/|||"} \; \forall f \; a \; b. \; map \; f \; (a \; ||| \; b) = map \; f \; a \; ||| \; map \; f \; b \; \#-\}$$

This pragma introduces a rule named "ft/|||" telling GHC to replace occurrences of the application $map\,f\,(a\,|||\,b)$ with $map\,f\,a\,|||\,map\,f\,b$. GHC does not perform any confluence checking on rewrite rules, so the programmer should ensure confluence or GHC might loop during compilation.

Optimisation of case statements. Case statements drive evaluation in GHC's core language, and give rise to many possible optimisations. Peyton Jones and Santos [12] provide a detailed account of these; in our derivation in Sect. 3.2 we used a "case of constant" rule to optimise a statement of the form:

case $(Left \; ())$ **of** $\{ \; Left \; () \; \rightarrow \; Ze; \; Right \; n \; \rightarrow \; Su \; n; \; \}$

Since we know what we are case-analysing, we can replace this case statement by the much simpler expression Ze. Similarly, in Sect. 3.1 we used a case-of-case transform to eliminate an inner case statement. Consider an expression of the form:

case (**case** x **of** $\{ \; p_1 \; \rightarrow \; e_2; \; \}$) **of** $\{ \; p_2 \; \rightarrow \; e_3; \; \}$

Here, p_1 and p_2 are patterns, e_2 and e_3 are expressions, and e_2 matches p_2. Taking care to avoid variable capture, we can often simplify this to:

case x **of** $\{ \; p_1 \; \rightarrow \; e_3; \; \}$

This rule naturally generalises to case statements with multiple branches.

---

[3] See the GHC User's Guide for more details: http://www.haskell.org/ghc/docs/7.4.1/ html/users_guide/pragmas.html.

4.2   Generic Equality

We have seen that we have a good number of tools at our disposal for directing the optimisation process in GHC: inline pragmas, rewrite rules, phase distinction, and all the standard optimisations for the functional core language. We will now annotate our generic functions and evaluate the quality of the core code generated by GHC.

We start by defining a *Generic* instance for the *Nat* type:

> **instance** *Generic Nat* **where**
> **type** *Rep Nat* = U_1 :+: K_1 *Nat*
>
> {−# *INLINE* [1] *to* #−}
> *to* (L_1 U_1)   = *Ze*
> *to* (R_1 (K_1 *n*)) = *Su n*
>
> {−# *INLINE* [1] *from* #−}
> *from Ze*   = L_1 U_1
> *from* (*Su n*) = R_1 (K_1 *n*)

We give inline pragmas for *to* and *from* to guarantee that these functions will be inlined. However, we ask the inliner to only inline them on phase 1 and after; this is to ensure that we first inline the generic function definitions, simplify those, and then inline the conversion functions and simplify again.

We can now provide a generic definition of equality for *Nat*:

> **instance** *GEq Nat*

Compiling this code with the standard optimisation flag -O gives us the following core code:

> $\$GEqNat_{geq}$ :: *Nat* → *Nat* → *Bool*
> $\$GEqNat_{geq}$ = λ(*x* :: *Nat*) (*y* :: *Nat*) →
>   **case** *x* **of**
>   *Ze* → **case** *y* **of** { *Ze* → *True*; *Su m* → *False*; }
>   *Su m* → **case** *y* **of** { *Ze* → *False*; *Su n* → $\$GEqNat_{geq}$ *m n*; }

The core language is a small, explicitly typed language in the style of System F [17]. The function $\$GEqNat_{geq}$ is prefixed with a $ because it was generated by the compiler, representing the *geq* method of the *GEq* instance for *Nat*. We can see that the generic representation was completely removed.

The same happens for lists, as evidenced by the generated core code:

$$\$GEq[]_{geq} :: \forall \alpha. GEq\ \alpha \Rightarrow [\alpha] \rightarrow [\alpha] \rightarrow Bool$$
$$\$GEq[]_{geq} = \lambda \alpha\ (eqA :: GEq\ \alpha)\ (l_1 :: [\alpha])\ (l_2 :: [\alpha]) \rightarrow$$
$$\textbf{case}\ l_1\ \textbf{of}$$
$$[] \qquad \rightarrow \textbf{case}\ l_2\ \textbf{of}\ \{[] \rightarrow True; (h:t) \rightarrow False;\ \}$$
$$(h_1 : t_1) \rightarrow \textbf{case}\ l_2\ \textbf{of}$$
$$[] \qquad \rightarrow False$$
$$(h_2 : t_2) \rightarrow \textbf{case}\ eqA\ h_1\ h_2\ \textbf{of}$$
$$False \rightarrow False$$
$$True \rightarrow \$GEq[]_{geq}\ \alpha\ eqA\ t_1\ t_2$$

Note that type abstraction and application is explicit in core. There is syntax to distinguish type and value application and abstraction from each other, but we suppress the distinction since it is clear from the use of Greek letters for type variables. Note also that constraints (to the left of the $\Rightarrow$ arrow) become just ordinary parameters, so $\$GEq[]_{geq}$ takes a function to compute equality on the list elements, eqA.[4]

Perhaps surprisingly, GHC performs all the required steps of Sect. 3.1 without requiring any annotations to the generic function itself. In general, however, we found that it is sensible to provide *INLINE* pragmas for each instance of the representation datatypes when defining a generic function. In the case of *geqRep*, the methods are small, so GHC inlines them eagerly. For more complicated generic functions, the methods may become larger, and GHC will avoid inlining them. Supplying an *INLINE* pragma tells GHC to inline the methods anyway.

4.3   Generic Enumeration

Generic consumers, such as equality, are, in our experience, more easily optimised by GHC. A generic producer such as enumeration, in particular, is challenging because it requires map fusion, and lifting auxiliary functions through maps using free theorems. As such, we encounter some difficulties while optimising enumeration. We start by looking at the natural numbers:

> **instance** *GEnum Nat* **where**
> $genum = map\ to\ genumRep$

Note that instead of using the default definition we directly inline its definition; this is to circumvent a bug in the current implementation of defaults that prevents later rewrite rules from applying. GHC then generates the following code:

---

[4] The type of *eqA* is $GEq\ \alpha$, but we use it as if it had type $\alpha \rightarrow \alpha \rightarrow Bool$. In the generated core there is also a coercion around the use of *eqA* to transform the class type into a function, but we elide these details as they are not relevant to the optimisation itself.

$$\$x_2 :: [\ U_1 :+: K_1\ Nat\,]$$
$$\$x_2 = map\ \$x_4\ \$GEnumNat_{genum}$$
$$\$x_1 :: [\ U_1 :+: K_1\ Nat\,]$$
$$\$x_1 = \$x_3 \;|||\; \$x_2$$
$$\$GEnumNat_{genum} :: [\ Nat\,]$$
$$\$GEnumNat_{genum} = map\ to\ \$x_1$$

We omit the definitions of $\$x_3$ and $\$x_4$ for brevity. To make progress we need to tell GHC to move the *map to* expression in $\$GEnumNat_{genum}$ through the ($|||$) operator. We use a rewrite rule for this:

$$\{-\#\ RULES\ \texttt{"ft/|||"}\ \forall f\ a\ b.\ map\ f\ (a\ |||\ b) = map\ f\ a\ |||\ map\ f\ b\ \#-\}$$

With this rule in place, GHC generates the following code:

$$\$x_2 :: [\ U_1 :+: K_1\ Nat\,]$$
$$\$x_2 = map\ \$x_4\ \$GEnumNat_{genum}$$
$$\$x_1 :: [\ Nat\,]$$
$$\$x_1 = map\ to\ \$x_2$$
$$\$GEnumNat_{genum} :: [\ Nat\,]$$
$$\$GEnumNat_{genum} = \$x_3 \;|||\; \$x_1$$

We now see that the $\$x_1$ term is *map* applied to the result of a *map*. The way *map* is optimised in GHC (by conversion to *build/foldr* form) interferes with our `"ft/|||"` rewrite rule, and map fusion is not happening. We can remedy this with an explicit map fusion rewrite rule:

$$\{-\#\ RULES\ \texttt{"map/map"}\ \forall f\ g\ l.\ map\ f\ (map\ g\ l) = map\ (f \circ g)\ l\ \#-\}$$

This rule results in much improved generated code:

$$\$x_3 :: [\ U_1 :+: K_1\ Nat\,]$$
$$\$x_3 = \$x_4 : []$$
$$\$x_2 :: [\ Nat\,]$$
$$\$x_2 = map\ to\ \$x_3$$
$$\$x_1 :: [\ Nat\,]$$
$$\$x_1 = map\ Su\ \$GEnumNat_{genum}$$
$$\$GEnumNat_{genum} :: [\ Nat\,]$$
$$\$GEnumNat_{genum} = \$x_2 \;|||\; \$x_1$$

The only thing we are missing now is to optimise $\$x_3$; note that its type is $[\ U_1 :+: K_1\ Nat\,]$, and not $[\ Nat\,]$. For this we simply need to tell GHC to eagerly map a function over a list with a single element:

$\{-\# \; RULES \; \texttt{"map/singleton"} \; \forall f \; x. \; map \; f \; (x : []) = (f \; x) : [] \; \#-\}$

With this, GHC can finally generate the fully specialised enumeration function on *Nat*:

$x_2 :: [\, Nat \,]$
$x_2 = Ze : []$
$x_1 :: [\, Nat \,]$
$x_1 = map \; Su \; \$GEnumNat_{genum}$
$\$GEnumNat_{genum} :: [\, Nat \,]$
$\$GEnumNat_{genum} = \$x_2 \; ||| \; \$x_1$

Compelling GHC to optimise generic enumeration for lists proves to be more difficult.[5] Since lists use products, we need to introduce a rewrite rule for the free theorem of *diag*, allowing *map* to be pushed inside *diag*:

$\{-\# \; RULES \; \texttt{"ft/diag"} \; \forall f \; l. \; map \; f \; (diag \; l) = diag \; (map \; (map \; f) \; l) \; \#-\}$

With this rule, and the extra optimisation flag `-fno-full-laziness` to maximise the chances for rewrite rules to apply, we get the following code:

$\$GEnum[]_{genum} :: \forall \alpha. GEnum \; \alpha \Rightarrow [\,[\, \alpha \,]\,]$
$\$GEnum[]_{genum} = \lambda(gEnumA :: GEnum \; \alpha) \rightarrow$
$\quad ([] : []) \; ||| \; \textbf{let} \; \$x_1 :: [\, K_1 \; [\, \alpha \,]\,]$
$\qquad\qquad\qquad \$x_1 = map \; K_1 \; (\$GEnum[]_{genum} \; gEnumA)$
$\qquad\qquad \textbf{in} \; diag \; (map \; (\lambda(\$x_3 :: \alpha) \rightarrow$
$\qquad\qquad\qquad\qquad map \; (\lambda(\$x_2 :: K_1 \; [\, \alpha \,]) \rightarrow \textbf{case} \; \$x_2 \; \textbf{of}$
$\qquad\qquad\qquad\qquad\qquad\qquad\qquad\qquad K_1 \; \$x_4 \rightarrow \$x_3 : \$x_4) \; \$x_1)$
$\qquad\qquad\qquad\qquad gEnumA)$

Most of the generic overhead is optimised away, but one problem remains: $\$x_1$ maps K_1 over the recursive enumeration elements, but this K_1 is immediately eliminated by a **case** statement. If $\$x_1$ was inlined, GHC could perform a map fusion, and then eliminate the use of K_1 altogether. However, we have no way to specify that $\$x_1$ should be inlined; the compiler generated it, so only the compiler can decide when to inline it. Also, we had to use the compiler flag `-fno-full-laziness` to prevent some let-floating, but the flag applies to the entire program and might have unintended side-effects.

Reflecting on our developments in this section, we have seen that:

---

[5] We believe, however, that this is only due to bugs in the inliner, and have filed bug reports #7109, #7112, and #7114 to address these issues.

- Convincing GHC to optimise *genum* for a simple datatype such as *Nat* requires the expected free theorem of (∥∥). However, due to interaction between phases of application of rewrite rules, we are forced to introduce new rules for optimisation of *map*.
- Optimising *genum* for a more complicated datatype like lists requires the expected free theorem of *diag*. However, even after further tweaking of optimisation flags, we are currently unable to derive a fully optimised implementation. In any case, the partial optimisation achieved is certainly beneficial.
- More generally, we see that practical optimisation of generic functions is hard because of subtle interactions between the different optimisation mechanisms involved, such as inlining, rewrite rule application, **let** floating, **case** optimisation, etc.

These experiments have been performed with GHC version 7.4.1. We have observed that the behavior of the optimiser changes between compiler versions. In particular, some techniques which resulted in better code in some versions (e.g. the use of *SPECIALISE* pragmas) result in worse code in other versions. We are working together with GHC developers to ensure that generic code, at least for the `generic-deriving` library, is specialised adequately, guaranteeing performance equivalent to type-specific code.

5   Benchmarking

We have confirmed the expected runtime behaviour of our code by benchmarking it. Benchmarking is, in general, a complex task, and a lazy language imposes even more challenges on the design of a benchmark. We designed a benchmark suite that ensures easy repeatability of tests, calculating the average running time and the standard deviation for statistical analysis. It is portable across different operating systems and can easily be run with different compiler versions. To ensure reliability of the benchmark we use profiling, which gives us information about which computations last longer. For each of the tests, we ensure that at least 50 % of the time is spent on the function we want to benchmark. A top-level Haskell script takes care of compiling all the tests with the same flags, invoking them a given number of times, parsing and accumulating results as each test finishes, and calculating and displaying the average running time at the end, along with some system information. To ensure the improvements are effective in practice, we have not used micro-benchmarking, and instead benchmark whole programs.

We have a detailed benchmark suite over different datatypes and generic functions.[6] It is, however, useless to show most of the benchmark figures; because we have inspected the resulting core code and concluded that it is equivalent to a hand-written variant, the benchmark is only a form of "sanity-check" on the optimisation. Confirming the findings of Sect. 4, the benchmark finds no difference between the running times of generic versus type-specific equality. We have also benchmarked a traversal that updates the values in a tree, and a conversion to

---

[6] https://bitbucket.org/dreixel/public/src/7d32c569e678/benchmark

String; in both cases, the generic function performs as fast as the handwritten code. The techniques used to optimise these functions were exactly the same as those for generic equality, and indeed we expect this to be the case for many common generic functions.

As for enumeration, we find no overhead for the *Nat* datatype. Enumeration for a binary tree datatype runs about 1.63 times slower than a type-specific variant, probably because the optimiser fails to remove all generic representation overhead (as predicted in Sect. 4.3). Even with the remaining problems in optimising generic enumeration, these results are a substantial improvement over our previous optimisation efforts [8], and rely on techniques that are far less likely to degrade performance in other parts of the code.

6   Conclusion

In this paper we have looked at the problem of optimising generic functions. With their representation types and associated conversions, generic programs tend to be slower than their type-specific handwritten counterparts, and this can limit adoption of generic programming in situations where performance is important. We have picked one specific library, `generic-deriving`, and investigated the code generation for generic programs, and the necessary optimisation techniques to fully remove any overhead from the library. We concluded that the overhead can be fully removed most of the time, using only already available optimisations that apply to functional programs in general. However, due to the difficulty of managing the interaction between several different optimisations, in some cases we are not able to fully remove the overhead. We are confident, however, that this is only a matter of further tweaking of GHC's optimisation strategies, and fixing some open bugs.

6.1   Automatic Inlining and Generation of Rewrite Rules

Some work remains to be done in terms of improving the user experience. We have mentioned that the *to* and *from* functions should be inlined; this should be automatically established by the mechanism for deriving *Generic* instances. Additionally, inserting *INLINE* pragmas for each case in the generic function is a tedious process, which should also be automated. Finally, it would be interesting to see if the definition of rewrite rules based on free theorems of auxiliary functions used could be automated; it is easy to generate free theorems, but it is not always clear how to use these theorems for optimisation purposes.

6.2   Optimising Other Libraries

The library we have used for the development in this paper, `generic-deriving`, is practical, realistic, and representative of many other libraries. In particular, our techniques readily apply to `regular` [9] and `instant-generics` [3], for instance.

Other approaches to generic programming, such as Scrap Your Boilerplate (SYB, [5,6]), use different implementation mechanisms and require different optimisation strategies. SYB, in particular, cannot be optimised using the same techniques we have seen, because it relies on (type-safe) runtime casts. Since type comparisons are performed at runtime, the compiler does not have enough information to automatically specialise generic functions. It remains to be seen how to optimise other approaches, and to establish general guidelines for optimisation of generic programs.

In any case, it is now clear that generic programs do not have to be slow, and their optimisation up to handwritten code performance is not only possible but also achievable using only standard optimisation techniques. This opens the door for a future where generic programs are not only general, elegant, and concise, but also as efficient as type-specific code.

References

1. Alimarine, A., Smetsers, S.: Optimizing generic functions. In: Kozen, D. (ed.) MPC 2004. LNCS, vol. 3125, pp. 16–31. Springer, Heidelberg (2004)
2. Alimarine, A., Smetsers, S.: Improved fusion for optimizing generics. In: Hermenegildo, M.V., Cabeza, D. (eds.) PADL 2004. LNCS, vol. 3350, pp. 203–218. Springer, Heidelberg (2005)
3. Chakravarty, M.M.T., Ditu, G.C., Leshchinskiy, R.: Instant generics: fast and easy. http://www.cse.unsw.edu.au/chak/papers/CDL09.html (2009)
4. Hinze, R., Jeuring, J., Löh, A.: Comparing approaches to generic programming in Haskell. In: Backhouse, R., Gibbons, J., Hinze, R., Jeuring, J. (eds.) SSDGP 2006. LNCS, vol. 4719, pp. 72–149. Springer, Heidelberg (2007)
5. Lämmel, R., Peyton Jones, S.: Scrap your boilerplate: a practical design pattern for generic programming. In: Proceedings of the 2003 ACM SIGPLAN International Workshop on Types in Languages Design and Implementation, pp. 26–37. ACM (2003). doi:10.1145/604174.604179
6. Lämmel, R., Peyton Jones, S.: Scrap more boilerplate: reflection, zips, and generalised casts. In: Proceedings of the 9th ACM SIGPLAN International Conference on Functional Programming, pp. 244–255. ACM (2004). doi:10.1145/1016850.1016883
7. Magalhães, J.P.: Less is more: generic programming theory and practice. Ph.D. thesis, Universiteit Utrecht (2012)
8. Magalhães, J.P., Holdermans, S., Jeuring, J., Löh, A.: Optimizing generics is easy! In: Proceedings of the 2010 ACM SIGPLAN Workshop on Partial Evaluation and Program Manipulation, pp. 33–42. ACM (2010). doi:10.1145/1706356.1706366
9. Van Noort, T., Rodriguez Yakushev, A., Holdermans, S., Jeuring, J., Heeren, B.: A lightweight approach to datatype-generic rewriting. In: Proceedings of the ACM SIGPLAN Workshop on Generic Programming, pp. 13–24. ACM (2008). doi:10.1145/1411318.1411321
10. Van Noort, T., Rodriguez Yakushev, A., Holdermans, S., Jeuring, J., Heeren, B., Magalhães, J.P.: A lightweight approach to datatype-generic rewriting. J. Funct. Program. 20(3–4), 375–413 (2010). doi:10.1017/S0956796810000183
11. Peyton Jones, S., Marlow, S.: Secrets of the Glasgow Haskell Compiler inliner. J. Funct. Program. 12(4&5), 393–433 (2002). doi:10.1017/S0956796802004331

12. Peyton Jones, S., Santos, A.L.M.: A transformation-based optimiser for Haskell. Sci. Comput. Program. **32**, 3–47 (1998). doi:10.1016/S0167-6423(97)00029-4

13. Jones, P., Tolmach, A., Hoare, T.: Playing by the rules: rewriting as a practical optimisation technique in GHC. In: Haskell Workshop 2001, pp. 203–233 (2001)

14. Rodriguez Yakushev, A., Jeuring, J., Jansson, P., Gerdes, A., Kiselyov, O., Oliveira, B.C.d.S.: Comparing libraries for generic programming in Haskell. In: Proceedings of the 1st ACM SIGPLAN Symposium on Haskell, pp. 111–122. ACM (2008). doi:10.1145/1411286.1411301

15. Sands, D.: Improvement theory and its applications. In: Gordon, A.D., Pitts, A.M. (eds.) Higher Order Operational Techniques in Semantics, Publications of the Newton Institute, pp. 275–306. Cambridge University Press, Cambridge (1998)

16. Wadler, P.: Theorems for free! In: Proceedings of the 4th International Conference on Functional Programming Languages and Computer Architecture, pp. 347–359. ACM (1989). doi:10.1145/99370.99404

17. Yorgey, B.A., Weirich, S., Cretin, J., Peyton Jones, S., Vytiniotis, D., Magalhães, J.P.: Giving Haskell a promotion. In: Proceedings of the 8th ACM SIGPLAN Workshop on Types in Language Design and Implementation, pp. 53–66. ACM (2012). doi:10.1145/2103786.2103795

A Type- and Control-Flow Analysis for System F

Matthew Fluet[✉]

Computer Science Department,
Rochester Institute of Technology, Rochester, NY 14623, USA
mtf@cs.rit.edu

Abstract. We present a monovariant flow analysis for System F (with recursion). The flow analysis yields both *control-flow* information, approximating the λ- and Λ-expressions that may be bound to variables, and *type-flow* information, approximating the type expressions that may instantiate type variables. Moreover, the two flows are mutually beneficial: the control flow determines which Λ-expressions may be applied to which type expressions (and, hence, which type expressions may instantiate which type variables), while the type flow filters the λ- and Λ-expressions that may be bound to variables (by rejecting expressions with static types that are incompatible with the static type of the variable under the type flow). As is typical for a monovariant control-flow analysis, control-flow information is expressed as an abstract environment mapping variables to sets of (syntactic) λ- and Λ-expressions that occur in the program under analysis. Similarly, type-flow information is expressed as an abstract environment mapping type variables to sets of (syntactic) types that occur in the program under analysis. Compatibility of static types (with free type variables) under a type flow is decided by interpreting the abstract environment as productions for a *regular-tree grammar* and querying if the languages generated by taking the types in question as starting terms have a non-empty intersection.

1   Introduction

Control-flow analysis is an important enabling technology for the compilation and optimization of functional languages. Because functional languages have first-class functions, the control flow of a functional program is not syntactically apparent: in an application expression, the function can itself be the result of a computation and may not be available until run time. Indeed, during the execution of a program, many different functions may be applied at the same (source-program) application expression. A control-flow analysis [16,22,26,34, 35] approximates, at compile time, the flow of first-class functions in a program: which first-class functions might be bound to a given variable or returned by a given expression at run time.

Control-flow analyses have typically been formulated for *dynamically*- or *simply*-typed functional languages.[1] However, most statically-typed functional

---

[1]   Although there are many *type-based* [27] control-flow analyses, where the analyses are expressed as a sophisticated type systems, the language under analysis is typically a simply-typed language.

R. Hinze (Ed.): IFL 2012, LNCS 8241, pp. 122–139, 2013.
DOI: 10.1007/978-3-642-41582-1_8, © Springer-Verlag Berlin Heidelberg 2013

languages have rich type systems that include polymorphic types. Indeed, System F [10,31], the polymorphic lambda calculus, and extensions thereof are commonly used as typed intermediate languages in compilers for functional languages [28,37,38]. Since optimizations are performed on a typed intermediate language and optimizations are enabled by control-flow analyses, it is natural to seek a control-flow analysis that is formulated for System F.

While one could naïvely adopt an existing control-flow analysis that is formulated for a dynamically- or simply-typed functional language and ignore the System F features of type abstraction and type application, such an approach fails to take advantage of the static information provided by a well-typed program. Intuitively, a control-flow analysis for System F should exploit the well-typedness of the program under analysis in order to obtain more precise control-flow information. For instance, if a control-flow analysis asserts that a variable x might be bound to a function of type int $\rightarrow$ int, a function of type bool $\rightarrow$ bool, and a function of type string $\rightarrow$ string (and no other functions), but the static type of x is int $\rightarrow$ int, then the type soundness of the language guarantees that x will only be bound to functions of type int $\rightarrow$ int at run time and the control-flow result may be soundly refined to assert that x might only be bound to the function of type int $\rightarrow$ int. However, if the static type of x is $\alpha \rightarrow \alpha$ (where the type variable α is bound by a type abstraction in the program under analysis), then it is unclear whether or not the control-flow result may be soundly refined, because the type variable α may be soundly instantiated at any type.

Given additional information that asserts that the type variable α might be instantiated at the type int and the type bool (and no other types), then the control-flow result may be soundly refined to assert that x might only be bound to the function of type int $\rightarrow$ int and the function of type bool $\rightarrow$ bool. This additional information may be obtained by a *type-flow analysis* that approximates, at compile time, the flow of types in a program: which types might instantiate a given type variable at run time. As demonstrated by the example above, this approximate type-flow information can be used to increase the precision of a control-flow analysis. Furthermore, this approximate type-flow information can be used to enable type-dependent optimizations, such as guiding the specialization of a polymorphic function that is used at a small number of distinct types or eliminating type operations in a language with intensional polymorphism [11]. Just as a control-flow analysis yields useful information because, for a given program, it is unlikely that a given variable is bound to *every* function during execution, a type-flow analysis yields useful information because it is unlikely that a given type variable is instantiated at *every* type during execution.

Although type-flow information and control-flow information might be obtained by independent analyses, the two kinds of information can be mutually beneficial, particularly for the higher-rank impredicative polymorphism of System F. Control-flow analysis supports type-flow analysis by yielding information about the type abstractions that may be applied at type applications and, hence, about the types at which type variables may be instantiated. The type-flow information soundly refines the control-flow information by rejecting flows that are incompatible with the static typing of the program under analysis; because the static typing may be expressed in terms of syntactic types with free type variables, the type-flow information is used to determine the compatibility of types. When the type-flow information refines the control-flow information by rejecting the flow of a type abstraction, the type-flow information itself may be refined because the type abstraction may be applied at fewer type applications, and, hence, there may be fewer types at which the type variable may be instantiated.

In a combined type- and control-flow analysis, the type-flow information soundly refines the control-flow information by determining when types are incompatible. In the presence of recursion and higher-rank impredicative polymorphism, the type-flow information must approximate complex relationships between type variables and types and the compatibility or incompatibility of types under the type-flow information may not be obvious. Indeed, during the execution of a program that is well-typed in System F with recursion, a type variable may be instantiated at an infinite number of types. In order to obtain a computable analysis, the type-flow information must use a finite representation that approximates the (potentially infinite) set of closed types that may instantiate a type variable and the compatibility of types under the type-flow information must be a decidable property.

Most control-flow analyses approximate the (potentially infinite) set of first-class functions that might be bound to a variable at run time by a (necessarily finite) set of function expressions (possibly with free variables) that occur in the program under analysis. Similarly, a type-flow analysis may approximate the (potentially infinite) set of closed types that may instantiate a type variable at run time by a (necessarily finite) set of type expressions (possibly with free type variables) that occur in the program under analysis. For instance, if a type-flow analysis asserts that a type variable α might be instantiated at the type expression int $\rightarrow$ int and the type expression int $\rightarrow$ α (and no other type expressions), then, by interpreting the type-flow information as productions for a *regular-tree grammar* [2,6,9], the type-flow analysis may be seen to be asserting that the type variable α might be instantiated at the infinite set of closed types {int $\rightarrow$ int, int $\rightarrow$ int $\rightarrow$ int, int $\rightarrow$ int $\rightarrow$ int $\rightarrow$ int, ...}. Furthermore, if the type-flow analysis asserts that a type variable β might be instantiated at the type expression int $\rightarrow$ bool and the type expression int $\rightarrow$ β (and no other type expressions) and a control-flow analysis asserts that a variable x might be bound to a function of type int $\rightarrow$ int, a function of type bool $\rightarrow$ int, a function of type string $\rightarrow$ int, a function of type int $\rightarrow$ α, and a function of type int $\rightarrow$ β (and no other functions), but the static type of x is α, then the control-flow result may be soundly refined to assert that x might only be bound to the function of type int $\rightarrow$ int and the function of type int $\rightarrow$ α, because the types of these two functions are compatible with the type α (under the type-flow information), while the types of the other three functions are incompatible with the type α.

Two types are compatible (under the type-flow information) if there exists a closed type that is a member of the sets of closed types at which the types might be instantiated; conversely, two types are incompatible if there does not exist a closed type that is a member of the sets of closed types at which the types might be instantiated. The type soundness of the language guarantees that a variable will only be bound to a well-typed closed function of a closed type at run time; hence, if there is no closed type at which both the static type of a variable and the static type of a function might be instantiated, then that variable will never be bound to that function at run time. For example, the types $\text{int} \to \alpha$ and α are compatible because the type $\text{int} \to \alpha$, interpreted as a starting term for the regular-tree grammar corresponding to the type-flow information, represents the infinite set of closed types $\{\text{int} \to \text{int} \to \text{int}, \text{int} \to \text{int} \to \text{int} \to \text{int}, \ldots\}$, which has a non-empty intersection with the infinite set of closed types that might instantiate the type variable α (given above). Similarly, the types $\text{int} \to \beta$ and α are incompatible because the type $\text{int} \to \beta$ represents the infinite set of closed types $\{\text{int} \to \text{int} \to \text{bool}, \text{int} \to \text{int} \to \text{int} \to \text{bool}, \ldots\}$, which has an empty intersection with the infinite set of closed types that might instantiate the type variable α. Since regular-tree grammars are closed under intersection and the emptiness of a regular-tree grammar is decidable, the compatibility of types under the type-flow information is a decidable property.

Overview. We present a monovariant type- and control-flow analysis for System F extended with recursive functions. Our flow analysis is a variation on 0CFA, the classic monovariant control-flow analysis [26]. For a given program, the flow analysis computes an abstract environment that maps variables to (finite) sets of λ- and Λ-expressions that occur in the program and maps type variables to (finite) sets of type expressions that occur in the program.

Our formulation of the type- and control-flow analysis as a refinement of the syntax-directed constraint-based formulation of 0CFA establishes that the combined type- and control-flow analysis can be more precise than 0CFA. Although not as precise as a type-directed polyvariant control-flow analysis [15], our monovariant type- and control-flow analysis nonetheless rejects some similar classes of spurious flows and, furthermore, has the benefits of handling full (i.e., impredicative) System F and terminating for all well-typed programs.

Soundness of the analysis is proven with respect to an operational semantics for System F given in the style of the administrative-normal-form (ANF) environment- and continuation-based $C_a EK$ abstract machine [7], where the (concrete) environment component of the abstract machine maps variables to closures (pairs of λ- or Λ-expressions and an environment, which captures the free variables and type variables of the λ- or Λ-expression) and maps type variables to *type closures* (pairs of type expressions and an environment, which captures the free type variables of the type expression). A sound flow analysis computes an abstract environment that approximates every concrete environment that arises during evaluation. We present the analysis-time type-compatibility predicate as a judgment; this yields a declarative specification of type compatibility, for which the regular-tree-grammar interpretation gives an algorithmic implementation. A companion technical report [8] provides additional commentary, technical details, and proofs.

Types	$Type \ni \tau ::= \tau_a \to \tau_b \mid \alpha \mid \forall \alpha.\, \tau_b$
Type variables	$TyVar \ni \alpha, \beta, \ldots$
Expressions	$Exp \ni e ::= x \mid \texttt{let } x{:}\tau_x = b \texttt{ in } e$
Binds	$Bnd \ni b ::= \mu f{:}\tau_f.\lambda z{:}\tau_z.e_b \mid x_f\, x_a \mid \mu f{:}\tau_f.\Lambda\beta.e_b \mid x_f\, [\tau_a]$
Variables	$Var \ni x, y, z, f, g, \ldots$

$$\lfloor \cdot \rfloor :: Exp \to Var$$
$$\lfloor x \rfloor = x$$
$$\lfloor \texttt{let } x{:}\tau_x = b \texttt{ in } e \rfloor = \lfloor e \rfloor$$

Fig. 1. Syntax of ANF System F

2 Language and Semantics

Our source language is a variant of System F, extended with recursive functions and presented in (a restriction of) administrative normal form (ANF). The operational semantics of the language is presented as an abstract machine. The static semantics of the language is entirely standard, but given for completeness.

Syntax. The syntax of our ANF variant of System F is given in Fig. 1.

Types include function types, type variables, and universal types; in the universal type $\forall \alpha.\, \tau_b$, the type variable α is bound in the type τ_b. Type equality is syntactic identity (up to α-conversion of bound type variables).

Expressions include variables, `let`-bindings of recursive functions, `let`-bindings of non-tail function applications, `let`-bindings of recursive type abstractions, and `let`-bindings of non-tail type applications. In the `let`-binding expression $\texttt{let } x{:}\tau_x = b \texttt{ in } e$, the variable x is bound in e; in the recursive function $\mu f{:}\tau_f.\lambda z{:}\tau_z.e_b$, the variables f and z are bound in the expression e_b and in the recursive type abstraction $\mu f{:}\tau_f.\Lambda\beta.e_b$, the variable f and the type variable β are bound in the expression e_b.

Finally, we define a function $\lfloor \cdot \rfloor$ on expressions, which extracts the variable that yields the expression's value.

The language is Church-style, in which every bound variable is annotated with its type. We restrict the constituents of function applications and type applications to variables, rather than allowing a larger class of "trivial" expressions, and we restrict function applications and type applications to non-tail calls, rather than allowing tail calls. Neither restriction is essential for the type- and control-flow analysis; we adopt them simply to reduce the number of inference rules in the operational semantics, static semantics, and flow analysis.

Operational Semantics. The operational semantics for our ANF-variant of System F is presented as an adaptation of the environment- and continuation-based $C_a EK$ machine [7] and is given in Fig. 2.

A machine state ς has four components: a control expression, a run-time type environment, a run-time value environment, and a continuation.

Run-time types	$RType \ni \pi ::= \langle \tau; \phi \rangle$
Run-time type environments	$RTEnv \ni \phi ::= \bullet \mid \phi, \alpha \mapsto \pi$
Run-time values	$RValue \ni w ::= \langle \mu f : \tau_f . \lambda z : \tau_z . e_b; \phi; \rho \rangle \mid \langle \mu f : \tau_f . \Lambda \beta . e_b; \phi; \rho \rangle$
Run-time value environments	$RVEnv \ni \rho ::= \bullet \mid \rho, x \mapsto w$
Continuations	$Kont \ni \kappa ::= \circ \mid \langle x; \tau_x; e; \phi; \rho \rangle :: \kappa$
States	$State \ni \varsigma ::= \langle e; \phi; \rho; \kappa \rangle$

$$\boxed{\varsigma \longrightarrow \varsigma}$$

$$\frac{\rho_r(x_r) = w_r}{\langle x_r; \phi_r; \rho_r; \langle z; \tau_z; e; \phi; \rho \rangle :: \kappa \rangle \longrightarrow \langle e; \phi; \rho, z \mapsto w_r; \kappa \rangle}$$

$$\frac{w_r = \langle \mu f : \tau_f . \lambda z : \tau_z . e_b; \phi; \rho \rangle}{\langle \texttt{let } x : \tau_x = \mu f : \tau_f . \lambda z : \tau_z . e_b \texttt{ in } e; \phi; \rho; \kappa \rangle \longrightarrow \langle e; \phi; \rho, x \mapsto w_r; \kappa \rangle} \qquad \frac{w_r = \langle \mu f : \tau_f . \Lambda \beta . e_b; \phi; \rho \rangle}{\langle \texttt{let } x : \tau_x = \mu f : \tau_f . \Lambda \beta . e_b \texttt{ in } e; \phi; \rho; \kappa \rangle \longrightarrow \langle e; \phi; \rho, x \mapsto w_r; \kappa \rangle}$$

$$\frac{\rho(x_f) = w_f \qquad w_f = \langle \mu f : \tau_f . \lambda z : \tau_z . e_b; \phi_f; \rho_f \rangle \qquad \rho(x_a) = w_a}{\langle \texttt{let } x : \tau_x = x_f \ x_a \texttt{ in } e; \phi; \rho; \kappa \rangle \longrightarrow \langle e_b; \phi_f; \rho_f, f \mapsto w_f, z \mapsto w_a; \langle x; \tau_x; e; \phi; \rho \rangle :: \kappa \rangle}$$

$$\frac{\rho(x_f) = w_f \qquad w_f = \langle \mu f : \tau_f . \Lambda \beta . e_b; \phi_f; \rho_f \rangle \qquad \pi_a = \langle \tau_a; \phi \rangle}{\langle \texttt{let } x : \tau_x = x_f \ [\tau_a] \texttt{ in } e; \phi; \rho; \kappa \rangle \longrightarrow \langle e_b; \phi_f, \beta \mapsto \pi_a; \rho_f, f \mapsto w_f; \langle x; \tau_x; e; \phi; \rho \rangle :: \kappa \rangle}$$

Fig. 2. Operational Semantics of ANF System F

A run-time type environment ϕ is a map from type variables to run-time types and a run-time value environment ρ is a map from variables to run-time values. A run-time type π is a "type closure": a pair of a (possibly open) type and a run-time type environment; the run-time type environment captures the free type variables of the type. A run-time value w is a "function closure" or a "type-abstraction closure": a triple of a (possibly open) value (a recursive function or a recursive type abstraction), a run-time type environment (that captures the free type variables of the value), and a run-time value environment (that captures the free variables of the value).

A continuation κ is a stack of frames, each of the form $\langle x; \tau_x; \phi; \rho; e \rangle$, where x is the variable receiving the result w of a non-tail function application or non-tail type application, τ_x is the (static, syntactic) type of x, and e is the expression to be evaluated in the environments ϕ and ρ extended with x bound to w to yield the result of the frame.

The first rule returns a result to the top-most frame of the continuation when the control expression has been reduced to a variable. The second and third rules create function closures and type-abstraction closures. The fourth and fifth rules extract the expression body, run-time type environment, and run-time value environment from an applied function closure or type-abstraction closure, extend the closure's run-time value environment with f bound to the closure (making the recursive function or recursive type-abstraction available to the expression body), extend the closure's run-time value environment with the run-time value argument (in the case of a function application) or extend the closure's run-time type environment with the run-time type argument (in the

$$\begin{array}{ll}
\textit{Type-variable contexts} & \textit{TCtxt} \ni \Delta ::= \bullet \mid \Delta, \alpha{:}\star \\
\textit{Variable contexts} & \textit{VCtxt} \ni \Gamma ::= \bullet \mid \Gamma, x{:}\tau
\end{array}$$

$$\boxed{\Delta \vdash \tau}$$

$$\frac{\Delta \vdash \tau_a \quad \Delta \vdash \tau_b}{\Delta \vdash \tau_a \to \tau_b} \qquad \frac{\Delta(\alpha) = \star}{\Delta \vdash \alpha} \qquad \frac{\Delta, \alpha{:}\star \vdash \tau_b}{\Delta \vdash \forall \alpha.\, \tau_b}$$

$$\boxed{\Delta; \Gamma \vdash e : \tau}$$

$$\frac{\Gamma(x) = \tau}{\Delta; \Gamma \vdash x : \tau} \qquad \frac{\Delta \vdash \tau_x \quad \Delta; \Gamma \vdash b : \tau_r \quad \tau_x = \tau_r \quad \Delta; \Gamma, x{:}\tau_x \vdash e : \tau}{\Delta; \Gamma \vdash \mathtt{let}\ x{:}\tau_x = b\ \mathtt{in}\ e : \tau}$$

$$\boxed{\Delta; \Gamma \vdash b : \tau}$$

$$\frac{\Delta \vdash \tau_f \quad \Delta \vdash \tau_z \quad \Delta; \Gamma, f{:}\tau_f, z{:}\tau_z \vdash e_b : \tau_b \quad \tau_f = \tau_a \to \tau_b \quad \tau_z = \tau_a}{\Delta; \Gamma \vdash \mu f{:}\tau_f . \lambda z{:}\tau_z . e_b : \tau_a \to \tau_b} \qquad \frac{\Delta \vdash \tau_f \quad \Delta, \beta{:}\star; \Gamma, f{:}\tau_f \vdash e_b : \tau_b \quad \tau_f = \forall \beta.\, \tau_b}{\Delta; \Gamma \vdash \mu f{:}\tau_f . \Lambda \beta . e_b : \forall \beta.\, \tau_b}$$

$$\frac{\Gamma(x_f) = \tau_a \to \tau_b \quad \Gamma(x_a) = \tau_a}{\Delta; \Gamma \vdash x_f\ x_a : \tau_b} \qquad \frac{\Gamma(x_f) = \forall \beta.\, \tau_b \quad \Delta \vdash \tau_a}{\Delta; \Gamma \vdash x_f\ [\tau_a] : [\beta \mapsto \tau_a]\tau_b}$$

Fig. 3. Static Semantics of ANF System F

case of a type application), and push a frame onto the continuation to receive the result of the function application or type application.

Static Semantics. The standard static semantics for System F, adapted to our ANF variant, is given in Fig. 3. A type-variable context Δ records free type variables and the judgment $\Delta \vdash \tau$ asserts that the type τ is well-formed in Δ. A variable context Γ records free variables and their types and the judgments $\Delta; \Gamma \vdash e : \tau$ and $\Delta; \Gamma \vdash b : \tau$ assert that the expression e and bind b have the type τ in Δ and Γ; in the rule for type applications, we write $[\alpha \mapsto \tau_a]\tau_b$ for the capture-avoiding substitution of τ_a for free occurrences of α in τ_b.

Type Soundness. A syntactic proof [39] of type soundness, using entirely standard Progress and Preservation theorems, is given in a technical report [8].

Theorem 1 (Type Soundness). *If $\bullet; \bullet \vdash e : \tau$ and $\langle e; \bullet; \bullet; \circ \rangle \longrightarrow^* \varsigma'$, then either $\varsigma' = \langle x'; \phi'; \rho'; \circ \rangle$ or $\varsigma \longrightarrow \varsigma'$.*

In addition to the judgments of Fig. 3, we introduce judgments that assert the "well-typedness" of run-time types ($\vdash \pi \Rightarrow \tau$), run-time type environments ($\vdash \phi : \theta$), run-time values ($\vdash w : \tau$), run-time value environments ($\vdash \rho : \Gamma$), continuations ($\vdash \tau \rightsquigarrow \kappa : \tau$), and states ($\vdash \varsigma : \tau$). Of note is the judgment $\vdash \phi : \theta$ that asserts that the run-time type environment ϕ corresponds to a substitution

θ; the domains of ϕ and θ are equal, but whereas ϕ maps a type variable to a run-time type (a pair of a (possibly open) type and a (closing) run-time type environment), θ maps a type variable to a closed type obtained by (recursively) expanding the (possibly open) type by its (closing) run-time type environment.

3   Type- and Control-Flow Analysis

Our type- and control-flow analysis is presented as an adaptation of the syntax-directed 0CFA, the classic monovariant control-flow analysis [26, Sect. 3.3], and is given in Fig. 4.

The result of our type- and control-flow analysis is a pair of abstract environments. An abstract type environment $\hat{\phi}$ is a map from type variables to sets of abstract types, where an abstract type is a (possibly open) type. An abstract

Abstract types	$AType \ni \hat{\pi} ::= \tau$	
Sets of abstract types	$\mathcal{P}(AType) \ni \hat{\Pi}$	
Abstract type environments	$ATEnv \ni \hat{\phi} \in TyVar \to \mathcal{P}(AType)$	
Abstract values	$AValue \ni \hat{w} ::= \mu f{:}\tau_f.\lambda z{:}\tau_z.e_b \mid \mu f{:}\tau_f.\Lambda\beta.e_b$	
Sets of abstract values	$\mathcal{P}(AValue) \ni \hat{W}$	
Abstract value environments	$AVEnv \ni \hat{\rho} \in Var \to \mathcal{P}(AValue)$	

$$\hat{\phi}_1 \sqsubseteq \hat{\phi}_2 \stackrel{def}{=} \forall\alpha \in TyVar.\hat{\phi}_1(\alpha) \subseteq \hat{\phi}_2(\alpha) \qquad \hat{\rho}_1 \sqsubseteq \hat{\rho}_2 \stackrel{def}{=} \forall x \in Var.\hat{\rho}_1(x) \subseteq \hat{\rho}_2(x)$$

$$\langle\hat{\phi}_1,\hat{\rho}_1\rangle \sqsubseteq \langle\hat{\phi}_2,\hat{\rho}_2\rangle \stackrel{def}{=} \hat{\phi}_1 \sqsubseteq \hat{\phi}_2 \wedge \hat{\rho}_1 \sqsubseteq \hat{\rho}_2$$

$\boxed{\hat{\phi};\hat{\rho} \vDash e}$

$$\frac{}{\hat{\phi};\hat{\rho} \vDash x} \qquad \frac{\hat{\phi};\hat{\rho} \vDash b \rightsquigarrow \hat{W}_r \quad \{\hat{w}_r \in \hat{W}_r \mid \boxed{\hat{\phi} \vdash \hat{w}_r :\approx \tau_x} \} \subseteq \hat{\rho}(x) \quad \hat{\phi};\hat{\rho} \vDash e}{\hat{\phi};\hat{\rho} \vDash \texttt{let } x{:}\tau_x = b \texttt{ in } e}$$

$\boxed{\hat{\phi};\hat{\rho} \vDash b \rightsquigarrow \hat{W}}$

$$\frac{\{\mu f{:}\tau_f.\lambda z{:}\tau_z.e_b\} \subseteq \hat{\rho}(f) \quad \hat{\phi};\hat{\rho} \vDash e_b}{\{\mu f{:}\tau_f.\lambda z{:}\tau_z.e_b\} \subseteq \hat{W}} \qquad \frac{\{\mu f{:}\tau_f.\Lambda\beta.e_b\} \subseteq \hat{\rho}(f) \quad \hat{\phi};\hat{\rho} \vDash e_b}{\{\mu f{:}\tau_f.\Lambda\beta.e_b\} \subseteq \hat{W}}$$

$$\frac{}{\hat{\phi};\hat{\rho} \vDash \mu f{:}\tau_f.\lambda z{:}\tau_z.e_b \rightsquigarrow \hat{W}} \qquad \frac{}{\hat{\phi};\hat{\rho} \vDash \mu f{:}\tau_f.\Lambda\beta.e_b \rightsquigarrow \hat{W}}$$

$$\frac{\bigwedge_{\mu f{:}\tau_f.\lambda z{:}\tau_z.e_b \in \hat{\rho}(x_f)} \left(\{\hat{w}_a \in \hat{\rho}(x_a) \mid \boxed{\hat{\phi} \vdash \hat{w}_a :\approx \tau_z} \} \subseteq \hat{\rho}(z) \wedge \hat{\rho}(\lfloor e_b \rfloor) \subseteq \hat{W} \right)}{\hat{\phi};\hat{\rho} \vDash x_f\, x_a \rightsquigarrow \hat{W}}$$

$$\frac{\bigwedge_{\mu f{:}\tau_f.\Lambda\beta.e_b \in \hat{\rho}(x_f)} \left(\{\tau_a\} \subseteq \hat{\phi}(\beta) \wedge \hat{\rho}(\lfloor e_b \rfloor) \subseteq \hat{W} \right)}{\hat{\phi};\hat{\rho} \vDash x_f\, [\tau_a] \rightsquigarrow \hat{W}}$$

Fig. 4. Type- and Control-Flow Analysis of ANF System F

value environment $\hat{\rho}$ is a map from variables to sets of abstract values, where an abstract value is a (possibly open) recursive function or recursive type abstraction. Pairs of abstract type and value environments form complete lattices with the usual partial orders for pairs, functions, and power sets.

The judgments $\hat{\phi}; \hat{\rho} \vDash e$ and $\hat{\phi}; \hat{\rho} \vDash b \leadsto \hat{W}$ assert that a pair of abstract environments $\hat{\phi}$ and $\hat{\rho}$ is an acceptable type- and control-flow analysis of the expression e and bind b, respectively. An acceptable type- and control-flow analysis is one that soundly approximates the run-time behavior of the program, in a sense made precise by Theorem 2; intuitively, acceptable abstract type and value environments must describe every run-time type and value environment that arises during the evaluation of the program. The judgment $\hat{\phi}; \hat{\rho} \vDash b \leadsto \hat{W}$ additionally asserts that the bind b is approximated by the set of abstract values $\hat{W}$.

Ignoring the shaded terms, the constraints asserted by the rules are standard for a monovariant control-flow analysis. The rule for a let-binding expression let $x : \tau_x = b$ in e asserts that the abstract environments are acceptable for the bind b and the expression e and that the set of abstract values that approximate the bind b are included in the set of abstract values mapped from the variable x. The rules for values (recursive functions and recursive type abstractions) assert that the value itself is included in both the set of abstract values approximating the bind and the set of abstract values mapped from the μ-bound variable f (corresponding to the $f \mapsto w_f$ binding in the operational semantics making the recursive function or recursive type-application available to the expression body) and that the abstract environments are acceptable for the body expression. The rule for a non-tail function application asserts that, for all functions in the set of abstract values mapped from the variable x_f, the abstract values mapped from the actual argument x_a flow to the formal argument z and the abstract values from the function result $\lfloor e_b \rfloor$ flow to the set of abstract values approximating the function application. Similarly, the rule for a non-tail type application asserts that, for all type abstractions in the set of abstract values mapped from the variable x_f, the actual type argument τ_a flows to the formal type argument β and the abstract values from the function result $\lfloor e_b \rfloor$ flow to the set of abstract values approximating the type application.

Now consider the shaded terms in the rules for a let-binding expression and a non-tail function application and the judgments and rules in Fig. 5. In essence, the shaded terms perform a kind of analysis-time type checking at the point where there is a non-local flow of abstract values. The judgment $\hat{\phi} \vdash \hat{w} :\approx \pi$ asserts that (the abstract type of) the abstract value $\hat{w}$ is compatible with the abstract type π under $\hat{\phi}$. Thus, in the rule for a let-binding expression, each abstract result $\hat{w}_r \in \hat{W}_r$ that flows from the bind to the receiving variable x must have an abstract type that is compatible with τ_x, the static type of the receiving variable. Similarly, in the rule for non-tail function applications, each abstract argument $\hat{w}_a \in \hat{\rho}(x_a)$ that flows from the actual argument to the formal argument z must have an abstract type that is compatible with τ_z, the static type of formal argument.

$$\boxed{\hat{\phi} \vdash \hat{w} :\not\approx \hat{\pi}}$$

$$\boxed{\hat{\phi} \vdash \hat{\pi} \approx \hat{\pi}}$$

$$\frac{\hat{\phi} \vdash \tau_f \approx \hat{\pi}}{\hat{\phi} \vdash \mu f : \tau_f . \lambda z : \tau_z . e_b :\not\approx \hat{\pi}} \qquad \frac{\hat{\phi} \vdash \tau_f \approx \hat{\pi}}{\hat{\phi} \vdash \mu f : \tau_f . \Lambda \beta . e_b :\not\approx \hat{\pi}} \qquad \frac{\bullet; \hat{\phi} \vdash \hat{\pi}_1 \Rrightarrow \tau \quad \bullet; \hat{\phi} \vdash \hat{\pi}_2 \Rrightarrow \tau}{\hat{\phi} \vdash \hat{\pi}_1 \approx \hat{\pi}_2}$$

$$\boxed{\Delta; \hat{\phi} \vdash \hat{\pi} \Rrightarrow \tau}$$

$$\frac{\Delta; \hat{\phi} \vdash \tau_a \Rrightarrow \tau_a' \quad \Delta; \hat{\phi} \vdash \tau_b \Rrightarrow \tau_b'}{\Delta; \hat{\phi} \vdash \tau_a \to \tau_b \Rrightarrow \tau_a' \to \tau_b'} \qquad \frac{\Delta(\alpha) = \star}{\Delta; \hat{\phi} \vdash \alpha \Rrightarrow \alpha} \qquad \frac{\Delta, \alpha : \star; \hat{\phi} \vdash \tau_b \Rrightarrow \tau_b'}{\Delta; \hat{\phi} \vdash \forall \alpha. \tau_b \Rrightarrow \forall \alpha. \tau_b'}$$

$$\frac{\alpha \notin \mathsf{dom}(\Delta) \quad \hat{\pi} \in \hat{\phi}(\alpha) \quad \bullet; \hat{\phi} \vdash \hat{\pi} \Rrightarrow \tau}{\Delta; \hat{\phi} \vdash \alpha \Rrightarrow \tau}$$

Fig. 5. Analysis-time Type Compatibility

The rules for the judgment $\hat{\phi} \vdash \hat{w} :\not\approx \hat{\pi}$ simply form the abstract type of the recursive function or recursive type abstraction from the (static, syntactic) type of the μ-bound variable. The judgment $\hat{\phi} \vdash \hat{\pi}_1 \approx \hat{\pi}_2$ asserts that the abstract types $\hat{\pi}_1$ and $\hat{\pi}_2$ are compatible under $\hat{\phi}$, by asserting that $\hat{\pi}_1$ and $\hat{\pi}_2$ expand to a common closed type. Finally, the judgment $\Delta; \hat{\phi} \vdash \hat{\pi} \Rrightarrow \tau$ asserts that the abstract type $\hat{\pi}$ expands under $\hat{\phi}$ to the type τ (which is well-formed in Δ). The first rule expands a function type by recursively expanding its argument and result types. The second rule expands a $\forall$-bound type variable to itself, while the third rule expands a universal type by recursively expanding its result type (in a type-variable context extended with α). The fourth rule expands a Λ-bound type variable to an abstract type according to the abstract type environment $\hat{\phi}$ and recursively expands the abstract type; the abstract type is expanded under the empty type-variable context, because it is not in the scope of the $\forall$-bound type variables appearing in Δ. Note that, when used in the context of the type compatibility judgment $\hat{\phi} \vdash \hat{\pi}_1 \approx \hat{\pi}_2$, this rule must "guess" a satisfying abstract type from among the set of abstract types mapped from the type variable.

Flow Soundness. We show that, with respect to a given program, every acceptable pair of abstract environments soundly approximates the run-time behavior of the program. To formalize the approximation, we introduce "shallow" abstraction functions that take run-time types and values to abstract types and values and that take run-time type and value environments to abstract type and value environments:[2]

---

[2] These abstraction functions are "shallow" in the sense that they do not abstract and join the embedded run-time type and value environments.

$$|\cdot| \; :: \; RType \rightarrow AType \qquad\qquad\qquad |\cdot| \; :: \; RValue \rightarrow AValue$$

$$|\langle \tau; \phi \rangle| = \tau \qquad\qquad |\langle \mu f{:}\tau_f.\lambda z{:}\tau_z.e; \phi; \rho \rangle| = \mu f{:}\tau_f.\lambda z{:}\tau_z.e_b$$

$$|\langle \mu f{:}\tau_f.\Lambda\beta.e_b; \phi; \rho \rangle| = \mu f{:}\tau_f.\Lambda\beta.e_b$$

$$|\cdot| \; :: \; RTEnv \rightarrow ATEnv \qquad\qquad |\cdot| \; :: \; RVEnv \rightarrow AVEnv$$

$$|\phi|(\alpha) = \begin{cases} \{\} & \text{if } \alpha \notin \mathsf{dom}(\phi) \\ \{|\pi|\} & \text{if } \phi(\alpha) = \pi \end{cases} \qquad |\rho|(x) = \begin{cases} \{\} & \text{if } x \notin \mathsf{dom}(\rho) \\ \{|w|\} & \text{if } \rho(x) = w \end{cases}$$

A proof of flow soundness for well-typed programs, using a Preservation (aka, subject reduction) theorem, is given in a technical report [8].

Theorem 2 (Flow Soundness). *If* $\bullet; \bullet \vdash e : \tau$, $\hat{\phi}; \hat{\rho} \vDash e$, *and* $\langle e; \bullet; \bullet; \circ \rangle \longrightarrow {}^{*}\langle e'; \phi'; \rho'; \kappa' \rangle$, *then* $\langle |\phi'|, |\rho'| \rangle \sqsubseteq \langle \hat{\phi}, \hat{\rho} \rangle$.

In addition to the judgments of Fig. 4, we introduce judgments that assert the acceptability of abstract environments with respect to run-time types ($\hat{\phi} \vDash \pi$), run-time type environments ($\hat{\phi} \vDash \phi$), run-time values ($\hat{\phi}; \hat{\rho} \vDash w$), run-time value environments ($\hat{\phi}; \hat{\rho} \vDash \rho$), continuations ($\hat{\phi}; \hat{\rho} \vDash \hat{W} \leadsto \kappa$), and states ($\hat{\phi}; \hat{\rho} \vDash \varsigma$). The judgments $\hat{\phi} \vDash \phi$ and $\hat{\phi}; \hat{\rho} \vDash \rho$ assert that the abstract environments are "deep" abstractions of the run-time environments.

A key lemma is the following, which establishes that two abstract types may be judged compatible if their expansions (induced by run-time type environments for which the abstract type environment is acceptable) are syntactically equal:

Lemma 3 (Syntactic Equality implies Analysis-Time Type Compatibility). *If* $\vdash \phi_1 : \theta_1, \hat{\phi} \vDash \phi_1, \bullet \vdash \theta_1(\tau_1)$, $\vdash \phi_2 : \theta_2, \hat{\phi} \vDash \phi_2, \bullet \vdash \theta_2(\tau_2)$, *and* $\theta_1(\tau_1) = \theta_2(\tau_2)$, *then* $\hat{\phi} \vdash \tau_1 \approx \tau_2$.

In the Preservation proof, the necessary preconditions for this lemma are obtained from the well-typedness of the machine state undergoing transition.

Existence of Minimum, Finite Flows. Although presented in constraint form, our type- and control-flow analysis can be presented in an equivalent fix-point form [5]. It is straightforward to read the analysis of Fig. 4 as defining a monotone function from pairs of abstract environments to pairs of abstract environments. For a given program, fixed points of this monotone function are acceptable pairs of abstract environments. Since pairs of abstract environments form complete lattices, Tarski's fixed point theorem establishes that:

Theorem 4 (Minimum Flows Exist). *For all expressions* e, *there exist minimum abstract environments* $\hat{\phi}_{\min}$ *and* $\hat{\rho}_{\min}$ *such that* $\hat{\phi}_{\min}; \hat{\rho}_{\min} \vDash e$.

Furthermore, for a given program e, the minimum abstract type environment must be an element of $ATEnv^e = TyVar^e \rightarrow \mathcal{P}(AType^e)$ (where $TyVar^e$ is the set of Λ-bound type variables that occur in the program and $AType^e$ is the set of (syntactic) types that occur in the program) and the minimum abstract value environment must be an element of $AEnv^e = Var^e \rightarrow \mathcal{P}(AValue^e)$ (where Var^e is the set of let-, μ-, and λ-bound variables that occur in the program and *AValue*^{e} is the set of (syntactic) values (recursive functions and recursive type abstractions) that occur in the program). These abstract environments are "finite", in the sense that they map finite domains to finite sets, and form complete lattices.

Decidability and Computability of Flows. While Theorems 2 and 4 establish that, for every program, there is a "best" pair of abstract environments that soundly approximates the run-time behavior of the program, we would like this pair of abstract environments to be computable. The key concern is the decidability of the $\hat{\phi} \vdash \hat{\pi}_1 \approx \hat{\pi}_2$ judgment. Even simply verifying that a pair of abstract environments is acceptable for a given program requires showing that constraints of the form $\{\hat{w}_a \in \hat{\rho}(x_a) \mid \hat{\phi} \vdash \hat{w}_a :\approx \tau_z\} \subseteq \hat{\rho}(z)$ are satisfied; this, in turn, requires showing, for each abstract value $\hat{w}_a$ that is an element of $\hat{\rho}(x_a)$ but is not an element of $\hat{\rho}(z)$, that the judgment $\hat{\phi} \vdash \hat{w}_a :\approx \tau_z$ is not derivable.

Due to "recursion" in the abstract type environment, whereby a type variable may be mapped to a set of abstract types in which the type variable itself occurs free, we cannot simply enumerate the (potentially infinite sets of) closed types τ_1 and τ_2 such that $\bullet; \hat{\phi} \vdash \hat{\pi}_1 \Rightarrow \tau_1$ and $\bullet; \hat{\phi} \vdash \hat{\pi}_2 \Rightarrow \tau_2$ in order to decide whether or not the judgment $\hat{\phi} \vdash \hat{\pi}_1 \approx \hat{\pi}_2$ is derivable. To address this issue, we take inspiration from the theory and implementation of regular-tree grammars [2,6,9], which has been used extensively for flow analysis [12,13,17,18] (including type inference [3,24]), but whereas previous work has applied regular-tree grammars to the analysis of values, we apply regular-tree grammars to the analysis of types.

Given a finite abstract type environment $\hat{\phi}$, we interpret it as a regular-tree grammar as follows: the set of non-terminals is dom($\hat{\phi}$) and the set of productions is $\{\alpha \Rightarrow \hat{\pi} \mid \alpha \in \text{dom}(\hat{\phi}) \wedge \hat{\pi} \in \hat{\phi}(\alpha)\}$. The language generated by the grammar $\hat{\phi}$ for the starting term $\hat{\pi}$ is $\mathcal{L}_{\hat{\phi}}(\hat{\pi}) \stackrel{\text{def}}{=} \{\tau' \in \textit{Type} \mid \bullet; \hat{\phi} \vdash \hat{\pi} \Rightarrow \tau'\}$; a derivation of $\bullet; \hat{\phi} \vdash \hat{\pi} \Rightarrow \tau'$ is exactly a parse tree witnessing the derivation of τ' from $\hat{\pi}$ by $\hat{\phi}$.

Consider deciding whether or not $\hat{\phi}_{\text{ex}} \vdash \text{int} \to \beta \approx \alpha$ is derivable, where $\hat{\phi}_{\text{ex}}(\alpha) = \{\text{int} \to \text{int}, \text{int} \to \alpha\}$ and $\hat{\phi}_{\text{ex}}(\beta) = \{\text{int} \to \text{bool}, \text{int} \to \beta\}$. Intuitively, it is not derivable because

$$\mathcal{L}_{\hat{\phi}_{\text{ex}}}(\text{int} \to \beta) = \{\text{int} \to \text{int} \to \text{bool}, \text{int} \to \text{int} \to \text{int} \to \text{bool}, \ldots\}$$
$$\mathcal{L}_{\hat{\phi}_{\text{ex}}}(\alpha) = \{\text{int} \to \text{int}, \text{int} \to \text{int} \to \text{int}, \text{int} \to \text{int} \to \text{int} \to \text{int}, \ldots\}$$

and $\mathcal{L}_{\hat{\phi}_{\text{ex}}}(\text{int} \to \beta) \cap \mathcal{L}_{\hat{\phi}_{\text{ex}}}(\alpha) = \emptyset$; there is no (closed) type that is generated by $\hat{\phi}_{\text{ex}}$ from both int $\to \beta$ and α. Simply unfolding definitions establishes that:

Theorem 5 (Analysis-Time Type Compatibility iff Languages Intersect). $\hat{\phi} \vdash \hat{\pi}_1 \approx \hat{\pi}_2$ *if and only if* $\mathcal{L}_{\hat{\phi}}(\hat{\pi}_1) \cap \mathcal{L}_{\hat{\phi}}(\hat{\pi}_2) \neq \emptyset$.

An immediate corollary of Theorem 5 is the decidability of type compatibility (under a finite abstract type environment), since regular-tree grammars are closed under intersection and the emptiness of a regular-tree grammar is decidable [9, 24]. In turn, we have that the acceptability of a pair of finite abstract environments for a given program is decidable. Finally, we have that the minimum acceptable pair of abstract environments for a given program is computable, either by enumerating the finite abstract environments for the program and checking acceptability or by defining the analysis as a monotone function and using a standard least fixed-point computation.

We briefly sketch implementations of testing emptiness and intersection of regular-tree grammars, based on those given by Aiken and Murphy [2]; both operations are (worst-case) quadratic time in the size of the regular-tree grammar. Recall that, for a given program e, it suffices to consider finite abstract type environments $\hat{\phi}^e \in ATEnv^e$, interpreted as (finite) regular-tree grammars.

To decide the emptiness of a language, we define the function Ψ as follows:

$$\Psi :: AEnv \to (TyVar \to \mathbb{B})$$
$$\Psi(\hat{\phi}) = \text{lfp}\, F$$
$$\text{where} \qquad F :: (TyVar \to \mathbb{B}) \to (TyVar \to \mathbb{B})$$
$$F(\psi)(\alpha) = \begin{cases} \top & \text{if } \exists \hat{\pi} \in \hat{\phi}(\alpha).\ \forall \beta \in \mathsf{FTV}(\hat{\pi}).\ \psi(\beta) = \top \\ \bot & \text{if } \forall \hat{\pi} \in \hat{\phi}(\alpha).\ \exists \beta \in \mathsf{FTV}(\hat{\pi}).\ \psi(\beta) = \bot \end{cases}$$

where $\mathbb{B} = \{\top, \bot\}$ with the usual partial order ($\bot \sqsubseteq \top$); $\bot$ (resp. $\top$) denotes an empty (resp. non-empty) language. The language $\mathcal{L}_{\hat{\phi}}(\hat{\pi})$ is non-empty if and only if $\forall \beta \in \mathsf{FTV}(\hat{\pi}).\ \Psi(\hat{\phi})(\beta) = \top$. If $\hat{\phi}$ is a finite abstract type environment, then $\Psi(\hat{\phi})$ is computable using a standard least fixed-point computation.

In order to intersect the languages generated by the regular-tree grammar $\hat{\phi}$ for the starting terms $\hat{\pi}_1$ and $\hat{\pi}_2$, we extend $\hat{\phi}$ with finitely many additional non-terminals and productions to obtain $\hat{\phi}^\star$ and generate a starting term $\hat{\pi}^\star$ such that $\mathcal{L}_{\hat{\phi}}(\hat{\pi}_1) \cap \mathcal{L}_{\hat{\phi}}(\hat{\pi}_2) = \mathcal{L}_{\hat{\phi}^\star}(\hat{\pi}^\star)$. The idea is that each new non-terminal represents the intersection of a type variable in $\mathsf{dom}(\hat{\phi})$ and a type; a global mapping from pairs of type variables and types to new non-terminals is maintained to ensure that the same new non-terminal is used whenever the same pair is encountered.

To illustrate the technique, consider intersecting the languages generated by $\hat{\phi}_{\mathsf{ex}}$ for the starting terms $\mathsf{int} \to \beta$ and α. First, extend the grammar with a new non-terminal Z and no productions (i.e., extend $\hat{\phi}_{\mathsf{ex}}$ with the mapping $Z \mapsto \{\}$); the non-terminal Z will serve as the starting term for an empty language. We are trying to intersect $\mathsf{int} \to \beta$ and α; since α is a non-terminal, generate a new non-terminal A_0 mapped from the pair $\langle \mathsf{int} \to \beta; \alpha \rangle$, add the triple $\langle A_0; \{\mathsf{int} \to \beta\}; \hat{\phi}_{\mathsf{ex}}(\alpha) \rangle$ to a work list, and return A_0 as the result of intersecting $\mathsf{int} \to \beta$ and α. The work list contains new non-terminals whose productions should be generated by intersecting all pairs of elements from the two sets. Therefore, add productions corresponding to $A_0 \Rightarrow \mathsf{int} \to \beta \oslash \mathsf{int} \to \mathsf{int}$ and $A_0 \Rightarrow \mathsf{int} \to \beta \oslash \mathsf{int} \to \alpha$. Intersecting $\mathsf{int} \to \beta$ and $\mathsf{int} \to \mathsf{int}$ generates a new non-terminal A_1 mapped from $\langle \beta; \mathsf{int} \rangle$, adds $\langle A_1; \hat{\phi}_{\mathsf{ex}}(\beta); \{\mathsf{int}\} \rangle$ to the work list, and returns $\mathsf{int} \to A_1$. Intersecting $\mathsf{int} \to \beta$ and $\mathsf{int} \to \alpha$ generates a new non-terminal A_2 mapped from $\langle \beta; \alpha \rangle$, adds $\langle A_1; \hat{\phi}_{\mathsf{ex}}(\beta); \hat{\phi}_{\mathsf{ex}}(\alpha) \rangle$ to the work list, and returns $\mathsf{int} \to A_2$. Therefore, extend with the mapping

$A_0 \mapsto \{\text{int} \to A_1\} \cup \{\text{int} \to A_2\}$. Returning to the work list, add productions corresponding to $A_1 \Rightarrow \text{int} \to \text{bool} \oslash \text{int}$ and $A_1 \Rightarrow \text{int} \to \beta \oslash \text{int}$. Intersecting $\text{int} \to \text{bool}$ and int returns Z (since clearly the intersection of the languages generated from these two starting terms is empty), as does intersecting $\text{int} \to \beta$ and int; therefore, extend with the mapping $A_1 \mapsto \{Z\} \cup \{Z\}$. Returning to the work list, add productions corresponding to $A_2 \Rightarrow \text{int} \to \text{bool} \oslash \text{int} \to \text{int}$ (returning Z), $A_2 \Rightarrow \text{int} \to \text{bool} \oslash \text{int} \to \alpha$ (generating a new non-terminal A_3 mapped from $\langle \text{bool}; \alpha \rangle$, adding $\langle A_3; \{\text{bool}\}; \hat{\phi}_{\text{ex}}(\alpha) \rangle$ to the work list, and returning $\text{int} \to A_3$), $A_2 \Rightarrow \text{int} \to \beta \oslash \text{int} \to \text{int}$ (returning $\text{int} \to A_1$, using the global map), and $A_2 \Rightarrow \text{int} \to \beta \oslash \text{int} \to \alpha$ (returning $\text{int} \to A_2$, using the global map); therefore, extend with the mapping $A_2 \mapsto \{Z\} \cup \{\text{int} \to A_3\} \cup \{\text{int} \to A_1\} \cup \{\text{int} \to A_2\}$. Finally, add productions corresponding to $A_3 \Rightarrow \text{bool} \oslash \text{int} \to \text{int}$ (returning Z) and $A_3 \Rightarrow \text{bool} \oslash \text{int} \to \alpha$ (returning Z); therefore, extend with the mapping $A_3 \mapsto \{Z\} \cup \{Z\}$. In summary, we have

Global map	New productions
$\langle \text{int} \to \beta; \alpha \rangle \mapsto A_0$	$A_0 \mapsto \{\text{int} \to A_1\} \cup \{\text{int} \to A_2\}$
$\langle \beta; \text{int} \rangle \mapsto A_1$	$A_1 \mapsto \{Z\} \cup \{Z\}$
$\langle \beta; \alpha \rangle \mapsto A_2$	$A_2 \mapsto \{Z\} \cup \{\text{int} \to A_3\} \cup \{\text{int} \to A_1\} \cup \{\text{int} \to A_2\}$
$\langle \text{bool}; \alpha \rangle \mapsto A_3$	$A_3 \mapsto \{Z\} \cup \{Z\}$

To conclude, return $\hat{\phi}_{\text{ex}}^{\star}$ equal to $\hat{\phi}_{\text{ex}}$ extended with the new productions and $\hat{\pi}^{\star}$ equal to A_0. Finally, note that $\Psi(\hat{\phi}_{\text{ex}}^{\star})(\hat{\pi}^{\star}) = \bot$, confirming that $\mathcal{L}_{\hat{\phi}_{\text{ex}}}(\text{int} \to \beta) \cap \mathcal{L}_{\hat{\phi}_{\text{ex}}}(\alpha) = \emptyset$ and that $\hat{\phi}_{\text{ex}} \vdash \text{int} \to \beta \approx \alpha$ is not derivable.

We conclude with a crude upper-bound on the time complexity of our type- and control-flow analysis. Consider a program of size n and the analysis defined in fixedpoint form. The two abstract environments are lattices of height $O(n^2)$. Each (naïve) iteration of the monotone function is syntax directed ($O(n)$) and dominated by the function-application bind, which loops over all of the elements of $\hat{\rho}(x_f)$ ($O(n)$), loops over all of the elements of $\hat{\rho}(x_a)$ ($O(n)$), and computes type compatibility via a regular-tree grammar intersection ($O(n^2)$) and emptiness test ($O((n^2)^2)$), because the regular-tree grammar representing the intersection may be of size $O(n^2)$. Hence, our analysis is computable in polynomial time: $O((n^2 + n^2) * (n * n * n * (n^2 + n^4))) = O(n^9)$. Further considerations regarding implementations of our type and control-flow analysis are given in Sect. 5.

4   Related Work

There is surprisingly little work on control-flow analyses for statically-typed languages with polymorphic types. Control-flow analyses have typically been formulated for dynamically- or simply-typed languages.[3] Production implementations of control-flow analyses for Standard ML, a language with rank-1 polymorphism (i.e., "let"-polymorphism), typically handle the polymorphism either

---

[3] Again, we draw a distinction between flow analyses expressed as sophisticated type systems and flow analyses of languages with sophisticated type systems.

by monomorphisation [4] (explicitly eliminating polymorphism before analysis) or by polyvariance [12] (implicitly eliminating polymorphism during analysis).

The most closely related work is the "Type-Directed Flow Analysis for Typed Intermediate Languages" of Jagannathan, Weeks, and Wright [15], which describes a framework for polyvariant flow analyses of Λ_i, the predicative subset of System F extended with recursive functions. A specific analysis called $S_{\mathcal{RT}}$ uses types to control polyvariance; essentially, $S_{\mathcal{RT}}$ introduces a distinct polyvariance context for each closed type at which a polymorphic function is applied, yielding an analysis more precise than our type- and control-flow analysis. Unfortunately, $S_{\mathcal{RT}}$ does not terminate on programs that use polymorphic recursion [14,19,25]; such programs may instantiate a polymorphic function at an infinite number of closed types during execution. In contrast, our type- and control-flow analysis is computable for all programs in (impredicative) System F extended with recursive functions.

Another closely related work is the "Type-sensitive Control-Flow Analysis" of Reppy [30], which describes an extension of Serrano's version of 0CFA [33] that uses a program's type information to compute more precise results. Serrano's and Reppy's analyses are modular and use an abstract value $\top$ to denote an unknown value; variables bound outside the unit of analysis are assigned $\top$, as are the parameters of functions that escape the unit of analysis. Reppy's insight is that values of an abstract type can only be created within their defining module; hence, "unknown" values of the abstract type can be soundly approximated by the known set of escaping values of the abstract type. This leads to a type-indexed family of abstract values for unknown values, in addition to the $\top$ abstract value. Reppy's analysis is formulated for a simply-typed language with top-level abstract types; he suggests extending the analysis to a language with polymorphism by mapping type variables to the $\top$ abstract value. Our type- and control-flow analysis is a whole-program analysis, but has a more precise treatment of type variables.

5   Future Work

While we have established the computability of the minimum, finite acceptable pair of abstract environments for every program, we would like our type- and control-flow analysis to be efficiently computable. A popular approach for computing control-flow analyses is as a constraint-based analysis [1]; an initial phase generates constraints that a solution to the analysis must satisfy, while a subsequent phase solves the constraints. The syntax-directed 0CFA that we adapt for our type- and control-flow analysis has an $O(n^3)$ algorithm following this approach [26, Sect. 3.4]. However, algorithms for solving a set of constraints are sensitive to the syntax of constraints; the filtering of sets by type compatibility may prove problematic, since the derivability of a type-compatibility judgment depends upon the abstract type environment, itself being solved for.

Independent of the overall approach, it seems clear that we will need to efficiently decide the derivability of a type-compatibility judgment under an abstract type environments. We have established that this decision can be made by intersecting and testing the emptiness of regular-tree grammars. Aiken and Murphy [2, Sect. 4] suggest maintaining a regular-tree grammar with an invariant that makes testing the emptiness (of a non-terminal) constant time. Aiken and Murphy [2, Sect. 5.3] also suggest that the algorithm given previously, which generates only the intersections necessary to express the result, performs well in the typical case. We further observe that, for a fixed abstract type environment, we can maintain the global map from pairs of type variables and types to new non-terminals across decisions of the derivability of type-compatibility. Hence, the (worst-case) quartic time bounds all queries under a given abstract type environment, not each query, and improves our crude upper-bound to $O(n^6)$. We may also be able to exploit the fact that we are only interested in the emptiness of an intersection of regular-tree grammars, and not the intersection itself.

Another direction of future work is to extend the type- and control-flow analysis to handle unknown and escaping values [36] and types [30]. It should be straightforward to introduce a $\top$ abstract type and a $\top$ abstract value; conservatively, the $\top$ abstract type should be judged compatible with any other abstract type. A more interesting direction is to consider primitives that make essential use of higher-rank polymorphism, such as Haskell's runST [20,21].

Yet another direction is to extend the monovariant type- and control-flow analysis to a polyvariant analysis.

Finally, we would like to extend type- and control-flow analysis to languages with even more sophisticated type systems. Of particular interest is System F with guarded algebraic data types (GADTs), as we would like to combine the flow-directed defunctionalization of Cejtin, Jagannathan, and Weeks [4] with the polymorphic typed defunctionalization of Pottier and Gauthier [29]. Also of interest is System F_ω, the higher-order polymorphic lambda-calculus: System F_ω has been used as a target language for the elaboration of a full-featured, higher-order ML-like module language [32] and System F_ω extended with type equality coercions [37] is used as a typed intermediate language in the Glasgow Haskell Compiler (GHC).

Acknowledgments. Many thanks to Jan Midtgaard for the excellent survey "Control-flow analysis of functional programs" [22] and companion bibliography and for valuable feedback on an earlier draft. Thanks to Jurriaan Hage, Fritz Henglein, and Peter Thiemann for thoughtful conversation at IFL'12. This material is based upon work supported by the National Science Foundation under Grant No. 1065099.

References

1. Aiken, A.: Introduction to set constraint-based program analysis. Sci. Comput. Program. **35**(2–3), 79–111 (1999)
2. Aiken, A., Murphy, B.R.: Implementing regular tree expressions. In: Conference on Functional Programming Languages and Computer Architecture (FPCA). LNCS, vol. 523, pp. 427–447, August 1991
3. Aiken, A., Murphy, B.R.: Static type inference in a dynamically typed language. In: Symposium on Principles of Programming Languages (POPL), pp. 279–290, January 1991

4. Cejtin, H., Jagannathan, S., Weeks, S.: Flow-directed closure conversion for typed languages. In: Smolka, G. (ed.) ESOP 2000. LNCS, vol. 1782, pp. 56–71. Springer, Heidelberg (2000)

5. Cousot, P., Cousot, R.: Compositional and inductive semantic definitions in fixpoint, equational, constraint, closure-condition, rule-based and game-theoretic form, invited paper. In: Conference on Computer Aided Verification (CAV). LNCS, vol. 939, pp. 293–308, July 1995

6. Cousot, P., Cousot, R.: Formal language, grammar and set-constraint-based program analysis by abstract interpretation. In: Conference on Functional Programming Languages and Computer Architecture (FPCA), pp. 170–181, June 1995

7. Flanagan, C., Sabry, A., Duba, B.F., Felleisen, M.: The essence of compiling with continuations. In: Conference on Programming Language Design and Implementation (PLDI), pp. 237–247, June 1993

8. Fluet, M.: A type- and control-flow analysis for System F. Tech. rep., Rochester Institute of Technology. https://ritdml.rit.edu/handle/1850/15920, February 2013

9. Gecseg, F., Steinby, M.: Tree Automata. Akademiai Kiado, Budapest (1984)

10. Girard, J.Y.: Une extension de l'interpretation de Gödel à l'analyse, et son application à l'élimination des coupures dans l'analyse et la théorie des types. In: Scandinavian Logic Symposium. Stud. Logic Found. Math. **63**, 63–92 (1971)

11. Harper, R., Morrisett, G.: Compiling polymorphism using intensional type analysis. In: Symposium on Principles of Programming Languages (POPL), pp. 130–141, Januay 1995

12. Heintze, N.: Set-based program analysis of ML programs. In: Conference on Lisp and Functional Programming (LFP), pp. 306–317, June 1994

13. Heintze, N., Jaffar, J.: A finite presentation theorem for approximating logic programs. In: Symposium on Principles of Programming Languages (POPL), pp. 197–209, January 1990

14. Henglein, F.: Type inference with polymorphic recursion. ACM Trans. Program. Lang. Syst. **15**(2), 253–289 (1993)

15. Jagannathan, S., Weeks, S., Wright, A.K.: Type-directed flow analysis for typed intermediate languages. In: International Symposium on Static Analysis (SAS). LNCS, vol. 1302, pp. 232–249, September 1997

16. Jones, N.D.: Flow analysis of lambda expressions (preliminary version). In: International Colloquium on Automata, Languages and Programming (ICALP). LNCS, vol. 115, pp. 114–128, July 1981

17. Jones, N.D.: Flow analysis of lazy higher-order functional programs. In: Abramsky, S., Hankin, C. (eds.) Abstract Interpretation of Declarative Languages, Chap. 4, pp. 103–122. Ellis Horwood, Chicheste (1987)

18. Jones, N.D., Muchnick, S.S.: Flow analysis and optimization of LISP-like structures. In: Symposium on Principles of Programming Languages (POPL), pp. 244–256, January 1979

19. Kfoury, A., Tiuryn, J., Urzyczyn, P.: Type reconstruction in the presence of polymorphic recursion. ACM Trans. Program. Lang. Syst. **15**(2), 290–311 (1993)

20. Launchbury, J., Peyton Jones, S.: Lazy functional state threads. In: Conference on Programming Language Design and Implementation (PLDI), pp. 24–35, June 1994

21. Launchbury, J., Peyton Jones, S.: State in Haskell. Lisp Symbolic Comput. **8**(4), 293–341 (1995)

22. Midtgaard, J.: Control-flow analysis of functional programs. ACM Comput. Surv. **44**(3), 10:1–10:33 (2012)

23. Midtgaard, J., Adams, M., Might, M.: A structural soundness proof for Shivers's escape technique. In: International Symposium on Static Analysis (SAS). LNCS, vol. 7460, pp. 352–369, September 2012

24. Mishra, P., Reddy, U.S.: Declaration-free type checking. In: Symposium on Principles of Programming Languages (POPL), pp. 7–21. ACM, January 1985

25. Mycroft, A.: Polymorphic type schemes and recursive definitions. In: International Symposium on Programming. LNCS, vol. 167, pp. 217–228, April 1984

26. Nielson, F., Nielson, H.R., Hankin, C.: Principles of Program Analysis. Springer, Heidelberg (1999)

27. Palsberg, J.: Type-based analysis and applications. In: Workshop on Programming Analysis for Software Tools and Engineering (PASTE), pp. 20–27 (2001)

28. Peyton Jones, S.: Compiling Haskell by program transformation: A report from the trenches. In: European Symposium on Programming (ESOP). LNCS, vol. 1058, pp. 18–44, April 1996

29. Pottier, F., Gauthier, N.: Polymorphic typed defunctionalization and concretization. Higher-Order Symbolic Comput. 19(1), 125–162 (2006)

30. Reppy, J.: Type-sensitive control-flow analysis. In: Workshop on ML (ML). pp. 74–83, September 2006

31. Reynolds, J.: Towards a theory of type structure. In: International Symposium on Programming. LNCS, vol. 19, pp. 408–425, April 1974

32. Rossberg, A., Russo, C., Dreyer, D.: F-ing modules. In: Workshop on Types in Language Design and Implementation (TLDI), pp. 89–102, January 2010

33. Serrano, M.: Control flow analysis: a functional languages compilation paradigm. In: Symposium on Applied Computing (SAC), pp. 118–122, Feburary 1995

34. Sestoft, P.: Replacing function parameters by global variables. In: Conference on Functional Programming Languages and Computer, Architecture (FPCA), pp. 39–53, September 1989

35. Shivers, O.: Control-flow analysis in Scheme. In: Conference on Programming Language Design and Implementation (PLDI), pp. 164–174, June 1988

36. Shivers, O.: Control-Flow Analysis of Higher-Order Languages or Taming Lambda. Ph.D. thesis, School of Computer Science, Carnegie Mellon University, Pittsburgh, Pennsylvania, Technical Report CMU-CS-91-145, May 1991

37. Sulzmann, M., Chakravarty, M.M.T., Peyton Jones, S., Donnelly, K.: System F with type equality coercions. In: Workshop on Types in Language Design and Implementation (TLDI), pp. 53–66, January 2007

38. Tarditi, D., Morrisett, G., Cheng, P., Stone, C., Harper, R., Lee, P.: TIL: a type-directed optimizing compiler for ML. In: Conference on Programming Language Design and Implementation (PLDI), pp. 181–192, May 1996

39. Wright, A.K., Felleisen, M.: A syntactic approach to type soundness. Inf. Comput. 115(1), 38–94 (1994)

Dependently-Typed Programming in Scientific Computing

Examples from Economic Modelling

Cezar Ionescu[1(✉)] and Patrik Jansson[2]

[1] Potsdam Institute for Climate Impact Research, Potsdam, Germany
ionescu@pik-potsdam.de
[2] Chalmers University of Technology, Göteborg, Sweden

Abstract. Computer simulations are essential in virtually every scientific discipline, even more so in those such as economics or climate change where the ability to make laboratory experiments is limited. Therefore, it is important to ensure that the models are implemented correctly, that they can be re-implemented and that the results can be reproduced. Typically, though, the models are described by a mixture of prose and mathematics which is insufficient for these purposes. We argue that using dependent types allows us to gradually reduce the gap between the mathematical description and the implementation, and we give examples from economic modelling. We discuss the consequences that our incremental approach has on programming style and the requirements it imposes on the dependently-typed programming languages used.

1 Introduction

In 2006, Herbert Gintis [10] announced the discovery of a mechanism that would explain price formation and disequilibrium adjustment without requiring the presence of a central authority or omniscience on part of the agents, as is currently assumed in mainstream economics. Gintis' results were, as he put it "empirical rather than theoretical: we have created a class of economies and investigated their properties for a range of parameters." They were obtained by computer simulations. Due to the importance of this result, two groups of researchers, one at PIK, the other at Chalmers [9], independently attempted to do something which should perhaps be routine, but is hardly ever done: to re-implement the model described in the paper and reproduce the results. After initial attempts failed and Gintis graciously provided the source code, both groups discovered several ways that his implementation diverged from the description in the paper, only one of which could be called a "bug". Much more problematic was the ambiguity left open by the model description given in the paper, which consisted of a mixture of prose and mathematical equations.

The example of the Gintis model was chosen because it is well documented in recent literature, not because it is unique. It is quite typical for scientists to believe that the mathematical equations used to develop a model are sufficient specification for the implementation of that model, but that is rarely the

R. Hinze (Ed.): IFL 2012, LNCS 8241, pp. 140–156, 2013.
DOI: 10.1007/978-3-642-41582-1_9, © Springer-Verlag Berlin Heidelberg 2013

case. Discretizations, approximations, choices of integration methods, and many other similar steps come between the mathematical description and the program. This is a gap that must be bridged if we are to be able to check correctness of implementations, re-implement models, or replicate results.

Sooner or later, everyone who considers this problem is bound to encounter constructive mathematics and Martin-Löf's type theory, which seems to be made to order for this purpose. Here is for example a quote from the programmatic article "Constructive Mathematics and Computer Programming" [12]:

> Now, it is the contention of the intuitionists (or constructivists, I shall use these terms synonymously) that the basic mathematical notions, above all the notion of function, ought to be interpreted in such a way that the cleavage between mathematics, classical mathematics, that is, and programming that we are witnessing at present disappears.

Specifications ("tasks that the programs are supposed to perform") are also mentioned explicitly:

> [Type theory] provides a precise notation not only, like other programming languages, for the programs themselves but also for the tasks that the programs are supposed to perform. Thus the correctness of a program written in the theory of types is proved formally at the same time as it is being synthesized.

The ideal of correctness put forward here is very enticing. There are many examples of such correct-by-construction development, for example [7, 14, 15, 17, 19, 20]. It seems natural to attempt to apply the same methodology in the context of scientific computing, for instance when building economic models such as the one we mentioned in the beginning.

A necessary (but far from sufficient) condition for that is that type theory has the expressive power to formulate the usual mathematical concepts which modelers use as specifications. In the next section we show that this is indeed the case. Together with economists at PIK, we have formalized basic building blocks of economic theory, used in almost all economic models today, concepts such as Pareto efficiency, Walrasian equilibrium, Nash equilibrium, and a host of others, together with the relations between them (for example, Walrasian equilibria are Pareto efficient). The resulting formalizations are pleasantly close to the mathematical formulations the modelers are used to, so we can hope they could use them in specifications.

The bad news is most of these concepts are classical in nature: economics is currently a non-constructive theory (and even the so-called "computable general equilibrium models" turn out to be non-computable, as pointed out by Velupillai in [25]). Therefore, the specifications turn out to be non-implementable and the gap between the mathematics and the programming is still there. But, as we argue in the third section, we are now in a better position to close it.

We close the paper with a discussion of some consequences of this approach.

2   Formalizing Economic Notions in Type Theory

The quintessential economic situation is that of exchange of goods, which we introduce via the simplest possible example: two agents and two goods. We have to assume at least two agents and two goods: if we had only one agent there would be no one to exchange with, and if there were only one kind of good then there would be nothing against which to exchange that good. We would then have a situation of gift-giving, rather than exchange.

For concreteness, let us call the first good "wine" and the second good "beer", assume they come in bottles and cans respectively, and that there are 5 bottles of wine and 10 cans of beer, distributed among our two agents: agent one has 3 bottles of wine and 3 cans of beer and agent two has 2 bottles of wine and 7 cans of beer. The bundle of goods each agent has is called its *endowment*, the distribution of the endowments is an *allocation*.

Let us assume that the agents have different preferences for beer and wine. For example, agent one likes beer more than wine, but needs to have at least one bottle of wine in case he has more sophisticated guests. Agent two, on the other hand, values wine over beer, but must have at least three cans of beer for watching football with friends. The agents are allowed to change their endowments by trading, but in the end there must be exactly as many bottles and cans as we started out with: there is no consumption and no production of goods, only pure exchange.

In our example, agents have preferences over their endowments (their own stocks only), but in general they could have them over allocations (including their competitors' endowments), allowing economists to model not just greed, but also envy. In most common examples, preferences, sometimes qualified with the adjective *weak*, are total preorders (reflexive and transitive, but not necessarily anti-symmetric). Thus, an agent can prefer x over y and y over x, without having x = y. We say that x is *strongly preferred* to y if x is weakly preferred to y, but y is not weakly preferred to x (in particular, nothing can be strongly preferred to itself).

An agent's preference over endowments can be extended to preference over allocations in the natural way (by just ignoring others' endowments).

An exchange leads to a re-allocation of goods, but the resulting allocation must be *feasible*: this includes the "no creation, no consumption"-condition, but also the constraints the agents have (at least one bottle of wine for the first agent and three cans of beer for the second one).

Under the assumptions we have made, we can expect that the two agents will indeed trade with each other, since each one stands to gain by an exchange. This would not be the case if we switched the two preferences (or, equivalently, the two endowments) because then the agent who prefers wine would not be able to trade any of his beer for it because of the 3-cans constraint. Coming back to the original setting, we can also see that intuitively a re-allocation of goods in which agent one has 1 bottle of wine and 7 cans of beer (and the rest goes to agent two) is optimal. The two agents are as well off as they can possibly be, given their initial endowments and their preferences. An allocation in which agent one has 2 bottles of wine and 7 cans of beer (and agent two therefore 3 and 3) is also feasible and preferred by both agents to the initial one, but is intuitively less satisfactory (since the first agent is indifferent to the second bottle of wine, it looks as though the second agent has not made a good deal, giving up four cans for just one bottle). Still, it is a possible end-result of an exchange between the agents.

The reader should now be in a position to understand the following definitions taken from the standard textbook on microeconomics:

Definitions of Pareto efficiency. A feasible allocation x is a **weakly Pareto efficient** allocation if there is no feasible allocation x' such that all agents strictly prefer x' to x. A feasible allocation x is a **strongly Pareto efficient** allocation if there is no feasible allocation x' such that all agents weakly prefer x' to x, and some agent strictly prefers x' to x.

Varian [23], *p. 323*

In our example, the first re-allocation, intuitively considered optimal, can be seen to be strongly Pareto efficient, while the second one, less satisfactory, but not leading necessarily to an exchange, is weakly Pareto efficient.

Pareto efficiency is fundamental in economics and easily formalized in constructive type theory, which makes it a good place to start. Since our economist colleagues were familiar with Haskell, we chose to work with implementations of type theory which offer a similar syntax, so we have used equally Agda and Idris (here we present the Agda version).

We were fortunate that we could assume familiarity with a functional programming language, which is not currently part of the standard training of economists. We were even more fortunate that we could assume familiarity with the ideas and practice of formalization, at the level of, for example, Chapter 12 of Suppes' *Introduction to Logic* [18]. The interdisciplinary nature of research at PIK, involving a mixture of natural and social sciences, has led to many inquiries into the meaning of words such as "sustainability", "resilience", or "vulnerability" in the context of climate change. There have been a number of projects, workshops, and seminars devoted to the topic of formalization and mathematical modeling of such concepts using classical logic and set theory.

Accordingly, our formalization of Pareto efficiency has a distinctively set-theoretical flavor. We assume a set Agent for the agents, a set Allocation for the allocations, a predicate Feasible on this set, and a ternary relation of strict preference. In Agda, the standard way of working with such assumptions is to pass them as parameters to the module encapsulating the formalization. Alternatively, we can explicitly express them as postulates:

```
postulate
    Agent    : Set
    Allocation : Set
    Feasible   : Allocation → Set
    _strictlyPrefers_to_  : Agent → Allocation → Allocation → Set
```

The formalization of weak Pareto efficiency as a predicate on allocations reads

```
WeakPareto x  =  Feasible x ∧
   ¬ (∃ [x' : Allocation] (Feasible x' ∧
                  (∀ [a : Agent] (a strictlyPrefers x' to x))))
```

We are using here Agda's flexible, Unicode-enabled syntax, to make the formalization readable to anyone familiar with the standard logical connectors and quantifiers. It is, we hope, clearly an ad-litteram translation of the definition cited above. To achieve this effect, we have sometimes used a different notation than that of the standard Agda library, for example we use ∃ where the standard library has Σ. The most important departures from the standard are noted in the Appendix, which also lists references for readers unfamiliar with Agda or the monomorphic version of Martin-Löf's type theory it implements.

The formalization of strong Pareto efficiency requires an additional ternary relation for weak preference, but is otherwise just as simple:

```
postulate
   _weaklyPrefers_to_  : Agent  →  Allocation  →  Allocation  →  Set
StrongPareto x  =  Feasible x ∧
   ¬ (∃ [x' : Allocation] (Feasible x' ∧
                  (∀ [a : Agent]  (a weaklyPrefers x' to x)) ∧
                  (∃ [a' : Agent] (a' strictlyPrefers x' to x))))
```

It is just as easy to formulate a simple relationship between weak and strong Pareto efficiency: namely, that strong Pareto efficiency is stronger than weak Pareto efficiency, i.e., the former implies the latter:

```
Strong⇒Weak : ∀ [x : Allocation] (StrongPareto x  →  WeakPareto x)
```

but this is as far as we can go without discussing the meaning of the connectives and quantifiers.

Until now, the formulas we have seen could have been written in classical logic. Typed predicate logic, for example, introduced by Raymond Turner in [22], has the same syntax as constructive type theory, but is a classical, multi-sorted predicate logic. What is different is the inferential system: what counts as a proof.

Constructively, the universal quantifier above is interpreted as a function which, to each allocation x, associates a proof of the statement "x is strongly Pareto efficient implies that x is weakly Pareto efficient". In turn, this implication is interpreted as a function which, given a proof that x is strongly Pareto efficient, produces a proof that x is weakly Pareto efficient. A proof that x is weakly Pareto efficient consists of a pair of proofs: one that x is feasible, the other that it is impossible to find an x' which is also feasible and strictly preferred by all agents to x. And so on.

It takes a bit of getting used to, but after that, and with a little help from the Agda proof assistant Agsy, it is easy to implement proofs such as the following:

```
postulate
    agent0        : Agent
    strict⇒weak  : ∀ {a x x'}  →  a strictlyPrefers x' to x  →
                                      a weaklyPrefers x' to x
Strong⇒Weak x (fx, spx)  =  (fx, wpx)
    where
    wpx  :  ¬ (∃ [x' : Allocation] (    Feasible x' ∧
                                        (∀ [a : Agent] (a strictlyPrefers x' to x))))
    wpx (x', (fx', prefx'))  =
        spx (x', (fx', ((λ a  →  strict⇒weak (prefx' a)),
                 (agent0, prefx' agent0))))
```

In fact, it is instructive to do so. Here, we can see that we need the assumption that strict preferences imply weak preferences (which holds in the common model of preferences as total preorders) and that the set of agents is not empty (and that we can actually pick an agent from it, whom we called agent0). As is often the case, assumptions are made explicit by formalization.

From Pareto efficiency we move on to one of the most important notions of economics: that of a Walrasian equilibrium.

In a first approximation, Walrasian equilibrium can be understood as a way of computing Pareto efficient allocations. This computation is difficult in general, among other reasons because it involves looking at all the agents simultaneously. It would be much easier if the agents could somehow be treated individually, instead of collectively.

In the model proposed by Walras in [27], goods have prices. Since each agent starts out with an initial endowment, the value of this endowment can be computed to yield the agent's budget. Each agent then computes the optimal endowment within this budget. Suppose these optimal endowments together make up a feasible allocation: this would surely be a good end-result for an exchange, since every agent gets the best it can afford. Whether this optimal allocation is in fact feasible depends on the prices. In our example above, if the price of a can of beer were the same as the price of a bottle of wine, say 1 cent each, then agent one would have as optimal endowment one bottle of wine and five cans of beer, while agent two could optimally afford six bottles of wine and three cans of beer. The resulting allocation is not feasible: it needs too many bottles of wine (seven, instead of the five available ones) and too few cans of beer (eight, instead of ten). On the other hand, if wine bottles cost twice as much as beer cans, say two cents to one, then the optimal endowments of the two agents make up the strongly Pareto allocation we have seen earlier. Prices for which the optimal endowments constitute a feasible allocation are called *equilibrium prices*, together with an optimal allocation they make up a *Walrasian equilibrium*. Here is the definition from Varian's classical textbook [23]:

An allocation-price pair (x, p) is a **Walrasian equilibrium** if (1) the allocation is feasible, and (2) each agent is making an optimal choice from its budget set. In equations:

1. $\sum_{i=1}^{n} x_i = \sum_{i=1}^{n} \omega_i$
2. If x'_i is preferred by agent i to x_i, then $px'_i > p\omega_i$.

Varian, Microeconomic Analysis, p. 325

Here, ω is the initial allocation. It is assumed that the endowments are vectors of non-negative real numbers, each component representing the quantity of the respective good, and that the value of an endowment is computed by a scalar product with the prices. In turn, an allocation is represented by a matrix, having the individual endowments as columns. Thus, the sum in the first point in the definition is column-wise and represents the conservation of goods condition. The second point states that if an allocation is preferred by an agent to the optimal one, the value of the agent's endowment in this allocation is greater than the value of the agent's initial endowment: the allocation is out of budget.

There is a level of detail in this definition which is more than we need for the moment. For the purpose of formalizing Walrasian equilibrium, it suffices to assume that we can compute an agent's endowment from an allocation and the value of that endowment at given prices, and that we can compare values with one another. This being granted, the precise nature of the sets of prices, endowments, values is not important and we can formalize a more general version of Walrasian equilibrium:

```
postulate
    Endowment : Set
    Price     : Set
    Value     : Set

    endmt     : Allocation → Agent → Endowment

    value     : Endowment → Price → Value

    _ > _     : Value → Value → Set

    ω         : Allocation
WalrasianEq (x, p) = Feasible x ∧
    (∀ [a : Agent] (∀ [x' : Allocation]
        ((a strictlyPrefers x' to x) →
            value (endmt x' a) p > value (endmt ω a) p)))
```

While a bit more abstract, this formalization is still just an almost literal translation of the definition given by Varian.

We have referred to the allocation in a Walrasian equilibrium as "optimal", but is it really Pareto efficient? In fact, it is easy to show that it is weakly Pareto efficient, a result known as the first theorem of welfare economics:

First theorem of welfare economics. If (x, p) is a Walrasian equilibrium, then x is [weakly] Pareto efficient.

Varian, *Microeconomic Analysis*, p. 326

We have explicitly added the qualifier *weakly*: Varian adopts the following convention "when we say 'Pareto efficient' we generally mean 'weakly Pareto efficient' " (p. 324).

The proof of the theorem is by contradiction and relies on the distributivity of multiplication over addition, on factor cancellation and on the assumption that prices are strictly positive (and therefore non-zero). We can abstract away from these properties by postulating that, for any prices p and any allocation x, if every agent's endowment in x is more valuable than in ω, then x is not feasible:

postulate
```
outOfBudget : ∀ [p : Price] (∀ [x : Allocation]
    (∀ [a : Agent] (value (endmt x a) p > value (endmt ω a) p) →
    ¬ (Feasible x)))
```

The formalization of the theorem is then short and simple, at least if one is accustomed to the computational reading of the logical connectives and quantifiers.

```
FirstTheorem : ∀ [x : Allocation] (∀ [p : Price] (WalrasianEq (x, p) →
                                                   WeakPareto x))
FirstTheorem x p (fx, weq) = (fx, wpe) where
    wpe : ¬ (∃ [x' : Allocation] (Feasible x' ∧
                            (∀ [a : Agent] (a strictlyPrefers x' to x))))
    wpe (x', (fx', prefx')) = outOfBudget p x'
                            (λ a → weq a x' (prefx' a)) fx'
```

More interestingly is that, while formalizing this proof, we hit upon the following question: if (x, p) is a Walrasian equilibrium, is then every endowment in x in the respective agent's budget? The answer, which even some of our economist colleagues found surprising, is no. Of course, if one has the idea of looking for them, counter-examples are easy to find. Consider our two-agent example, with the same initial allocation, but removing the constraints on the preferences: agent one no longer needs to have at least one bottle of wine, and agent two no longer cares about beer.

The former equilibrium prices, two cents for a bottle of wine and one for a can of beer, are still equilibrium prices for the new situations. The allocation which gives agent one an endowment of no wine and nine cans of beer, and agent two all five bottles of wine and one can of the beer is optimal. Any allocation strictly preferred by agent one would have more cans of beer than it can afford, and the same for agent two in terms of wine (no half-bottles accepted!). Therefore, the Walrasian equilibrium condition is satisfied.

Now consider the allocation that gives agent one all ten cans of beer, and agent two the five bottles of wine. This allocation is certainly feasible: it contains five bottles of wine and ten cans of beer, just like ω. If another allocation is preferred by agent one, it has to give it at least ten cans of beer: more than it can afford. If it is preferred by agent two, it has to give it six bottles of wine, but agent two can only afford five. Therefore, this allocation is also a Walrasian equilibrium for these prices. But, as we see, it is out of budget for agent one.

We have said that Walrasian equilibrium can be approached as a way of computing Pareto efficient allocation, an idea that we found useful but which might make some of our economist colleagues cringe. Before going further, we should point out that the importance of the Walrasian model lies in that it serves to explain prices as arising from desirability of goods, from the preferences of the agents and their initial endowments, as opposed to the Marxist theory of value, where prices appear as a measure of the labor involved in the production of goods.

This model admits many extensions: one can add to it production and consumption of goods, a labor market (treating labor as a good to be exchanged by the workers), exchanges in several steps (adding a temporal dimension to the problem), and so on. Most mainstream economic models, including such as are used for policy advice (for example ReMIND [4] and GEM-E3 [3]) are *general equilibrium models* based on extensions of the Walrasian ideas formalized in this section.

A general criticism of all these models is that they neglect the dynamical aspect of reaching the equilibrium situation. There is no known plausible mechanism which explains exactly how equilibrium prices can arise in practice. Walras' own proposal for such a price-formation mechanism involved an *auctioneer*. This is a central entity who can see all supply-demand imbalances and adjust prices accordingly, raising the prices of goods for which there is too great demand, and lowering those for which there is too little, in an iterative process. Even if one accepts that in some situations one could have an authority that might act as auctioneer, there is no general proof that the iterative process will eventually converge.

This, in fact, was the problem that Gintis attempted to solve, and the reason the papers we referred to in the previous section found an immediate echo in the economics community. This shows that even non-mainstream models like his can actually benefit from having formal specifications of the classical economic concepts.

We have formalized much more than just what we have shown here: the detailed definitions in Varian's book, but also the notions of Nash equilibria, correlated equilibria, and several others. They are all more complex, but not more complicated than what we have been able to show here. All in all, we can say that constructive type theory as embodied by Agda or Idris has passed our test for expressiveness: we were able to formulate in it fundamental notions of economics and relationships between them in such a way that they can be read, and with some exercise even used, by our colleagues.

That was the good news. The bad news is that most of these concepts are not constructive. Specifications of programs that take as input agents characterized by preference relations and initial endowments and return a Walrasian (or Nash, or correlated, ...) equilibrium can in general not be fulfilled. In fact, as mentioned in the introduction, even the so-called computable general equilibrium models are not, in fact, computable.

We started with the problem that the mathematical descriptions employed in scientific computing are too far from the implementation to serve as specifications. Constructive type theory promised to be a bridge across this gulf. However, it now appears that we have not made any progress. The simplicity of the translation from informal mathematical definitions to formal ones, which we interpreted as proof of the expressiveness of constructive type theory, turns out to have been deceptive. We appear to have the same unsatisfactory specifications, only in slightly fancier notation. The gap has not been bridged, after all.

However, the translational effort has brought us something essential, as we shall see in the next section.

3   Increasingly Correct Scientific Computing

There are general reasons for wanting to formalize the kind of mathematical specifications used in scientific programming. For one thing, formalization can help us understand the informal definitions better. We have seen this in the case of Walrasian equilibrium, where optimal allocations are allowed by the standard definition to be "out of budget" for some agents. For another, having formal specifications makes them checkable by computer: we can be fairly confident that the syntactic errors are going to be signalled by it, as well as some of the more glaring semantical errors, such as inverting quantifier order.

Still, why choose constructive type theory as the vehicle for the formalization, over, for example, classical higher-order logic and set theory (which also have the advantage of being more familiar to non-computer scientists)?

The reason is that the only way one can decrease the distance between mathematics and programming is to make the mathematical side more constructive: computation cannot become more classical. There are many efforts underway aiming to use constructive mathematics in the context of scientific computing. For example, Velupillai's program for computable economics [24, 26], or various projects for developing constructive numerical methods [2, 11].

Using constructive type theory both for formalizing specifications and for the implementations enables us to take advantage of these developments as they occur, by gradually replacing the non-constructive concepts with their constructive counterparts. This is an increase of correctness "from above": we are improving the specifications, becoming more precise about what we are "really" computing and what relationship there is between this and what we think we should be computing.

We can already implement the constructive parts, and isolate the ones that depend on classical theory in *postulates*. For example, the kind of inter-temporal

optimization that many economic models are based on can be solved by applying Bellman's dynamic programming algorithm [5,6], thus reducing the inter-
temporal optimization to the successive application of local optimizations. This
works if the Bellman principle can be applied, and the proof is constructive.
Thus, we can have a verified implementation of the dynamic programming algorithm, *if* we can implement the local maximization.

Few modelers are going to implement their own optimization routine. Rather,
they are going to use an external one, with an interface which in its simplest
form can be expressed as

maxUtil : {n : Nat} → (Vect Float n → Float) → Float

so that maxUtil u returns the maximum of the utility function u defined over $\mathbb{R}^n$.
(For brevity, we ignore here that a function such as maxUtil should also return
the input vector for which the utility reaches its maximum). The modeler will
often use maxUtil as if it implemented the specification

postulate maxSpec : {n : Nat} →
  ∀ [u : (Vect Float n → Float)]
    (∀ [x : Vect Float n]
      (so (u x ⩽ maxUtil u)))

In this usage, postulates express a condition relative to which the correctness
of the implementation is to be judged. In particular, this is always the case
when using external routines which do not have a type theoretical interface. The
typechecker can at least verify that we are using the postulated properties in a
correct way. Another advantage is that we have clearly signalled the spots where
further refinement is necessary, where constructive mathematics can help.

There is another usage of postulates which points to further refinements in
a different, simpler way. The scientists involved in the modeling process are
usually not experts in giving formal proofs, let alone constructive formal proofs.
Sometimes, it is useful to just defer the proof to the experts, or to a later stage
of development. For example, while maximizing utility functions is in general
not computable, it is computable when the domain of the utility is a finite set.
Therefore, the following specification

postulate maxFinSpec : {n : Nat} →
  ∀ [u : (Fin (S n) → Float)]
    (∀ [i : Fin (S n)]
      (so (u i ⩽ maxUtil u)))

is implementable, but the proof might be tricky for the beginner.

In fact, beginners, even under the somewhat ideal conditions of familiarity
with Haskell, tend to paint themselves into a corner. For example, to implement

maximization by enumeration, one might try to translate the following Haskell code:

```
maxUtil :: Nat -> (Nat -> Float) -> Float
maxUtil 0       u  = u 0
maxUtil (n + 1) u  = maxUtil' (n + 1) u (u 0) 0

maxUtil' :: Nat -> (Nat -> Float) -> Float -> Nat -> Float
maxUtil' n u best c' =
  let c  = c' + 1 in  -- c is the candidate new best
  let uc = u c   in  -- uc is potential new optimum
  let bU = max uc best in
     if  c == n       -- is c the last candidate?
         then bU
         else maxUtil' n u bU c
```

in the following somewhat exaggeratedly literal manner. We hasten to say that we are not presenting this example as a model of good style, instead, it's main merit is that it has actually arisen in practice and is a somewhat typical and instructive case:

```
maxUtil : {n : Nat} → (Fin (S n) → Float) → Float
maxUtil {O} u   = u fO
maxUtil {S n} u = maxUtil' u (u fO) fO
maxUtil' :   {n : Nat} →
             (Fin (S n) → Float) → Float → Fin n → Float
maxUtil' {n} u bestU c' =
  let c  = fS c' in        -- c is the candidate
  let uc = u c in          -- uc is potential new optimum
  let bU = max uc bestU in
    if (c =F= toFin n)     -- is c the last candidate?
      then bU
      else (maxUtil' u bU c)   -- !
```

But this code does not type check! The reason is that the type of the last argument to maxUtil', namely c, is Fin (S n) instead of Fin n, as required by our use of it (namely to increment it in order to obtain a new candidate). We know that, in fact, c could be cast to a valid value of type Fin n, since we have just tested that it is not maximal in Fin (S n), but we are going to have a very hard time convincing the type checker of it, let alone prove that the resulting max satisfies maxFinSpec. On top of it all, the termination checker also complains it does not see why maxUtil' is not just going to loop forever. Unfortunately, this situation is quite common when attempting to just write Haskell in Agda.

At this point, many a scientific programmer can feel like throwing their hands up and returning to Haskell or Fortran. Which is why it is important that the language provides some form of unsafe cast. In Agda, this takes the form of trustMe, on the basis of which one can write an unsafe function coerce (see the Appendix) which can be used to eliminate the type error. We can get the above code to work by replacing the last line with else (maxUtil' u bU (coerce c)) and adding a no-termination-check option for the compiler.

But, in so doing we have lost all additional safety provided by the dependently-typed system: we are just writing Haskell in Agda. Again, the same question arises: why not just write Haskell then? And, again, the same answer: because here we can improve. It is an instructive exercise to repair the maxUtil function, eliminating the unsafe elements, while still keeping it tail-recursive. In doing so, one discovers that the main culprit is the boolean test, where work is done to determine if the candidate is maximal, only to immediately discard that work so that it is unavailable when we need it only a couple of lines later. This will also help with the proof that maxUtil satisfies the specification, leading to the realization that proving "the correctness of a program ... at the same time as it is being synthesized" is sometimes the simplest way to go.

The usage of unsafe coercions leads to the possibility of increasing the correctness of our programs "from below". They indicate the key points we need to address to improve the implementations and prove they meet the specifications. As an intermediate step, one can eliminate "brutal" coercions in favor of applications of non-constructive principles, such as the law of double negation. In interval analysis, for example, it is often much easier to show that the interval returned by a given method cannot possibly fail to contain the solution, than that it actually does contain the solution.

In summary, formulating the current specifications and implementations in constructive type theory does not result in immediate ideal correctness for our programs, which is perhaps disappointing. On the other hand, it leaves us no worse off than before, and it offers a clear path for improvement: we can better our specifications by making them more constructive, and we can refine our implementations by removing unsafe features and postulates.

4   Conclusions

The approach to increasing the correctness of scientific computing presented here requires us to formalize the current typical mixture of classical and constructive mathematics within an implementation of constructive type theory, using the kind of brute-force mechanisms that the dependently-typed programming community rightly frowns upon. Nevertheless, the possibility to use unsafe features and postulates, together with a good foreign-function interface, is essential if we want to take advantage of what we can do *now*, in our less than ideal circumstances.

The results of such a formalization are, as we have seen in the previous section, not very pretty, but they have the advantage of explicitly flagging the points where improvements can be made. We are then in a better position to move towards the Martin-Löf ideal of correctness, by replacing unsafe coercions and postulates.

In many cases, this requires a shift in the programming style we adopt. There are (at least) two ways of specifying a computation with inputs of type A and outputs of type B which have to satisfy a relation R:

1. as a member of the type

$$\forall\,[a : A]\,(\exists\,[b : B]\,(R\ a\ b))$$

   that is, a function which, for every input a : A returns a pair consisting of a value b : B together with a proof that R a b. This is the approach presented in the textbook of Nordström et al. [15];
2. or as a member of the type

$$\exists\,[f : (A \rightarrow B)]\,(\forall\,[a : A]\,(R\ a\ (f\ a)))$$

   that is, as a pair consisting of a function f : A → B and a proof that for every a : A we have R a (f a). This is the approach of the other major textbook on programming and type theory, that of Thompson [20].

The two approaches are logically equivalent (see also Thompson [21]), in the sense that a member of one can always be turned in a member of the other, but they encourage a different practice: the Nordström et al. style suggests developing the proof *within* the implementation, while the Thompson style advocates developing the proof *alongside* the implementation.

The Thompson approach fits very well the current state of affairs in scientific computing, where implementations are generally considered separately from specifications, and is therefore easier for newcomers to type theory to understand. This is the style we saw in the previous section, when we translated the Haskell function maxUtil more or less literally in Agda, and postulated that it fulfills the specification maxFinSpec. This approach is also forced on us whenever we use an external function without a type-theoretical interface.

However, this style usually leads to duplication of effort: the same kind of operations needed to implement the computation turn out to be useful for proving that it fulfills the specification. Moreover, in the absence of a powerful reflection mechanism, the proof cannot be formulated at all. This was the case in the example from the previous section, where, after the boolean test, we "lost" the information necessary to prove the type-correctness of our program and had to appeal to unsafe coercion.

Once these difficulties are encountered in practice, the newcomers quickly start to appreciate the value of developing the proof and the program in the same context.[1] The increase in correctness is accompanied by a gradual shift from the Thompson-style to the Nordström-style. This is not so surprising, after all the observation that correct-by-construction programming is easier than separating proof and program predates Martin-Löf's type theory (e.g. Dijkstra [8]).

---

[1] And explore environments that could assist them in this task, such as Coq.

5   Appendix

We have summarized here the definitions of the datatypes and functions we have used in this article and which are not part of the standard Agda syntax or library. For more information on the latter, the reader is referred to the Agda wiki [1], where a wealth of material is available, starting with the ever-growing reference manual. For an introduction to the Martin-Löf type theory that Agda is based on we recommend, besides the standard textbooks referred to in Sect. 4, also the chapter by Nordström et al. in the *Handbook of logic in computer science* [16]. The various video lectures and associated materials of Conor McBride, such as [13], are an excellent and entertaining introduction to programming with dependent types.

Back to the Agda definitions: these fall in three categories. The first comprises datatypes and functions designed to maximize the amount of cut-and-paste we can do between Agda and Idris programs:

```
data ⊥ : Set where

data One : Set where
   one     : One

so : Bool → Set
so true = One
so false = ⊥

data _∧_ (A : Set) (B : Set) : Set where
   _,_ : A → B → A ∧ B

fst : {A B : Set} → A ∧ B → A
fst (a, b) = a

snd : {A B : Set} → A ∧ B → B
snd (a, b) = b
```

The second category consists of definitions and syntax declarations meant to increase the similarity of Agda and standard logic notations:

```
data Σ (A : Set) (B : A → Set) : Set where
   _,_ : (a : A) → (b : B a) → Σ A B

syntax Σ A (λ x → B) = ∃ [x : A] B

Π : (A : Set) → (B : A → Set) → Set
Π A B = (a : A) → B a

syntax Π A (λ x → B) = ∀ [x : A] B
```

The third category is that of function definitions that are meant to facilitate the usage of unsafe features and the literal translation of Haskell programs. The only such function we have used here is

```
coerce' : {A B : Set}  →  A ≡ B  →  A  →  B
coerce' refl a  =  a
coerce : {A B : Set}  →  A  →  B
coerce  =  coerce' trustMe
```

Note that the intended use of **postulate**s and trustMe is to mark the spots where assumptions are made and improvements are needed.

References

1. Agda wiki page. http://wiki.portal.chalmers.se/agda/
2. Formalisation of Mathematics. http://wiki.portal.chalmers.se/cse/pmwiki.php/ForMath/ForMath
3. GEM-E3 Website. http://www.gem-e3.net/
4. ReMIND-R. http://www.pik-potsdam.de/research/sustainable-solutions/models/remind
5. Bellman, R.E.: Dynamic Programming. Princeton University Press, Princeton (1957)
6. Bertsekas, D.P.: Dynamic Programming and Optimal Control, 2nd edn. Athena Scientific, Belmont (2000)
7. Brady, E., Hammond, K.: Correct-by-construction concurrency: using dependent types to verify implementations of effectful resource usage protocol. Fundamenta Informaticae **102**, 145–176 (2010)
8. Dijkstra, E.W.: A constructive approach to the problem of program correctness. BIT Numer. Math. **8**(3), 174–186 (1968)
9. Evensen, P., Märdin, M.: An extensible and scalable agent-based simulation of barter economics. Master's thesis 2009/04a, Chalmers University of Technology and University of Gothenburg (2009)
10. Gintis, H.: The emergence of a price system from decentralized bilateral exchange. B.E. J. Theor. Econ. **6**(1), 13 (2006)
11. Kreinovich, V.: Designing, understanding, and analyzing unconventional computation: the important role of logic and constructive mathematics. Appl. Math. Sci. **6**(13–16), 645–649 (2012)
12. Martin-Löf, P.: Constructive mathematics and computer programming. Philos. Trans. R. Soc. Lond. **312**(1522), 501–518 (1984)
13. McBride, C.: Dependently typed programming. http://www.cs.uoregon.edu/Research/summerschool/summer10/curriculum.htm
14. Mu, S.-C., Ko, H.-S., Jansson, P.: Algebra of programming in Agda: dependent types for relational program derivation. J. Funct. Program. **19**, 545–579 (2009)
15. Nordström, B., Petersson, K., Smith, J.: Programming in Martin-Löf's Type Theory. Oxford University Press, Oxford (1990)
16. Nordström, B., Petersson, K., Smith, J.: Martin-Löf type theory. In: Handbook of Logic in Computer Science, vol. 5, pp. 1–37. Oxford University Press, Oxford (2000)
17. Nordström, B., Smith, J.: Propositions and specifications of programs in Martin-Löf's type theory. BIT Numer. Math. **24**, 288–301 (1984)
18. Suppes, P.: Introduction to Logic. Dover Books on Mathematics Series. Dover, New York (1999). (Reprint of the 1957 edition from Van Nostrand)

19. Swierstra, W.: A Hoare logic for the state monad. In: Berghofer, S., Nipkow, T., Urban, C., Wenzel, M. (eds.) TPHOLs 2009. LNCS, vol. 5674, pp. 440–451. Springer, Heidelberg (2009)

20. Thompson, S.: Type Theory and Functional Programming. Addison-Wesley, Redwood (1991)

21. Thompson, S.: Are subsets necessary in Martin-Löf type theory? In: Myers Jr, J.P., O'Donnell, M.J. (eds.) Constructivity in CS 1991. LNCS, vol. 613. Springer, Heidelberg (1992)

22. Turner, R.: Computable Models. Springer, London (2009)

23. Varian, H.R.: Microeconomic Analysis. Norton, New York (1992)

24. Velupillai, K.: Computable Economics: The Arne Ryde Memorial Lectures. Oxford University Press, Oxford (2000)

25. Velupillai, K.V.: Algorithmic foundations of computable general equilibrium theory. Appl. Math. Comput. **179**, 360–369 (2006)

26. Velupillai, K.V.: Taming the incomputable, reconstructing the nonconstructive and deciding the undecidable in mathematical economics. New Math. Nat. Comput. (NMNC) **8**(01), 5–51 (2012)

27. Walras, L.: Elements of Pure Economics: Or the Theory of Social Wealth. Routledge Library Editions-Economics. Taylor & Francis Group, London (1954)

Engineering Proof by Reflection in Agda

Paul van der Walt[(✉)] and Wouter Swierstra

Department of Computer Science, Utrecht University, Utrecht, The Netherlands
paul@denknerd.org, w.s.swierstra@uu.nl

Abstract. This paper explores the recent addition to Agda enabling *reflection*, in the style of Lisp and Template Haskell. It gives a brief introduction to using reflection, and details the complexities encountered when automating certain proofs with *proof by reflection*. It presents a library that can be used for automatically quoting a class of concrete Agda terms to a non-dependent, user-defined inductive data type, alleviating some of the burden a programmer faces when using reflection in a practical setting.

Keywords: Dependently-typed programming · Reflection · Agda · Proof by reflection · Metaprogramming

1 Introduction

The dependently typed programming language Agda [1,2] has recently been extended with a *reflection mechanism* [3] for compile time metaprogramming in the style of Lisp [4], MetaML [5], Template Haskell [6], and C++ templates. Agda's reflection mechanisms make it possible to convert a program fragment into its corresponding abstract syntax tree (AST) and vice versa. In tandem with Agda's dependent types, this has promising new programming potential.

This paper addresses the following central questions:

> "What practical issues do we run into when trying to engineer automatic proofs in a dependently typed language with reflection? Are Agda's reflective capabilities sufficient and practically usable, and if not, which improvements might make life easier?"

Contributions. This paper reports on the experience of using Agda's reflection mechanism to automate certain categories of proofs. This is a case study, illustrative of the kind of problems that can be solved using reflection. More specifically:

- We give a very brief introduction to Agda's reflection mechanism (Sect. 2). Previously, these features were only documented in the release notes and comments in Agda's source files. A detailed tutorial is available elsewhere [3].
- We present Autoquote, an Agda library that does a declaratively-specified translation of a quoted expression to a representation in a user-defined non-dependent datatype (Sect. 3).

R. Hinze (Ed.): IFL 2012, LNCS 8241, pp. 157–173, 2013.
DOI: 10.1007/978-3-642-41582-1_10, © Springer-Verlag Berlin Heidelberg 2013

– We show how to use Agda's reflection mechanism to automate certain categories of proofs (Sect. 4). The idea of *proof by reflection* is certainly not new, but still worth examining in the context of this technology.

The code presented in this paper compiles using Agda version 2.3.2.[1]

1.1   Introducing Agda

Agda is an implementation of Martin-Löf's type theory [7], extended with records and modules. It is developed at the Chalmers University of Technology [1]; in accordance with Curry–Howard isomorphism, it can be viewed as both a functional programming language and a proof assistant for intuitionistic logic. It is comparable to Coq, which is based on Coquand's calculus of constructions [8]. There are many excellent tutorials on Agda [1,2,9].

Since version 2.2.8, Agda includes a reflection API [10], which allows the conversion of parts of a program's code into an abstract syntax tree, a data structure in Agda itself, that can be inspected or modified like any other. The idea of reflection is old: in the 1980s Lisp included a similar feature, then already called *quoting* and *unquoting*, which allowed run time modification of a program's code.

2   Using Reflection

We will now introduce the reflection API with some small examples.

The Keywords. There are several keywords that can be used to quote and unquote terms: **quote**, **quoteTerm**, **quoteGoal**, and **unquote**. The **quote** keyword allows the user to access the internal representation of any identifier. This internal representation, a Name value, can be used to query the type or definition of the identifier. We refer to the release notes [10] for a listing of the data structures involved; most important is Term : Set, representing concrete Agda terms.

The simplest example of quotation uses the keyword **quoteTerm** x : Term, where x is a fragment of concrete syntax. Note that **quoteTerm** reduces like any other function in Agda. As an example, the following unit test type checks:

```
example₀ : quoteTerm (λ (x : Bool) → x) ≡ lam visible (var 0 [])
example₀ = refl
```

In dissecting this, we find the lam constructor, since we introduced a lambda abstraction. Its one argument is visible (as opposed to implicit), and the body of the lambda abstraction is just a reference to the nearest-bound variable, thus var 0, applied to an empty list of arguments. Variables are referred to by their De Bruijn indices.

---

[1] All supporting code, including this paper in Literate Agda format, is available on GitHub. https://github.com/toothbrush/reflection-proofs

Furthermore, **quoteTerm** type checks its argument before returning the Term. Since type checking a term necessitates normalisation, the returned Term is always in normal form, as $example_1$ demonstrates.

```
example₁ : quoteTerm ((λ x → x) 0) ≡ con (quote zero) []
example₁ = refl
```

The identity function is applied to zero, resulting in just the value zero. The quoted representation of a natural zero is con (**quote** zero) [], where con means that we are introducing a constructor. The constructor zero takes no arguments, hence the empty list.

The **quoteGoal** keyword is different. We cannot assign **quoteGoal** an informal type, since it is really a syntactic construct that depends on the context. See the following example.

```
example₂ : ℕ
example₂ = quoteGoal e in { }₀
```

The **quoteGoal** keyword binds the variable e to the Term representing the type expected at the position of **quoteGoal**. In this example, the value of e in the hole will be def ℕ [], i.e., the Term representing the type ℕ, which is a definition, hence def.

The **unquote** keyword takes one argument – a Term – and converts it back to a concrete expression. Just as **quoteTerm** and **quoteGoal**, **unquote** type checks and normalises the Term before splicing it into the program text. Note that it is not yet possible to introduce top-level declarations using **unquote**. This is a technical limitation.

The **quote** x : Name keyword returns the representation of an identifier x as a value in the primitive type Name, if x is the name of a definition (function, datatype, record, or a constructor). Unfortunately, we cannot simply pattern match on constructor names. The reason pattern matching on Names is not supported, is that the elimination principle is not clear, since Name is a built-in, non-inductive type. The only mechanism we have to distinguish Names is decidable equality,[2] which results in code as presented below – a lot less concise than the pattern matching equivalent would be. Agda does allow matching on String (which similarly only exposes decidable equality), so the limitation is a technical one, which might be solved in the future.

```
whatever : Term → ...
                        ?
whatever (con c args) with c =-Name quote foo
... | yes p  = { }₀   -- foo applied to arguments
... | no ¬p  = { }₁   -- not foo, try another Name, etc.
```

---

[2] using the function _ $\stackrel{?}{=}$ -Name_

This short introduction should already be enough to start developing simple programs using reflection. For a more detailed description of the reflection API in Agda, the reader is referred to Van der Walt's thesis ([3], Chap. 3).

3   Automatic Quoting

In the previous section, we saw how to recover values of type Term, representing concrete Agda terms. This is a start, but we rarely want to directly manipulate Terms: often it is much more useful to use our own AST for computations. It should be a minor task to write a function to convert a Term into another AST, but this often turns out to become a mess.

When pattern matching is possible, converting elements of one AST to another is a simple task. Unfortunately, Agda functions are required to be total, which means they must have a case for each possible pattern. Since Term covers all quotable terms, it has many alternatives. Furthermore, for Names, we only have decidable equality. This is why such conversion functions tend to become verbose, as in the code snippet of Fig. 1, an excerpt of a conversion function used before a better solution was developed.

```
term2boolexpr n (con tf [ ]) pf with tf ≟-Name quote true
term2boolexpr n (con tf [ ]) pf | yes p  =  Truth

...

term2boolexpr n (def f [ ]) ()
term2boolexpr n (def f (arg v r x :: [ ])) pf with f ≟-Name quote ¬_
... | yes p  =  Not (term2boolexpr n x pf)
... | no ¬p with f ≟-Name quote _∧_
...
```

Fig. 1. The gist of a naïve conversion function, from Term into some more specific data type.

A (partial) solution – something which at least mitigates the agony – is presented in this section, in the form of the Autoquote library.

The Autoquote Library. We will use Expr, presented in Fig. 2, as a running example of a toy AST. It is a simple non-dependent inductive data structure representing terms with Peano-style natural numbers, variables represented using De Bruijn indices, and additions.

We might want to convert an expression, such as $5 + x$, to this AST using reflection. In an ideal world, we would just pattern match on concrete constructs such as the _+_ function and return elements like Plus of our AST. The Autoquote library allows just this, exposing an interface which, when provided with such a mapping, automatically quotes expressions that fit. Here, *fitting* is defined as only containing names that are listed in the mapping, or variables

```
data Expr : Set where
   Var  : ℕ              → Expr
   Plus : Expr → Expr → Expr
   S    : Expr           → Expr
   Z    :                   Expr
```

Fig. 2. The toy expression language Expr. Quoting such terms is now easier.

with De Bruijn indices, and respecting constructor arities. Trying to convert other terms results in a type error. The user provides a straightforward mapping, such as in Fig. 3, and Autoquote converts Agda terms to values in the AST. Currently only non-dependent inductive types are supported.

```
exprTable : Table Expr
exprTable = (Var, (quote _+_ ) ↦ Plus ::
                  (quote zero) ↦ Z    ::
                  (quote suc ) ↦ S    :: [])
```

Fig. 3. The mapping table for converting to the Expr AST.

This table should be interpreted as follows: any variables encountered should be stored in Vars, and the _+_ operator should be mapped to a Plus constructor. A zero, from the Data.Nat standard library, should be treated as our Z constructor, etc. Note that the first item in the table (Var in this case) is special, and should be a constructor for De Bruijn-indexed variables. The rest of the table is an arbitrary list of constructors.

We will not say much about the implementation of this library, since it is not groundbreaking. For more details, we again refer to ([3], Sect. 3.3). Using the library is simple; it exposes a function called doConvert which takes the conversion table, a (hidden, automatically inferred) proof that the conversion is possible, and a Term to convert, and produces an inhabitant of the desired data type, where possible. The implicit proof technique is outlined in Sect. 4.1.

The use of doConvert is illustrated in Fig. 4. The hidden assumption that the conversion is possible causes a type error if an incompatible term is given. The utility of the Autoquote library is clear if you compare this relatively straightforward code to the verbose term2boolexpr snippet in Fig. 1.

Usually, the result from doConvert will require some post-processing – for example, turning all naturals into Fin n values, or scope checking a resulting expression – as we will see in the Boolean tautologies example (Sect. 4.2). However, for now it suffices to say that Autoquote eases converting Terms into other ASTs.

```
example₃ : {x : ℕ} → doConvert exprTable (quoteTerm (x + 1))
                 ≡                      Plus (Var 0) (S Z)
example₃ = refl
```

Fig. 4. An example of Autoquote in use. See Fig. 3 for the definition of exprTable, a declarative Name-to-constructor mapping.

A mechanism like Autoquote is actually an ad-hoc workaround for a more general difficulty in Agda, namely that currently, a watered-down version of pattern matching on data types exposing decidable equality is unreasonably awkward. If this were possible in general, like it is for String, the Autoquote library would be redundant.

4   Proof by Reflection

The idea behind proof by reflection is simple: given that type theory is both a programming language and a proof system, it is possible to define functions that compute proofs. Reflection in the proof technical sense is the method of mechanically constructing a proof of a theorem by inspecting its shape. The proof by reflection technique we describe here is not new – see for example Chap. 16 of Coq'Art [11] – but instead combines a number of existing methods into a usable package. The following two case studies illustrate proof by reflection and how Agda's reflection mechanism can make the technique more accessible. The first example is a closed example and sets the stage for the second, an open expression type extended to include variables.

4.1   Closed Example: Evenness

To illustrate the concept of proof by reflection, we will follow Chlipala's example of even naturals [12]. Our objective is to be able to automatically prove evenness of certain naturals. To this end, we first write a test function which decides if a natural is even, then prove the soundness of this predicate. This results in a proof generator.

We start by defining the property Even.

```
data Even  : ℕ  →  Set where
  isEven0  :                          Even 0
  isEven+2 : {n : ℕ}  →  Even n  →  Even (2 + n)
```

Using these rules to produce the proof that some large number n is even is tedious: it requires $n/2$ applications of the isEven+2 constructor.

To automate this, we will show how to *compute* the proof required. We define a predicate even? that returns the unit type (top) when its input is even and the empty type (bottom) otherwise. In this context, $\top$ and $\bot$ can be seen as the analogues of true and false, since there exists a proof that some number is even, if it is 0 or $2 + n$, for even n. Otherwise, no proof exists.

```
even? : ℕ → Set
even? 0           = ⊤
even? 1           = ⊥
even? (suc (suc n)) = even? n
```

Next we need to show that the even? function is *sound*. To do so, we prove that if and only if even? n returns $\top$, the type Even n is inhabited. Since we are working in a constructive logic, the only way to show this is to give a witness. This is done in the function soundnessEven. Note that we are actually giving a recipe for constructing proof trees.

```
soundnessEven : {n : ℕ} → even? n → Even n
soundnessEven {0}         tt = isEven0
soundnessEven {1}         ()
soundnessEven {suc (suc n)} s = isEven+2 (soundnessEven s)
```

In the case of $n = 1$, we do not need to provide a right-hand side of the function definition. The assumption even? 1 is uninhabited, and we discharge this branch using Agda's absurd pattern, ().

If we need a proof that some arbitrary n is even, soundnessEven builds it. Note that the value of n is inferred. The only argument we must to provide to soundnessEven is proof that even? n is inhabited. For any closed term, such as the numbers 28 or 8772, this proof obligation reduces to $\top$, which is proven by its single constructor, tt.

```
isEven8772 : Even 8772
isEven8772 = soundnessEven tt
```

Now we can easily get a proof term for arbitrary even numbers, without having to explicitly write down the proof tree. Note that it is not possible to give a term with type Even 27, or any other uneven number, since the parameter even? n is equal to $\bot$, which is uninhabited. Providing tt anyway will produce a type error stating that the types $\top$ and $\bot$ cannot be unified.

Implicit Proofs. Since the type $\top$ is a simple record type, Agda can infer the tt argument. This means we can turn the assumption even? n into an implicit argument, so a user could just write soundnessEven as the proof, letting Agda fill in the missing proof. This trick works because Agda supports eta expansion for record types. Concretely, Agda will automatically fill in implicit arguments of the unit type. Here, the type system is doing more work than for general data types; for records eta expansion is safe, since recursion is not allowed. This trick will be used from here on to ameliorate our proof generators' interfaces.

Friendlier Errors. It is possible to generate a descriptive "error" of sorts, by replacing the ⊥ with an empty type that has a friendly name:

```
data IsOdd : ℕ → Set where
```

This makes the soundness proof a little less straightforward, but in return the type error generated if an odd number is used becomes more informative. When a user tries to use the soundnessEven lemma to generate a proof of the statement Even 7, Agda will complain about a missing implicit argument of type IsOdd 7. An unsolved implicit argument is marked yellow in Agda, which looks less dire than a type error in a visible argument, but no spurious proofs are being generated.

Limitations. This is a very simple, closed example. In particular, it would not work in the presence of quantifications, for example to define a lemma like Even x → Even (x + 100). Why this is the case, and how it could be solved, is discussed at the end of Sect. 4.2.

The next step will be to use the same approach for a problem involving variables.

4.2   Open Example: Boolean Tautologies

We will now apply the same steps as above to a different problem, clarifying the relationship to the previous example at each step. This example of proof by reflection will be lifting a predicate that checks if a Boolean expression with indexed variables is a tautology under all possible assignments, to a proof generator.

Take as an example the following proposition.

$$(p_1 \lor q_1) \land (p_2 \lor q_2) \Rightarrow (q_1 \lor p_1) \land (q_2 \lor p_2) \tag{1}$$

If we squint, we see that (1) is a tautology, but explicitly proving this in Agda would be rather tedious. Assuming we want to check if the formula always holds by trying all possible variable assignments, this would require 2^n pattern matching cases, where n is the number of variables.

To automate this process, we start by defining an inductive data type to represent Boolean expressions with at most n free variables (see Fig. 5).

```
data BoolExpr (n : ℕ) : Set where
    Truth Falsehood :                                        BoolExpr n
    And Or Imp      : BoolExpr n → BoolExpr n → BoolExpr n
    Not             : BoolExpr n                → BoolExpr n
    Atomic          : Fin n                     → BoolExpr n
```

Fig. 5. Modelling boolean expressions with n free variables.

We use the type Fin n to ensure that variables (represented by Atomic and identified by their De Bruijn index) are in scope. If we want to evaluate the expression, we will need some way to map variables to values. For this we use Env n: a vector of n Boolean values.

Now we can define an interpretation function, which tells us if an expression is true or not, given some assignment of variables. It does this by evaluating the formula's AST, filling in for Atomic values the concrete values which are looked up in the environment. For example, And is evaluated to the Boolean function $\_\wedge\_$, and its two arguments in turn are recursively interpreted.

```
[_⊢_] : ∀ {n : ℕ} (e : Env n)  →  BoolExpr n  →  Bool
[ env ⊢ Truth      ]  =  true
[ env ⊢ And be be₁ ]  =  [ env ⊢ be ] ∧ [ env ⊢ be₁ ]
[ env ⊢ Atomic n   ]  =  lookup n env
...
```

Recall our test function even? in the previous section. It returned ⊤ if the proposition was valid, ⊥ otherwise. Looking at $[\_\vdash\_]$, we see that we should just translate true to the unit type and false to the empty type, to get the analogue of the even? function. We therefore define a function P, mapping Booleans to types (see Fig. 6). As before we decorate the empty type, this time with a string, to give more informative error messages.

```
data Error (e : String) : Set where
P : Bool → Set
P true  = ⊤
P false = Error "Argument expression does not evaluate to true."
```

Fig. 6. Empty type Error, facilitating clearer errors.

Now that we have these helper functions, it is easy to define what it means to be a tautology. We quantify over a few Boolean variables and wrap the formula in the function P. If the resulting type is inhabited, the argument to P is a tautology, i.e., for each assignment of the free variables the entire equation still evaluates to true. An example encoding of such a theorem is Fig. 7 – notice how similar it looks to the version expressed in mathematical notation, in (1).

Here a complication arises, though. We are quantifying over a list of Boolean values *outside* of the function P, so proving P to be sound will not suffice. We just defined the function $[\_\vdash\_]$ to take one environment and one expression. In Fig. 7, though, we effectively quantified over all possible environments. We are going to need a way to lift the function P over arbitrary environments.

The function forallsAcc, in Fig. 8, performs this lifting. This function represents the real analogue of even? in this situation: it returns a type which is

exampletheorem = $(p_1\ q_1\ p_2\ q_2\ :\ \mathsf{Bool}) \rightarrow$
$P\ ((p_1 \vee q_1) \wedge (p_2 \vee q_2) \Rightarrow (q_1 \vee p_1) \wedge (q_2 \vee p_2))$

Fig. 7. The term exampletheorem : Set encodes (1).

only inhabited if the argument Boolean expression is true under all variable assignments. This is done by cumulatively generating a full binary tree – the truth table – of $\top$ or $\bot$ types, depending on the result of $[\![\_\vdash\_]\!]$ under each assignment. This corresponds precisely to the expression being a tautology if and only if the tree is inhabited. The function foralls simply bootstraps forallsAcc with an empty environment – it is omitted for brevity. The Diff argument makes forallsAcc produce a tree with depth equal to the number of free variables in an expression, putting a bound on the recursion.

forallsAcc : $\{n\ m\ :\ \mathbb{N}\} \rightarrow \mathsf{BoolExpr}\ m \rightarrow \mathsf{Env}\ n \rightarrow \mathsf{Diff}\ n\ m \rightarrow \mathsf{Set}$
forallsAcc b acc (Base) = $P\ [\![\ acc \vdash b\ ]\!]$
forallsAcc b acc (Step y) =
    forallsAcc b (true :: acc) y $\times$ forallsAcc b (false :: acc) y

Fig. 8. The function forallsAcc, which decides if a proposition is a tautology. Compare to the even? function in Sect. 4.1

Soundness. Now we finally know our real decision function foralls, we can set about proving its soundness. Following the soundnessEven example, we want a function with a type something like in Fig. 9.

soundness : $\{n\ :\ \mathbb{N}\} \rightarrow (b\ :\ \mathsf{BoolExpr}\ n) \rightarrow \mathsf{foralls}\ b \rightarrow ...$

Fig. 9. The informal type of soundness, taking an expression and its truth table.

But what should the return type of the soundness lemma be? We would like to prove that the argument b is a tautology, and hence, the soundness function should return something of the form $(b_1 \ldots b_n\ :\ \mathsf{Bool}) \rightarrow P\ B$, where B is an expression in the image of the interpretation $[\![\_\vdash\_]\!]$. For instance, the statement exampletheorem is a proposition of this form.

The function proofGoal takes a BoolExpr n as its argument and generates the proposition that the expression is a tautology, by giving back the type equal to the theorem under scrutiny. It first introduces n universally quantified Boolean variables. These variables are accumulated in an environment. Finally, when n binders have been introduced, the BoolExpr n is evaluated under this environment.

```
proofGoal : (n m : ℕ) → Diff n m → BoolExpr m → Env n → Set
proofGoal  .m m (Base ) b acc = P ⟦ acc ⊢ b ⟧
proofGoal  n  m (Step y) b acc =
          (a : Bool) → proofGoal (1 + n) m y b (a :: acc)
```

Now that we can interpret a BoolExpr n as a theorem using proofGoal, and we have a way to decide if something is true for a given environment, we need to show the soundness of our decision function foralls. That is, we need to be able to show that a formula is true if it holds for every possible assignment of its variables to true or false.

This is done in the function soundness, of which we only provide the type signature. It requires the predicate foralls which is only satisfied when a proposition is a tautology, and gives back a proof which has the type computed by proofGoal. It uses the predicate to safely extract the leaf from foralls corresponding to any given environment resulting from the binders introduced by proofGoal.

```
soundness : {n : ℕ} → (b : BoolExpr n) → {p : foralls b}
                    → proofGoal 0 n (zero-least 0 n) b []
```

Now, we can prove theorems by a call of the form soundness b {p}, where b is the representation of the formula under consideration, and p is the evidence that all branches of the proof tree are true. We do not give p explicitly since the only valid values are nested pairs of tt, which can be inferred automatically. This once again exploits the fact that Agda supports eta expansion for record types.

If the module type checks, we know that the representation of the formula corresponds to the concrete expression, soundness gave a valid proof, and that the formula is in fact a tautology. We also have the corresponding proof object at our disposal, as in someTauto (Fig. 10).

If one were to give as input a formula which is not a tautology, Agda would not be able to infer the proof foralls, since it would be an uninhabited type. As before, this would result in an unsolved meta-variable (a type error stating

```
rep        : BoolExpr 2
rep        = Imp (And (Atomic (suc zero)) (Atomic zero))
                  (Atomic zero)
someTauto : (p q : Bool) → P (p ∧ q ⇒ q)
someTauto = soundness rep
```

Fig. 10. An example Boolean formula, along with the transliteration to a proposition and the corresponding proof.

Error and ⊤ cannot be unified). Agda disallows importing modules with unsolved meta-variables, which means such an unfulfilled proof obligation would not be usable elsewhere in a real-life development.

Limitations. Unfortunately, this approach is only possible using variables with a finite type. If we wanted to prove properties about naturals, for example, we would not be able to enumerate all possible values. Also, not all problems are decidable. In the ring solver example [13] a canonical representation is used, but this does not always exist. One way forward would be if a proof search system could be implemented, going beyond simple reflection. By inspecting the shape of the obligation it might be possible to find a lemma which sufficiently reduces the goal to something we can easily generate. This is motivated by the evenness example: we could imagine it being possible to automatically prove lemmas like Even n → Even (n + 100), given a list of usable lemmas. On inspecting the goal and finding the Plus (Var n) 100 term, we might be able to learn that this lemma (which would have a particularly tedious proof) is an instance of Even x → Even y → Even (x + y), which might be an existing library proof. However, this would require a rather advanced way of recognising structures in proof goals, and a reliable proof search for useful lemmas in a database. This would correspond to implementing an analogue of Coq's auto tactic in Agda. The Agda synthesizer Agsy already implements such a proof search, but is built directly into the compiler. This is definitely an avenue for future work.

Summary. The only thing we still have to do manually is convert the Agda representation of the formula (p ∧ q ⇒ q, for example) into our abstract syntax (rep). This is unfortunate, as we end up typing out the formula twice. We also have to count the number of variables ourselves and convert them to De Bruijn indices. This is error-prone given how cluttered the abstract representation can get for formulae containing many variables.

   We would like this transliteration process to be automated. Luckily Autoquote is available for precisely this purpose, and we show this now.

4.3 Adding Reflection

It might come as a surprise that in a paper focusing on reflection – in the programming language technology sense – we have not yet presented a convincing use for reflection. We can get rid of the duplication seen in Fig. 10 using Agda's reflection API. Using the **quoteGoal** keyword to inspect the current goal would give us the Agda representation, and passing that to Autoquote, we can convert it to its corresponding BoolExpr.

   The conversion between a Term and BoolExpr is achieved in two phases, necessary because Autoquote only supports non-dependent data types, and BoolExpr n has an argument of type Fin n to its constructor Atomic (see Fig. 5). To work around this, we introduce a simpler, intermediary data structure, to which we will convert from Term. This type, called BoolInter, is not shown here, but the only difference with BoolExpr n is that its variables are represented by Nats instead of Fins.

The Autoquote library uses a lookup table, mentioning which constructor represents variables and how names map to constructors. This way only Terms containing variables or the usual operators are accepted. Using the mapping presented in Fig. 11, we can construct a function that, for suitable Terms, gives us a value in BoolInter.

```
boolTable  :  Table BoolInter
boolTable  =  (Atomic, (quote _∧_ )  ↦  And       :: (quote _∨_ )  ↦  Or
   ::                  (quote ¬_  )  ↦  Not       :: (quote true )  ↦  Truth
   ::                  (quote false)  ↦  Falsehood :: (quote _⇒_)  ↦  Imp :: [])
```

Fig. 11. The mapping table for quoting to BoolInter.

Once we have a BoolInter expression, the second phase is to check that its variables are all in scope (this means that $\forall$ Atomic $x : x < n$, if we want to convert to a BoolExpr n), and replace all $\mathbb{N}$ values with their Fin n counterparts. We can now write a function proveTautology, which uses the automatic quoter and calls soundness on the resulting term. An approximation of proveTautology's type is given here. In summary, it takes a term (as bound in the body of **quoteGoal**), quotes it with Autoquote, passes it to soundness, which returns a term fulfilling the proofGoal type.

```
proveTautology : (t : Term)  →  let  t' = doConvert boolTable t
                                in ... {i : foralls t'}  →  proofGoal n t'
```

That is all we need to automatically prove that formulae are tautologies. The following snippet illustrates the use of the proveTautology function; we can omit all arguments except e, since they can be inferred.

```
peirce :  (p q : Bool)  →  P (((p ⇒ q) ⇒ p) ⇒ p)
peirce = quoteGoal e in proveTautology e
```

With that, we have automatically converted propositions in Agda to our own AST, generated a proof of their soundness, and converted that back into a proof term for the concrete formula.

5 Discussion

Related Work. Our main innovations are novel combinations of existing techniques. As a result, quite a number of subjects are relevant to mention here.

As far as reflection in general goes, Demers and Malenfant [14] provide an informative historical overview. What we are referring to as reflection dates back to work by Smith [15] and was initially presented in Lisp in the 80s. Since then, many developments in the functional, logic as well as object-oriented programming worlds have emerged – systems with varying power and scope [16,17]. Unfortunately, reflection is often unsafe: in Smalltalk and Objective-C, for example, calling non-existent functions causes exceptions, to name just one pitfall.

These systems have inspired the reflection mechanism introduced in Agda, which is lacking in a number of fundamental capabilities – most notably type awareness of **unquote**, type preservation when using **quoteTerm** and inability to introduce top-level definitions. Nevertheless, it does provide the safety of a strong type system.

Evaluation. If we look at the taxonomy of reflective systems in programming language technology written up by Sheard [18], we see that we can make a few rough judgements about the metaprogramming facilities Agda currently supports.[3]

- Agda's current reflection API leans more towards analysis than generation,
- it supports encoding of terms in an algebraic data type (as opposed to a string, for example),
- it involves manual staging annotations (by using keywords such as **quote** and **unquote**),
- it is homogeneous, because the object language is the metalanguage. The object language's representation is a native data type.
- It is only two-stage: we cannot as yet produce an object program which is itself a metaprogram. This is because we rely on keywords such as **quote**, which cannot be represented.

As far as the proof techniques used in Sect. 4 are concerned, Chlipala's work [12] proved an invaluable resource. One motivating example for doing this in Agda was Jedynak's ring solver [13], which is the first example of Agda's reflection API in use that came to our attention. Compared to Jedynak's work, the proof generator presented here is marginally more refined in terms of the interface presented to the user. We expect that approaches of this kind will become commonplace for proving mundane lemmas in large proofs. The comparison to tactics in a language like Coq is a tempting one, and we see both advantages and disadvantages of each style. Of course, the tactic language in Coq is much more specialised and sophisticated, but it is a pity that it is separate. This paper explores an alternative, with metaprograms written directly in the object language. Some people might also appreciate the fact that proof generation in Agda is explicit.

---

[3] Of course, having been implemented during a single Agda Implementors' Meeting [19], the current implementation is more a proof-of-concept, and is still far from being considered finished, so it would be unfair to judge the current implementation all too harshly. In fact, we hope that this work might motivate the Agda developers to include some more features, to make the system truly useful.

Performance is another possible area of improvement. Introducing reflective proofs requires a lot of compile time computation, and for this approach to scale, Agda would need a more efficient static evaluator than the current call-by-name implementation. The extensive use of proof by reflection in Coq and SSReflect [20], for example for proving the four colour theorem [21], has motivated a lot of recent work on improving Coq's compile time evaluation. We hope that Agda will be similarly improved.

Conclusions. Returning to our research question, repeated here, a summary of findings is made.

> "What practical issues do we run into when trying to engineer automatic proofs in a dependently typed language with reflection? Are Agda's reflective capabilities sufficient and practically usable, and if not, which improvements might make life easier?"

This paper shows that the reflection capabilities recently added to Agda are quite useful for automating tedious tasks. For example, we now need not encode expressions manually: using **quoteTerm** and Autoquote, some AST conversion can be done automatically. Furthermore, by using the proof by reflection technique, we have shown how to automatically generate a simple class of proofs, without loss of general applicability. Constraining ourselves to (pairs of) unit types as predicates, we can let Agda infer them, and by tagging an empty type with a string, we can achieve more helpful errors if these predicates are invalid. These simple tools were sufficient to engineer relatively powerful and – more importantly – easily usable proof tools. Unfortunately, these proofs are limited to finite domains, and are still not very scalable or straightforward to implement. In particular, quantifying over variables with infinite domains should not be a great conceptual difficulty, but would necessitate a lot of extra machinery: a smarter goal inspector, and a generalised lemma searching or matching algorithm. Simple pattern matching on Names would also be a useful feature.

It seems conceivable that in the future, using techniques such as those presented here, a framework for tactics might be within reach. Eventually we might be able to define an embedded language in Agda, in the style of Coq's tactic language, then inspect the shape of the proof obligation, and look at a database of predefined proof recipes to see if one of them might discharge or simplify the obligation. An advantage of this approach versus the tactic language in Coq, would be that the language of the propositions and tactics is the same.

Acknowledgements. We would like to thank each of the four anonymous reviewers for taking the time to provide detailed and constructive comments that greatly improved the article.

References

1. Norell, U.: Towards a practical programming language based on dependent type theory. Ph.D. thesis, Department of Computer Science and Engineering, Chalmers University of Technology, SE-412 96 Göteborg, Sweden (2007)
2. Norell, U.: Dependently typed programming in Agda. In: Proceedings of the 4th International Workshop on Types in Language Design and Implementation, TLDI '09, pp. 1–2. ACM, New York (2009)
3. van der Walt, P.: Reflection in Agda. Master's thesis, Department of Computer Science, Utrecht University, Utrecht, The Netherlands. http://igitur-archive.library.uu.nl/student-theses/2012-1030-200720/UUindex.html (2012)
4. Pitman, K.M.: Special forms in Lisp. In: Proceedings of the ACM Conference on LISP and Functional Programming, pp. 179–187. ACM (1980)
5. Taha, W., Sheard, T.: Multi-stage programming with explicit annotations. In: Proceedings of the 1997 ACM SIGPLAN Symposium on Partial Evaluation and Semantics-Based Program Manipulation, PEPM '97 (1997)
6. Sheard, T., Peyton Jones, S.: Template meta-programming for Haskell. In: Proceedings of the 2002 ACM SIGPLAN Workshop on Haskell, pp. 1–16 (2002)
7. Martin-Löf, P.: Constructive mathematics and computer programming. In: Proceedings of a Discussion Meeting of the Royal Society of London on Mathematical Logic and Programming Languages, pp. 167–184. Prentice-Hall Inc., Upper Saddle River (1985)
8. Coquand, T., Huet, G.P.: The calculus of constructions. Inf. Comput. **76**(2/3), 95–120 (1988)
9. Oury, N., Swierstra, W.: The power of pi. In: Proceedings of the 13th ACM SIGPLAN International Conference on Functional Programming, ICFP '08, pp. 39–50. ACM, New York (2008)
10. Agda Developers: Agda release notes, regarding reflection. The Agda Wiki: http://wiki.portal.chalmers.se/agda/agda.php?n=Main.Version-2-2-8 and http://wiki.portal.chalmers.se/agda/agda.php?n=Main.Version-2-3-0 (2013). Accessed 9 Feb 2013
11. Bertot, Y., Castéran, P.: Interactive Theorem Proving and Program Development, Coq'Art: The Calculus of Inductive Constructions. Texts in Theoretical Computer Science. Springer, Heidelberg (2004)
12. Chlipala, A.: Certified Programming with Dependent Types. MIT Press, New York (2011)
13. Jedynak, W.: Agda ring solver using reflection. GitHub. https://github.com/wjzz/Agda-reflection-for-semiring-solver (2012). Accessed 26 June 2012
14. Demers, F., Malenfant, J.: Reflection in logic, functional and object-oriented programming: a short comparative study. In: Proceedings of the IJCAI, vol. 95, pp. 29–38 (1995)
15. Smith, B.C.: Reflection and semantics in LISP. In: Proceedings of the 11th ACM SIGACT-SIGPLAN Symposium on Principles of Programming Languages, POPL '84, pp. 23–35. ACM, New York (1984)
16. Stump, A.: Directly reflective meta-programming. High. Order Symbolic Comput. **22**(2), 115–144 (2009)
17. Goldberg, A., Robson, D.: Smalltalk-80: The Language and Its Implementation. Addison-Wesley Longman Publishing Co. Inc., Boston (1983)
18. Sheard, T.: Staged programming. http://web.cecs.pdx.edu/~sheard/staged.html. Accessed 20 Aug 2012

19. Altenkirch, T.: [Agda mailing list] More powerful quoting and reflection? mailing list communication. https://lists.chalmers.se/pipermail/agda/2012/004127.html (2012). Accessed 14 Sept 2012

20. Gonthier, G., Mahboubi, A.: An introduction to small scale reflection in Coq. J. Formalized Reasoning **3**(2), 95–152 (2010). (RR-7392 RR-7392)

21. Gonthier, G.: The four colour theorem: engineering of a formal proof. In: Kapur, D. (ed.) ASCM 2007. LNCS (LNAI), vol. 5081, p. 333. Springer, Heidelberg (2008)

Agda Meets Accelerate

Peter Thiemann[1]([⊠]) and Manuel M. T. Chakravarty[2]

[1] University of Freiburg, Freiburg, Germany
thiemann@informatik.uni-freiburg.de
[2] University of New South Wales, Sydney, Australia
chak@cse.unsw.edu.au

Abstract. Embedded languages in Haskell benefit from a range of type extensions, such as type families, that are subsumed by dependent types. However, even with those type extensions, embedded languages for data parallel programming lack desirable static guarantees, such as static bounds checks in indexing and collective permutation operations.

This observation raises the question whether an embedded language for data parallel programming would benefit from fully-fledged dependent types, such as those available in Agda. We explored that question by designing and implementing an Agda frontend to Accelerate, a Haskell-embedded language for data parallel programming aimed at GPUs. We discuss the potential of dependent types in this domain, describe some of the limitations that we encountered, and share some insights from our preliminary implementation.

Keywords: Programming with dependent types · Data parallelism

1 Introduction

Generative approaches to programming parallel hardware promise to combine high-level programming models with high performance. They are particularly attractive for targeting restricted architectures that cannot efficiently execute code aimed at conventional multicore CPUs. One prime example are GPUs (graphics processor units), which require a high degree of data parallelism, restricted control flow, and custom tailored data access patterns to be efficient. Previous work —for example, Accelerator [17], Copperhead [2], and Accelerate [3]— demonstrates that embedded array languages with a custom code generator can meet those GPU constraints with carefully designed language constructs.

Given a host language with an expressive type system, it is attractive to leverage that type system to express static properties of the embedded language. For example, Accelerate, an embedded array language for Haskell, uses Haskell's recent support for type-level programming like GADTs and type families in that manner [3]. This design choice is desirable for approaches relying on run-time code generation: each potential fault at application run time should be discovered by a compile-time fault in the embedded language. Moreover, static guarantees hold the potential to improve the predictability of parallel performance.

R. Hinze (Ed.): IFL 2012, LNCS 8241, pp. 174–189, 2013.
DOI: 10.1007/978-3-642-41582-1_11, © Springer-Verlag Berlin Heidelberg 2013

Dependent types [9] are an established approach to certified programming, where invariants are established in the form of types and proven at compile time. Many of Haskell's type-level extensions used in Accelerate approximate aspects of dependently-typed programming. Hence, it is natural to ask whether fully-fledged dependent types, such as those provided by Agda, improve the specification of an embedded language like Accelerate, whether they increase the scope of static guarantees, and whether they may be leveraged to predict performance more accurately.

This paper is a first investigation into this topic. It reports on a partial port of Accelerate to a new, dependently-typed host language, Agda [1,10]. Agda is particularly suited to this port because of its foreign function interface to Haskell, which enables it to directly invoke the functionality of Accelerate. The main contributions of this paper are the following:

- We identify and discuss the challenges of combining generative embedded languages with dependent typing (Sect. 4).
- We propose predicated arrays to overcome some of these challenges (Sect. 5).
- We outline an implementation of the main parts of Accelerate in Agda using the Agda-Haskell FFI for code execution (Sect. 6).

Overall, our investigation has the following structure. After recalling some background on Agda and Accelerate in Sect. 2 and describing related work in Sect. 3, Sect. 4 discusses potential uses of dependent types in an array-oriented data parallel language and how they were realized in our implementation. Section 5 considers conceptual problems and limitations that we ran into when constructing the Agda frontend for Accelerate. Section 6 explains some technical details of the implementation and discusses some example code.

Source code is available at https://github.com/mchakravarty/accelerate-agda.

2   Background

2.1   Agda

Agda [1,10] is a dependently-typed functional programming language. Its basis is a dependently-typed lambda calculus extended with inductive data type families, dependent records, and parameterized modules. At the same time, Agda is also a proof assistant for interactively constructing proofs in an intuitionistic type theory based on the work of Per Martin-Löf [9].

One attractive feature of Agda's inductive data type families is the ability to construct indexed data types. A familiar example for such an indexed data type is the type Vec A n of vectors of fixed length n and elements of type A. This vector data types can be equipped with an access operation that restricts the index to the actual length of the vector at compile time.[1]

---

[1] An identifier can be an almost arbitrary string of Unicode characters except spaces, parentheses, and curly braces. Agda also supports mixfix syntax with the position of arguments indicated by underscores in the defining occurrence of an identifier.

```
data Nat : Set where
  zero : Nat
  suc  : Nat -> Nat

data Vec (A : Set) : Nat -> Set where
  []   : Vec A zero
  _::_ : {n : Nat} -> A -> Vec A n -> Vec A (suc n)
```

The above defines the type Nat of natural numbers and an indexed data type Vec A n where A is a type and n is a natural number. The latter type comes with two constructors, [] for the vector of length zero and _ :: _ for the infix cons operator that increases the length by one.

One way of writing a safe access operation first defines an indexed type that encodes the required less-than relation on natural numbers.

```
data _<_ : Nat -> Nat -> Set where
  z<s : {n : Nat} -> zero < suc n
  s<s : {m n : Nat} -> m < n -> suc m < suc n
```

Lines two and three of the definition encode named inference rules for the cases that $0 < n + 1$ (for all n) and that $m + 1 < n + 1$ if $m < n$ (for all m, n).

The access operation takes a vector of length n, an index m, and a proof of $m < n$ (a derivation tree) to produce an element of the vector.

```
get : {A : Set} {n : Nat} -> Vec A n -> (m : Nat) -> m < n -> A
get []          _           ()          -- impossible case
get (x :: xs) zero      z<s       = x
get (x :: xs) (suc m) (s<s p) = get xs m p
```

This code cannot fail at run time because a caller has to construct the proof tree for $m < n$ before invoking get. Thus, an "index out of bounds" error cannot happen. (In Agda, arguments in curly braces are *implicit arguments* that will be inferred if omitted in an application.)

2.2   Accelerate

Accelerate [3] is a *generative* data-parallel array language embedded into Haskell, which targets GPUs. Being generative, its data-parallel array operations are not executed directly. Instead, Accelerate constructs abstract syntax trees (AST) representing an entire data-parallel subcomputation. These *computation representations* are executed using a run operation that accepts such a representation (of type Acc a), compiles it to GPU kernels, uploads it to a device, executes it, and retrieves the results.[2]

```
CUDA.run :: Arrays a => Acc a -> a
```

---

[2] To distinguish Haskell code from Agda code, we display Haskell code in a framed boxes.

The type class constraint `Arrays a` restricts the result type to a single array or a tuple of arrays.

As computation representations of type `Acc a` are compiled at application run time, all `Acc` compilation errors are effectively *run-time errors* of the application. Hence, Accelerate uses a range of Haskell type system extensions to statically type Accelerate expressions, such that these run-time errors are avoided where possible. In particular, Accelerate uses GADTs [7], associated types [4], and type families [14].

As a simple example of an Accelerate program, consider a function implementing a dot product:

```
dotp :: Vector Float -> Vector Float -> Acc (Scalar Float)
dotp xs ys = let { xs' = use xs; ys' = use ys }
             in  fold (+) 0 (zipWith (*) xs' ys')
```

The types `Vector` and `Scalar` represent one- and zero-dimensional arrays. Plain arrays, such as `Vector Float` are conventional Haskell arrays, using an unboxed representation to improve performance. However, when they are wrapped into the constructor `Acc`, such as in `Acc (Scalar Float)`, they represent arrays of the embedded language and are allocated in GPU memory, which in current high-performance GPUs is physically separate from CPU memory.

The `use` operation makes a Haskell array available in the embedded language by wrapping it into the `Acc` constructor. It amounts to copying it to GPU memory.[3] The operations `fold` and `zipWith` represent collective operations on Accelerate arrays, effectively producing a representation of an array computation yielding a single float value (`Scalar Float`). The code relies on (type class) overloading: `0`, `(+)`, and `(*)` are overloaded to construct abstract syntax.

The types `Scalar` and `Vector` are type synonyms instantiating a shape-parameterised array type to the special case of zero and one dimensional arrays:

```
type Scalar e = Array DIM0 e
type Vector e = Array DIM1 e
```

In the general type for `use`, the class `Elt` characterizes all types that may be held in Accelerate arrays. These are currently primitive types and tuples.

```
use :: Elt e => Array sh e -> Acc (Array sh e)
```

Common dimensions, such as `DIM0`, `DIM1`, and so on, are predefined, but to enable shape polymorphic computations, along the lines pioneered in the Haskell array library Repa [8], shapes are inductively defined using type-level snoc lists built from the data types `Z` and `:..`. The use of snoc lists simplifies the type signatures of fold operations that reduce or abstract over the least significant dimensions.

---

[3] Accelerate employs caching to avoid the transfer of arrays that are already available in GPU memory.

```
data Z       = Z
data sh :. i = sh :. i
-- Types for often used dimensions
type DIM0 = Z
type DIM1 = DIM0 :. Int
-- and so on
```

3   Related Work

Peebles formalizes parts of the Repa API using Agda [11]. The formalisation relies on the same shape structure as Accelerate, but array computations are neither embedded nor can parallel high-performance code be generated.

Swierstra and Altenkirch investigated the use of dependent types for *distributed* array programming [15, 16]. Their notation for distributed arrays is inspired by the X10 language [13]. They focus on expressing locality awareness.

Dependent ML is an ML dialect with a restricted form of dependent types, which, among other applications, may be used to statically check array bounds [18]. However, only simple indexing and array updating are considered and not aggregate array operations, such as those provided by Accelerate.

Accelerator [17] enables embedded GPU computations in C# programs; it subsequently also added F# support. However, no attempt is made to track properties of array programs statically. Similarly, Copperhead [2] embeds an array language into Python, but does not attempt to track information statically.

4   Dependent Types for Accelerate

In this section, we investigate the potential uses of dependent typing in a language like Accelerate and point out how they may be implemented in Agda. First, we review some basics of the embedding.

4.1   Embedding of Haskell Types

Accelerate supports a wide range of numeric types, characterized by the type class Elt, as base types for array computations. Almost all of these types lack a suitable counterpart in Agda, which only supplies computationally expensive encodings for natural and rational numbers. For that reason, our embedding keeps the Haskell types abstract in Agda. To specify the types of functions that are polymorphic in such a Haskell type or depend on it in some way, we have reified the possible element types as an Agda type Elt:

```
data Elt : Set where
  Bool   : Elt
  Int    : Elt
```

```
Float   : Elt
Double  : Elt
Pair    : Elt -> Elt -> Elt
-- and so on
```

Corresponding to Haskell type classes that are used in Accelerate, our embedding supplies predicates that characterize subsets. For example, the set of numeric types is defined by a predicate `Numeric`[4]:

```
Numeric : Elt -> Set
Numeric Int = ⊤
Numeric Float = ⊤
Numeric Double = ⊤
Numeric _ = ⊥
```

The embedding declares further subsets all in the same style.

4.2   Array Types

To demonstrate the Agda embedding in action, we translate the dot product example from Sect. 2.2 to Agda.[5]

```
dotp : forall {E : Elt} {{p : Numeric E}} {n : Nat}
    -> PreVector n E -> PreVector n E -> Scalar E
dotp{E} xs ys =
  let xs' = use xs
      ys' = use ys
  in  fold _+_ ("0" ::: E) (zipWith _*_ xs' ys')
```

Unlike the Accelerate code, this function is polymorphic with respect to the array element type, provided it is numeric. The length parameter n ensures that the two input vectors have the same size. The `PreVector` type of the arguments corresponds to the plain `Vector` type in Accelerate, whereas the result type `Scalar E` corresponds to `Acc (Scalar E)`—a piece of abstract syntax.

The `use` function works as before, but its type includes more information:

```
use : {sh : Shape}{E : Elt} -> PreArray sh E -> Array sh E
```

Like E, the index `sh` is now an element of an ordinary type instead of having to rely on type-level snoc lists[6]:

```
data Shape : Set where
  Z     : Shape
  _:<_> : Shape -> Nat -> Shape
```

---

[4] ⊤ is a one-element type, whereas ⊥ is a type without elements. These types customarily represent truth and falsity.

[5] In Agda, arguments in double curly braces are *instance arguments* [5] that are aggressively inferred. We use them like type class constraints in Haskell.

[6] Recent work on Haskell's type system manages to avoid this issue [19].

Asking for arrays of equal shape, as in the signature of use, means that the arrays have to have the exact same layout. The PreVector and Vector types are just synonyms as in Haskell:

```
PreVector n E = PreArray (Z :< n >) E
Vector n E    = Array    (Z :< n >) E
```

The functions fold, zipWith, and ::: are discussed in the subsequent subsections. The functions _+_ and _*_ both have the same type:

```
_+_ _*_ : {E : Elt} {{p : Numeric E}} -> Exp E -> Exp E -> Exp E
```

They are restricted to arguments of numeric type and construct abstract syntax for an addition or a multiplication by delegating to the corresponding Accelerate functions. The type Exp E denotes an AST of an expression of type E.

4.3   Exact Checking of Array Bounds

Accelerate's API features expressive type constraints that describe the shape of the array arguments and results. These constraints ensure that no shape mismatches occur (e.g., a 1D array cannot be considered 2D), but they do not ensure at compile time that the sizes of the dimensions match up. Such a mismatch results in a run-time error.

As an example, consider the function reshape. It takes a target shape sh and an array of source shape sh' and changes the layout of that array to sh.

```
reshape :: Exp sh -> Acc (Array sh' e) -> Acc (Array sh e)
```

For this reshaping to work correctly, the underlying number of elements must remain the same. For example, while it makes sense to reshape a two-dimensional 3×4-array to a vector of size 12 or to a three-dimensional $3 \times 2 \times 2$-array, an attempt to reshape to a 2×5-array should be rejected at compile time.

As Shape is an ordinary data type in Agda, we can define a size function that computes the number of elements stored in an array of a certain shape.

```
size : Shape -> Nat
size Z = 1
size (sh :< n >) = size sh * n
```

Now we can state an accurate type for reshape in Agda, which involves an extra argument with a proof that the source and target shapes have the same size.

```
reshape : {sh : Shape} {E : Elt}
        -> (sh' : Shape) -> Array sh E -> (size sh ≡ size sh')
        -> Array sh' E
```

There is a subtle difference to the original signature. In Accelerate, the first argument is an *expression* that produces a value of type sh at run time, whereas the Agda reshape requires a Shape as its first argument. Hence, Agda reshape computes the shape in the host language on the CPU, whereas the original signature admits to compute the new shape in the embedded language as part of a GPU computation. In other words, we slightly restrict expressiveness here to gain more static information, we will get back to that issue when discussing filtering.

In Agda, functions like `map` and `zipWith` obtain more precise types. The type of `map` tells us that the input shape is identical to the output shape:

```
map : {A B} {sh} -> (Exp A -> Exp B) -> Array sh A -> Array sh B
```

Similarly, the type of `zipWith` restricts its input arrays to identical shapes:

```
zipWith : {A B C} {sh} -> (Exp A -> Exp B -> Exp C)
          -> Array sh A -> Array sh B -> Array sh C
```

The latter type is more restrictive than the Accelerate implementation of `zipWith`. Instead of checking the sizes of the input arrays, it truncates them to the respective minima. We also developed an Agda type that directly corresponds to this implementation. It requires a binary function `isect` that computes the minimum of two shapes of the same rank, which we leave as an exercise to the reader.

```
zipWith' : {A B C} {shA shB} {p : rank shA ≡ rank shB}
           -> (A -> B -> C)
           -> Array shA A -> Array shB B -> Array (isect shA shB p) C
```

4.4 Associativity of Operations

Some parallel reduction operations require their base operation to be associative to return a predictable result. Here are two examples from Accelerate.

```
fold   :: (Shape ix, Elt a) =>
          (Exp a -> Exp a -> Exp a) -> Exp a ->
          Acc (Array (ix :. Int) a) -> Acc (Array ix a)
fold1  :: (Shape ix, Elt a) =>
          (Exp a -> Exp a -> Exp a) ->
          Acc (Array (ix :. Int) a) -> Acc (Array ix a)
```

In both cases, the text of the documentation says that "the first argument needs to be associative" and furthermore the `fold1` documentation "requires the reduced array to be non-empty". The second requirement can be enforced by asking for a suitable proof object on each call of `fold1`:

```
fold1 : ... -> Array (sh :< n >) E -> (size sh * n > 0)
              -> Array sh E
```

The first requirement can be rephrased to saying that the first two parameters of `fold` together form a monoid, which requires an associative operation with a unit element. The concept of a monoid can be formalized in Agda, which has indeed been done in the standard library. Unfortunately, the formalization from the library cannot be used because Accelerate deals with ASTs, not with values. So, a formalization is required that states that the meaning of an AST-encoded function is associative and the meaning of another AST-encoded constant is its unit element. Given that Accelerate encodes AST construction using higher-order abstract syntax, such a formalization is not straightforward. Moreover, even given expressions with a fixed meaning, associativity has to be proved on a case by case basis.

In any case, providing such information would be done by including an additional argument that holds a suitable proof object, as in

```
fold : forall {E}{sh}{n}
    -> (f : Exp E -> Exp E -> Exp E) -> (e : Exp E)
    -> Array (sh :< n >) E -> IsMonoid f e -> Array sh E
```

where

```
IsMonoid : forall {E} -> (Exp E -> Exp E -> Exp E) -> Exp E -> Set
IsMonoid f e = ( IsAssociative f , IsUnit f e)
```

Some readers may object that neither addition nor multiplication of floating point numbers is associative [6]. However, for advanced optimizations, the exploitation of algebraic laws is a necessity and the involved degradation of precision or change of result is accepted or accounted for in the error estimates. Moreover, there are other operations, like min or max, that are commonly used with fold-like operations, which are truly associative. Last, but not least, the associativity declarations serve as important documentation that passing an inherently non-associative function will produce unpredictable, implementation-dependent results.

4.5   Embedding of Constants

Accelerate relies on Haskell's built-in support for the type classes Num and Fractional to embed constants. The Haskell compiler reads each integer literal as a value of type Integer, which is a built-in type of arbitrary precision integers. To this value, Haskell applies the function fromInteger that converts to the type expected by the context. Similarly, floating point constants are read as values of type Rational (Integer fractions) and then converted using fromRational. Accelerate provides instances of these type classes that define fromInteger and fromRational to produce suitable AST fragments.

Because of Agda's lack of support for overloaded numeric literals, we embed numeric literals for integers and floating point numbers using a string with an explicit type annotation that determines the parsing of the string. Here are some example embeddings:

```
"3.1415926" ::: Float
"6.0221415E23" ::: Double
```

Recall that `Float` and `Double` are not types, but rather values of type `Elt`. The
: : : operation is the workhorse of the embedding:

```
_:::_ : (s : String) -> (E : Elt)
     -> {{nu : Numeric E}} -> {p : T (s parsesAs E)} -> Exp E
s ::: E = Ex (constantFromString (EltDict E) (ReadDict E) s)
```

The arguments s and E are explicit, but the remaining ones are inferred by Agda.
As mentioned, the argument nu is an instance argument; it is automatically filled-
in with a suitably typed value in scope [5]. As before, the predicate `Numeric` plays
the role of a type class that characterizes the numeric types.

The function `parsesAs` dispatches on its "type" argument and parses the
string to check whether it is an acceptable literal of the expected type. The
function `constantFromString` is imported from Accelerate. It is an overloaded
function that requires two type dictionaries, which are computed from E using
the functions `EltDict` and `ReadDict`. This results in a flexible way of handling
literals, which worked well in our examples.

5   Limitations

In a number of places, Accelerate's generativity limits the applicability of dependent typing. We already mentioned that the formalization of associativity or
of the concept of a monoid cannot be verified in Agda because such properties
have to be asserted for abstract syntax.

For a related problem, consider an implementation of the `filter` operation
that takes a predicate and a source array and returns an array that only contains
the elements of the source array fulfilling the predicate. First of all, filtering only
makes sense for one-dimensional arrays, that is, for vectors. To see the second
catch, let's try to write down a dependent type signature for `filter`.

```
filter : forall {n m : Nat}{E : Elt}
        -> Vector n E -> (Exp E -> Exp Bool) -> Vector m E
```

The problem is that the size of the result cannot be determined statically — that
is, we cannot simplify define a type-level function that determines the length of
a vector. Why? `Vector m E` is not a representation of a vector. Instead, it is a
representation of a computation that, *once run,* produces a vector.

Similarly, we cannot define a function that uses the predicate passed to
`filter` to count the number of elements that will appear in `filter`'s result.
Such a function would need access to the elements of the `filter`ed vector, but,
as discussed, we cannot even get its length. Moreover, such a counting function would need to evaluate the predicate. We cannot do that as the predicate
of type `Exp E -> Exp Bool` maps abstract syntax to abstract syntax; it *does
not* directly implement a Boolean predicate. We might consider to include an
evaluator for abstract syntax to lift these restrictions. However, that evaluator
would not be the code actually executed on the GPU, and hence, it doesn't seem
to be any more valuable than simply asserting an axiom concerning the size of

`filter`'s result. That is the price we pay for a generative approach, where at program runtime, we dynamically generate the code to be executed on the GPU.

We encounter similar restrictions if we try to, at least, establish that m must be less than or equal to n for `filter`. We cannot prove this constraint as the GPU code of `filter` is not available to us — it is generated by the underlying Haskell library. Even if we had access to that code, any statements about its properties would need to be based on the semantics of CUDA (i.e., NVIDIA's C dialect for GPU programming).

We might contemplate employing an existential type like

```
exists Nat (\ m -> m <= n -> Vector m E)
```

but it is not possible to build such an existential package because the evidence m is not available when the existential package has to be constructed.

However, we may use an alternative encoding of arrays that is compatible with filtering. The idea is to keep all elements but mark those which are no longer present because they have been filtered out. There are several ways of implementing this idea. The simplest approach is to pair up each element with a boolean flag that indicates its presence, which we call *predicated arrays*[7]:

```
FVector : Nat -> Elt -> Set
FVector n E = Vector n (Pair Bool E)
```

In this encoding, filtering is quite simple because the length of the FVector does not change. Furthermore, filtering could be extended to multi-dimensional arrays, although the result might require careful interpretation.

```
filterF : forall {n : Nat}{E : Elt}
        -> (Exp E -> Exp Bool) -> FVector n E -> FVector n E
filterF {n}{E} pred vec = map g vec
   where g : Exp (Pair Bool E) -> Exp (Pair Bool E)
         g bx = pair ((fst bx) && p (snd bx)) x
```

Mapping, which applies a function to each element of an array, becomes more complicated as it either has to materialize a dummy result for each absent element in the argument vector or apply the function to absent elements, too. This makes `filter` reminiscent of the `where` statement of the SIMD language C* [12].

```
mapF : forall {n : Nat}{E F : Elt}
      -> Exp F -> (Exp E -> Exp F) -> FVector n E -> FVector n F
mapF {n}{E}{F} defaultF f vec = map g vec
   where g : Exp (Pair Bool E) -> Exp (Pair Bool F)
         g bx = if (fst bx) then (pair (fst bx) (f (snd bx)))
                            else (pair (fst bx) defaultF)
```

Some operations can get rid of absent elements. A fold operation which reduces a filtered vector with a monoid returns a single value. In Accelerate, such a value has type `Scalar`, which is a synonym for an array of dimension 0.

---

[7] Accelerate currently does not support `Maybe` types as array elements.

```
foldF : forall {n : Nat}{E : Elt}
      -> (Exp E -> Exp E -> Exp E) -> Exp E
      -> FVector n E -> Scalar E
foldF f e vec =
  fold f e (map (\ bx -> if (fst bx) then (snd bx) else e) vec)
```

Operations like foldl and the scan operations extend to this representation, but they cannot revert to a non-filtered representation.

In the end, such a representation may not even lead to reduced efficiency on a GPU. As long as all computations take the same path, all processing elements work in unison. As soon as there are different paths in the same computation step, then some elements will be idle for part of the computation step. So it would be most advantageous to organize work as uniformly as possible by reorganizing the array so that the present and the absent elements are grouped together. A segmented array might be a suitable representation.

6   Implementation

Ordinarily, Agda is an interactive tool for constructing proofs and verified programs. Programs may be run, which amounts to normalizing Agda expressions, but this process is not very efficient.

Alternatively, an interactively developed program may be compiled to Haskell using the Alonzo compiler. It supports a Haskell foreign function interface (FFI), for Agda programs to invoke Haskell functions. Using this interface amounts to declaring a typed identifier in Agda and then binding the identifier to a suitably typed Haskell function. As an example, consider the import of the use function.

```
postulate
  useHs : {E : Set}
        -> HsEltDict E -> HsArray HsDIM1 E -> Acc (AccArray HsDIM1 E)
  {-# COMPILED useHs        (\ _ -> Accel.use) #-}
```

The first three lines introduce the typed identifier useHs and the last line is a pragma for the Alonzo compiler that binds the Agda identifier useHs to the Haskell expression on the right. But wait, this type looks very unpleasant and quite different to the one mentioned in Sect. 4.2. This difference arises as the type translation of Alonzo is unable to cope with the index type Shape. Hence, the interface uses a simplified array type and adapter functions are required, in the worst case, both on the Agda side and on the Haskell side of the interface.

At the foreign function interface level, all arrays are considered as one-dimensional arrays. Additional arguments are passed to encode the shape information as far as it is needed. The Agda adapter provides the encoding of this structure and the Haskell adapter decodes it again.

We believe that these adaptations only have a minor performance impact because (1) most functions just manipulate abstract syntax, so that only AST construction is affected, and (2) internally, Accelerate considers all arrays as one-dimensional so that operations like reshape are no-ops at run time.

Here is the Agda adapter for use:

```
use : forall {sh : Shape}{E : Elt} -> PreArray sh E -> Array sh E
use {sh}{E} (PA y) = Ar (useHs (EltDict E) y)
```

It makes use of two wrapper types. PreArray wraps a one-dimensional Haskell array using the constant HsDIM1 (the DIM1 type shown in Sect. 2.2 imported from Haskell via FFI) and the function EltType (not shown), which interprets a value of type Elt as a Haskell type. The latter types are also imported via FFI.

```
data PreArray (E : Elt) : Shape -> Set where
  PA : {sh : Shape} -> HsArray HsDIM1 (EltType E) -> PreArray sh E
```

The Array type wraps an AST reference for an Accelerate array, where Acc and AccArray are types imported from Haskell.

```
data Array (E : Elt) : Shape -> Set where
  Ar : {sh : Shape} -> Acc (AccArray HsDIM1 (EltType E)) -> Array sh E
```

The EltDict function translates a value (E : Elt) into a Haskell expression that evaluates to a dictionary for the Haskell type of E for the Haskell type class Elt. Such a dictionary is passed, whenever the corresponding Haskell function has type class constraints.

```
EltDict : (E : Elt) -> HsEltDict (EltType E)
```

The Haskell side of the adapter has several purposes. First, it materializes the type class dictionaries from the encoding that we just discussed. Second, it reconstructs sufficient information about the array shape so that the intended operation can execute. Here is the code for Accel.use, where the module name A is a shorthand for Data.Array.Accelerate.

```
use :: EltDict e -> Array A.DIM1 e -> A.Acc (A.Array A.DIM1 e)
use EltDict (ARRAY ar) = (A.use ar)
```

It does not have to reconstruct any information except the type class constraint. This constraint is materialized using the type EltDict below.

```
data EltDict e where
  EltDict :: (A.Elt e) => EltDict e
```

This datatype is built such that each value captures the Elt dictionary of type e. It remains to build such values for all types that we want to transport across the FFI. These are the values used by the (Agda) EltDict function. Here are two examples.

```
eltDictBool :: EltDict Bool
eltDictBool = EltDict

eltDictInt :: EltDict Int
eltDictInt = EltDict
```

As an example for a function that requires more work on both sides, consider the fold operation.

```
fold : forall {E}{sh}{n}
       -> (Exp E -> Exp E -> Exp E)
       -> Exp E
       -> Array (sh :< n >) E
       -> Array sh E
fold {E}{sh}{n} f (Ex e) (Ar a) =
  Ar (foldHs (EltDict E) (toHsInt (size sh)) (toHsInt n)
             (unwrap2 f) e a)
```

As values of type Exp also need a wrapper type in Agda (it is not possible to import type constructors via the FFI), there is some unwrapping going on for the e and f arguments. The implementation of fold just calls the foldHs function and encodes the information about the shape in two integer arguments. Here, size sh is the size of the result and n is the size of the dimension that is folded. As these values are initially available as Agda natural numbers, they need to be converted to Haskell numbers using the function toHsInt.

The foldHs function is defined via the FFI.

```
postulate
  foldHs : {A : Set}
           -> HsEltDict A
           -> HsInt
           -> HsInt
           -> (AccExp A -> AccExp A -> AccExp A)
           -> AccExp A
           -> Acc (AccArray HsDIM1 A)
           -> Acc (AccArray HsDIM1 A)
  {-# COMPILED foldHs      (\_ -> Accel.fold) #-}
```

The Haskell adapter reconstructs the Elt dictionary as before, but it also needs to reshape the one-dimensional array representation into a two-dimensional one for executing the fold operation. The two size arguments are required for exactly this reshape operation. With that insight, the code is straightforward.

```
fold :: EltDict a
     -> Int -> Int
     -> (A.Exp a -> A.Exp a -> A.Exp a)
     -> A.Exp a
     -> A.Acc (A.Array A.DIM1 a)
     -> A.Acc (A.Array A.DIM1 a)
fold EltDict size2 size1 f e a =
    (A.reshape (A.lift (A.Z A.:. size2))
      (A.fold f e
        (A.reshape (A.lift (A.Z A.:. size2 A.:. size1)) a)))
```

Fortunately, the `fold` example is about as complicated as the adapter code gets. There are also many cases where at least one side of the adapter code is trivial. However, each case must be considered separately.

7   Conclusion

We have built an experimental Agda frontend for the Accelerate language. The goal of this experiment was to explore potential uses of dependently-typed programming for data-parallel languages.

At the moment, the outcome of the experiment is mixed. It is successful, because we have been able to construct Agda functions for a representative sample of Accelerate's functionality. However, there was less scope for encoding extra information in the dependent types than we had hoped for. Exact matching of array bounds works, but results in restrictions (like the problems with `zipWith` and filtering) that were not anticipated.

Exploiting algebraic properties did not work out in the intended way, mainly because it boils down to asserting that some AST denotes an associative function. However, these assertions cannot be proven: the proof would have to apply the semantics to the AST, but the AST is an abstract type in our implementation. An AST representation in Agda might give us a better handle at this problem.

In some places, the Agda frontend is less dynamic than Accelerate. In a number of places, Accelerate accepts a run-time value of type `Exp sh` for a shape argument, where the Agda frontend requires a value of type `Shape`. To address this problem, we would have to include a `Shape`-indexed encoding of the `Shape` type in the `Elt` type so that we can describe the type of an expression whose value has a certain shape.

Finally, the type translation of Agda's FFI has a number of shortcomings that cause problems when transporting information between Agda and Haskell. One part of the problem is, unfortunately, the rich type structure of Accelerate's API which already encodes many useful constraints. An alternative, untyped (or less-typed) interface to Accelerate would make the adaptation to an Agda frontend simpler.

References

1. Bove, A., Dybjer, P., Norell, U.: A brief overview of agda - a functional language with dependent types. In: Berghofer, S., Nipkow, T., Urban, C., Wenzel, M. (eds.) TPHOLs 2009. LNCS, vol. 5674, pp. 73–78. Springer, Heidelberg (2009)
2. Catanzaro, B., Garland, M., Keutzer, K.: Copperhead: Compiling an embedded data parallel language. Technical Report UCB/EECS-2010-124. University of California, Berkeley (2010)
3. Chakravarty, M.M.T., Keller, G., Lee, S., McDonell, T.L., Grover, V.: Accelerating Haskell array codes with multicore GPUs. In: Carro, M., Reppy, J.H. (eds.) Workshop on Declarative Aspects of Multicore Programming, DAMP 2011, Austin, TX, USA, January 2011, pp. 3–14. ACM (2011)

4. Chakravarty, M.M.T., Keller, G., Peyton Jones, S.: Associated type synonyms. In: Pierce, B.C. (ed.) Proceedings International Conference on Functional Programming 2005, Tallinn, Estonia, September 2005, pp. 241–253. ACM Press, New York (2005)

5. Devriese, D., Piessens, F.: On the bright side of type classes: Instance arguments in Agda. In: Danvy, O. (ed.) Proceedings International Conference on Functional Programming 2011, Tokyo, Japan, September 2011, pp. 143–155. ACM Press, New York (2011)

6. Goldberg, D.: What every computer scientist should know about floating-point arithmetic. ACM Comput. Surv. **23**(1), 5–48 (1991)

7. Jones, S.L.P., Vytiniotis, D., Weirich, S., Washburn, G.: Simple unification-based type inference for GADTs. In: Lawall, J. (ed.) ICFP, Portland, Oregon, USA, September 2006, pp. 50–61. ACM Press, New York (2006)

8. Keller, G., Chakravarty, M.M., Leshchinskiy, R., Peyton Jones, S., Lippmeier, B.: Regular, shape-polymorphic, parallel arrays in Haskell. In: Proceedings of the 15th ACM SIGPLAN International Conference on Functional Programming, ICFP 2010. ACM (2010)

9. Martin-Löf, P.: Intuitionistic Type Theory. Bibliopolis, Napoli (1984)

10. Norell, U.: Dependently typed programming in Agda. In: Koopman, P., Plasmeijer, R., Swierstra, D. (eds.) AFP 2008. LNCS, vol. 5832, pp. 230–266. Springer, Heidelberg (2009)

11. Peebles, D.: A dependently typed model of the Repa library in Agda. https://github.com/copumpkin/derpa (2011)

12. Rose, J.R., et al.: C*: An extended c language for data parallel programming. In: Proceedings of the Second International Conference on Supercomputing, pp. 2–16 (1987)

13. Saraswat, V.: Report on the programming language X10. http://dist.codehaus.org/x10/documentation/languagespec/x10-200.pdf. October 2009. Version 2.0

14. Schrijvers, T., Peyton Jones, S.L., Chakravarty, M.M.T., Sulzmann, M.: Type checking with open type functions. In: Thiemann, P. (ed.) Proceedings International Conference on Functional Programming 2008, Victoria, BC, Canada, October 2008, pp. 51–62. ACM Press, New York (2008)

15. Swierstra, W.: More dependent types for distributed arrays. Higher-Order Symbolic Comput., pp. 1–18 (2010)

16. Swierstra, W., Altenkirch, T.: Dependent types for distributed arrays. In: Trends in Functional Programming, vol. 9 (2008)

17. Tarditi, D., Puri, S., Oglesby, J.: Accelerator: using data parallelism to program GPUs for general-purpose uses. In: ASPLOS-XII: Proceedings of the 12th International Conference on Architectural Support for Programming Language and Operating Systems, pp. 325–335. ACM (2006)

18. Xi, H.: Dependent ML: An approach to practical programming with dependent types. J. Funct. Program. 12(2) (2007)

19. Yorgey, B.A., Weirich, S., Cretin, J., Jones, S.L.P., Vytiniotis, D., Magalhães, J.P.: Giving Haskell a promotion. In: Pierce, B.C. (ed.) Proceedings of TLDI 2012, Philadelphia, PA, USA, January 2012, pp. 53–66. ACM (2012)

An Embedded Type Debugger

Kanae Tsushima[(⊠)] and Kenichi Asai

Ochanomizu University, Tokyo, Japan
tsushima.kanae@is.ocha.ac.jp, asai@is.ocha.ac.jp

Abstract. This paper presents how to build a type debugger *without* implementing any dedicated type inferencer. Previous type debuggers required their own type inferencers apart from the compiler's type inferencer. The advantage of our approach is threefold. First, by *not* implementing a type inferencer, it is guaranteed that the debugger's type inference never disagrees with the compiler's type inference. Secondly, we can avoid the pointless reproduction of a type inferencer that should work precisely as the compiler's type inferencer. Thirdly, our approach is robust to updates of the underlying language. The key observation of our approach is that the interactive type debugging, as proposed by Chitil, does not require a type inference tree but only a tree with a certain simple property. We identify the property and present how to construct a tree that satisfies this property using the compiler's type inferencer. The property guides us how to build a type debugger for various language constructs. In this paper, we describe our idea and first apply it to the simply-typed lambda calculus. After that, we extend it with let-polymorphism and objects to see how our technique scales.

1 Introduction

To write a well-typed program is not always easy. Although a compiler gives us an error message when a type error occurs, it is not straightforward to understand why the type error arose. Furthermore, the source of a type error can be far from the place reported by the compiler as a type error. In this paper, we define the source of a type error to be a part of an ill-typed program which programmers want to fix. Our purpose is to construct a way to find it in a strongly typed functional language. In this paper, we use OCaml's syntax for examples.

1.1 Locating the Source of a Type Error

Two Conflicting Expressions. A type error occurs when types of two expressions conflict with each other. Let us consider the following example:

```
let rec f g lst = match lst with
  | [] -> []
  | fst :: rest -> (g fst) :: (f g rest) in
(f 1 [2;3;4]) @ [5;6;7]
```

R. Hinze (Ed.): IFL 2012, LNCS 8241, pp. 190–206, 2013.
DOI: 10.1007/978-3-642-41582-1_12, © Springer-Verlag Berlin Heidelberg 2013

In this program, the two boxed expressions have a type conflict causing a type error. The first argument g of the function f is used as a function in (g fst), but an integer 1 is passed as g in (f 1 [2;3;4]). Because a function type 'a -> 'b cannot be unified with int, a type error occurs. To locate these two conflicting expression is useful when one of these conflicting expressions is the source of a type error. Unfortunately, it is not always the case.

The Source of a Type Error. The source of a type error cannot be determined solely from the conflict of types. For example, suppose that a call to f in the previous example is wrapped by a call to h.

```
let rec f g lst = match lst with
  | [] -> []
  | fst :: rest -> (g fst) :: (f g rest) in
let h n lst = f n lst in
(h 1 [2;3;4]) @ [5;6;7]
```

In this program, although (g fst) and (h 1 [2;3;4]) are the conflicting expressions, the source of the type error may be in the definition of h: if we replace the boxed expression with (f (fun x -> x + n) lst), the program is well-typed. Because which of these expressions is the source of the type error depends on the programmer's intention, we cannot locate the source of the type error automatically.

A Standard Type Inference Tree. To locate the source of a type error, we basically detect the difference between an inferred type and a programmer's intended type. Let us consider a small example:

$$(fun\ x\ \text{->}\ x\ +\ x)\ true$$

This program is ill-typed, because true is passed to x, but x is consumed by an integer addition +. Let us assume that the programmer wrote this program, because he mistakenly thought that + was the logical *or* operator.[1] Since the logical *or* operator in OCaml is ||, the programmer's intended program is (fun x -> x || x) true.

We show a standard type inference tree for this example constructed by the compiler in Fig. 1 and programmer's intended type tree in Fig. 2. By detecting the difference between these two type inference trees, we can locate an expression that includes the source of a type error. For example, since types of expressions in the boxed part differ in Figs. 1 and 2, the source of the type error resides in the expression (fun x -> x + x). However, we cannot further identify which subexpression of this expression is the root cause of the type error, as long as we use a compiler's type inference tree.

The standard type inference tree is not suited for type debugging, because a type of an expression can depend on the types of other expressions. In the above

---

[1] This is an example of the source of this type error. If the programmer has a different intention, other fixes are possible, such as replacing true with 1.

```
{x:int} ⊢x:int   {x:int} ⊢(+):int -> int -> int   {x:int} ⊢x:int
─────────────────────────────────────────────────────────────
              {x:int} ⊢ x + x:int
─────────────────────────────────────────────────────────────            ──────────────
         {} ⊢(fun x -> x + x):int -> int                                  {} ⊢true:bool
──────────────────────────────────────────────────────────────────────────────────────
                    (fun x -> x + x) true ···Type Error
```

Fig. 1. A standard type inference tree

```
{x:bool} ⊢x:bool   {x:bool} ⊢(+):bool -> bool -> bool   {x:bool} ⊢x:bool
──────────────────────────────────────────────────────────────────────
                  {x:bool} ⊢ x + x:bool
──────────────────────────────────────────────────────────────────────            ──────────────
         {} ⊢(fun x -> x + x):bool -> bool                                         {} ⊢true:bool
────────────────────────────────────────────────────────────────────────────────────────────────
                       {} ⊢(fun x -> x + x) true:bool
```

Fig. 2. Programmer's intended type tree

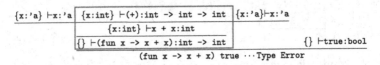

```
{x:'a} ⊢x:'a │ {x:int} ⊢(+):int -> int -> int │{x:'a}⊢x:'a
             ├───────────────────────────────┤
             │        {x:int} ⊢ x + x:int     │
             ├───────────────────────────────┤            ──────────────
             │ {} ⊢(fun x -> x + x):int -> int│            {} ⊢true:bool
─────────────────────────────────────────────────────────────────────────
                    (fun x -> x + x) true ···Type Error
```

Fig. 3. The most general type tree

example, the type of x does not have to be int if it appears independently. It becomes int, because it is used as an argument of +. Such information is lost in the standard type inference tree, because the type of x becomes int throughout, once it is unified with the argument type of +.

The Most General Type Tree. To break the dependency between expressions, we introduce the most general type tree. We show the most general type tree for our example in Fig. 3. The most general type tree holds the most general type for each subexpression. For example, x has a typing {x:'a} ⊢x:'a for any type 'a, because x alone does not require any constraints on its type. The type of x is constrained only when it is used in a context. For example, x + x has a typing {x:int} ⊢ x + x:int, because + requires that x has type int. Using this most general type tree, we can exactly locate the source of a type error by detecting difference between inferred types and intended types. By comparing Figs. 3 and 2, we find that the type conflict occurs in the boxed part of Fig. 3. We can then locate the source of the type error to be +. Note that the type of x (at the two leaves of the tree) does not contradict with programmer's intended type, because bool is an instance of 'a.

Algorithmic Debugging. Of course, a tree with programmer's intended types exists only in programmer's mind. To extract programmer's intention, we use algorithmic debugging proposed by Shapiro [11]. Algorithmic debugging is used to identify the location of an error in a tree by traversing over the tree according to oracles. For oracles, questions for the programmer are often used. It is originally used for Prolog, but algorithmic debugging can be used for any tree structures and is applied to various areas, to locate run-time errors [9], semantic errors [12], etc. To debug Fig. 3 using algorithmic debugging, we start from the root of the tree where a type error occurs. The type debugger first asks if the two child nodes are correctly typed according to programmer's intention. Since the programmer's intended type for (fun x -> x + x) is not int -> int but bool -> bool, the programmer answers no to the first question. From this answer, the type debugger determines that the source of the type error resides within this expression. Next, the type debugger asks whether the intended type of x + x is int. Again, the answer is no, and the type debugger moves into the subexpression. By repeating this process, the type debugger locates the source of the type error as +.

1.2   Problems

Chitil [1] constructed the most general type tree by inferring types compositionally, and located the source of a type error interactively using algorithmic debugging. Using his type debugger, one can locate the source of a type error by simply answering questions.

Following Chitil's work, we implemented a type debugger for a subset of OCaml together with some improvements [15] and used it in a course in our university. However, due to the need to implement a tailor-made type inferencer, we encountered at least three problems.

Implementation of a Type Inferencer. First, to implement a type inferencer that returns exactly the same type as the compiler's type inferencer is tedious and error-prone. Even for a small language, we had to fully understand the behavior of the compiler's type inferencer. For example, a compiler has an initial environment for typing. If a tailor-made type inferencer lacks a part of the initial environment, it cannot infer the same type as the compiler's type inferencer. Furthermore, the discrepancy between the two type inferencers becomes apparent only when we find unexpected debugging behavior. It makes it hard to detect errors in the tailor-made type inferencer.

Support for Advanced Features. Secondly, to implement a type inferencer for advanced features, such as objects and modules, is difficult and takes time. In our previous type debugger [15], we could implement the main subset of OCaml, including functions, lists, and pattern matching, but not the advanced features, such as user-defined data structures, objects, and modules. This is unfortunate: a type debugger would be particularly useful in the presence of such advanced features.

Compiler's Updates. Thirdly, to reimplement the type inferencer every time the compiler is updated is costly. In the last three years, the OCaml compiler had two major updates and two minor updates. It is not realistic to follow all these updates and reimplement the type inferencer.

To solve these problems, we propose *not* to implement a tailor-made type inferencer but to use the compiler's own type inferencer as is to construct the most general type tree.

1.3 Our Approach

Rather than implementing our own type inferencer, we use a compiler's type inferencer to construct the most general type tree. Construction consists of two stages. First, the erroneous program to be debugged is decomposed into subprograms. This decomposition determines the overall shape of the tree. Then, the type of each subprogram is inferred by passing the subprogram to the compiler's type inferencer. For example, if a program M is decomposed into subprograms, $M_1, \ldots, M_n$, we first construct the left tree below.

$$\frac{M_1 \quad \ldots \quad M_n}{M} \quad \Rightarrow \quad \frac{M_1 : \tau_1 \quad \ldots \quad M_n : \tau_n}{M : \tau}$$

We then infer their types (possibly an error) by passing each of M_i (and M) to the compiler's type inferencer to obtain its type τ_i (and τ). Note that unlike the standard type inference, types of subexpressions are *not* determined by applying typing rules to the parent expression. Rather, they are determined by executing the compiler's type inferencer for each subexpression independently.

The above explanation is somewhat simplistic, because we did not consider bindings. To cope with bindings properly, we actually maintain a context C of an expression M, treating $C[M]$ as a complete closed program (where $C[M]$ is the expression C whose hole is filled with M, possibly capturing free variables of M). We call M in $C[M]$ the *focused* expression.

Overview. In the rest of this paper, we first show a type debugger for the simply-typed lambda calculus in Sect. 2 and a necessary property for decomposition in Sect. 3. We then extend it with let polymorphism (Sect. 4), and objects (Sect. 5) to see how our technique scales. Finally, we describe our implementation of a type debugger for OCaml that uses OCaml's own type inferencer (Sect. 6). We compare our work with related work in Sect. 7, and the paper concludes in Sect. 8.

2 The Simply-Typed Lambda Calculus

In this section, we introduce a type debugger for the simply-typed lambda calculus. Although simple, it is enough to explain the basic behavior of our type debugger.

The Language. We show the syntax of lambda calculus $\lambda_\rightarrow$ in Fig. 4. It includes constants, variables, abstractions, and applications. We assume that basic primitive operations (such as $+$ that we will use in examples) are predefined as constants. Types include type variables, type constants, and function types.

Tree Structure Determined by Decomposition. Let us consider a type inference tree for $\lambda x.x + 1$. Since the only subprogram of $\lambda x.x + 1$ is $x + 1$ and it is further decomposed into three subprograms, x, $(+)$, and 1, the overall structure of the tree should look like:

$$\frac{\dfrac{\Gamma_0 \vdash x \quad \Gamma_0 \vdash (+) \quad \Gamma_0 \vdash 1}{\Gamma_0 \vdash x + 1}}{\Gamma_0 \vdash \lambda x.x + 1}$$

$$(M : term) ::= c \qquad \text{(constant)}$$
$$|\quad x \qquad \text{(variable)}$$
$$|\quad \lambda x.M \qquad \text{(abstraction)}$$
$$|\quad M_1\ M_2 \qquad \text{(application)}$$
$$(\tau : typ) ::= b \qquad \text{(type variable)}$$
$$|\quad \text{int, bool, ...} \quad \text{(type constants)}$$
$$|\quad \tau_1 \rightarrow \tau_2 \qquad \text{(function type)}$$
$$(C : context) ::= \square \qquad \text{(empty context)}$$
$$|\quad \lambda x.C \qquad \text{(lambda context)}$$

Fig. 4. The syntax of simply-typed lambda calculus $\lambda_\rightarrow$

where Γ_0 is the initial environment used by the type inferencer of the underlying compiler and contains all the bindings for the supported constants. However, the above subprograms are not directly typable using the compiler's type inferencer, because they include free variables (such as x).

Decomposition with Contexts. To make a subprogram typable, we enclose it with a context that supplies necessary bindings for free variables. In this language, a context is defined as either an empty context $\square$ or a lambda binding $\lambda x.C$ (Fig. 4). The most general type tree of $\lambda x.x + 1$ becomes as follows:

$$\frac{\Gamma_0 \vdash \lambda x.[x] : \text{'a} \rightarrow \text{['a]} \quad \Gamma_0 \vdash \lambda x.[(+)] : \text{'a} \rightarrow \text{[int -> int -> int]} \quad \Gamma_0 \vdash \lambda x.[1] : \text{'a} \rightarrow \text{[int]}}{\dfrac{\Gamma_0 \vdash \lambda x.[x + 1] : \text{int} \rightarrow \text{[int]}}{\Gamma_0 \vdash [\lambda x.x + 1] : \text{[int -> int]}}}$$

Looking at the focused expressions filled in the context, we see that it has the same structure as the previous tree. Thanks to the contexts, all the subprograms are now typable under Γ_0. The types enclosed by [...] correspond to the types of focused expressions.

Although the above tree is similar to the standard type inference tree for $\lambda_\rightarrow$:

$$\frac{\Gamma_0, x : \text{int} \vdash x : \text{int} \quad \Gamma_0, x : \text{int} \vdash (+) : \text{int -> int -> int} \quad \Gamma_0, x : \text{int} \vdash 1 : \text{int}}{\dfrac{\Gamma_0, x : \text{int} \vdash x + 1 : \text{int}}{\Gamma_0 \vdash \lambda x.x + 1 : \text{int -> int}}}$$

they have two important differences. First, the type of x is *not* constrained to int at the leaf nodes. Since we treat all the subderivations independently, each judgement depends only on its subexpressions. It enables us to locate where the type of x is first forced to int. Secondly, the type environment contains only the predefined constants. It enables us to use the compiler's type inferencer to infer the type of each expression. We simply pass it to the compiler's type inferencer and obtain its type. This is in contrast to the standard type inference tree where the environment contains free variables.

Other Approach. A compiler's type inferencer is usually designed to accept an open expression and an environment for its free variables. Although we could use this extra flexibility for the type debugger, it does not lead to a simpler type debugger. In this paper, we chose to use contexts, to avoid going into the underlying compiler implementation together with the representation of environments.

$$Dec : context * term \rightarrow (context * term) \; list$$
$$Dec[\![(C, c)]\!] = [\,]$$
$$Dec[\![(C, x)]\!] = [\,]$$
$$Dec[\![(C, \lambda x.M)]\!] = [(C[\lambda x.\Box], M)]$$
$$Dec[\![(C, M_1 \; M_2)]\!] = [(C, M_1); (C, M_2)]$$

Fig. 5. The decomposition function Dec for $\lambda_\rightarrow$

$$env = (var * typ) \; list$$
$$Collect : context \rightarrow typ \rightarrow env \rightarrow (env * typ)$$
$$Collect_\Box[\![\tau]\!]\mu = (\mu, \tau)$$
$$Collect_{\lambda x.C}[\![\tau_1 \rightarrow \tau_2]\!]\mu = Collect_C[\![\tau_2]\!]\mu[x \mapsto \tau_1]$$

Fig. 6. The function $Collect$ to obtain types of free variables for $\lambda_\rightarrow$

If we want to implement type debuggers for various languages, it would require substantial investigation of the underlying compiler. The method proposed here has an advantage that we can treat the compiler's type inferencer completely as a black box that accepts an expression and returns its type.

Construction of the Most General Type Tree. The most general type tree is built as follows. A program to be debugged $C[M]$ is first decomposed into subprograms using the decomposition function Dec defined in Fig. 5. It basically decomposes M and returns a list of its subprograms, but it maintains its contexts properly so that the resulting subprograms (pairs of a context and a decomposed term) are always closed. When the decomposition of $C[M]$ is $[C_1[M_1]; \ldots; C_n[M_n]]$, all the subprograms become the children of $C[M]$ in the tree.

The type of each subprogram $C[M_i]$ is determined using the compiler's type inferencer by passing $C[M_i]$ to it. When the context C is empty $\Box$, the returned type is the type of the expression. When the context is not empty, we split the obtained type into two: types for free variables and the type for the focused expression. If we obtain the type of $\lambda x.[x + 1]$ as `int -> int`, for example, we associate the type of x to be `int` (the argument part of `int -> int`) and the type of $x + 1$ to be `int` (the body part of `int -> int`). This is done by the function $Collect$ in Fig. 6.

Using Dec and $Collect$, we construct a judgement for $C[M]$ in the tree as shown in Fig. 7. First, we construct a closed term M' by plugging M into C. It is then passed to the compiler's type inferencer written as **typing** here. When we obtain a type τ of M', we split it into an environment γ holding types of variables in the context and a type τ' for M. Using them, we can construct a judgement for (possibly open) M (in the context C) as $\Gamma_0, \gamma \vdash M : \tau'$. For $\lambda x.[x + 1]$, for example, we have $\Gamma_0, x : \mathtt{int} \vdash x + 1 : \mathtt{int}$.[2]

---

[2] Before, we wrote $\Gamma_0 \vdash \lambda x.[x + 1] : \mathtt{int}$ `-> [int]` to emphasize that we are using the compiler's type inferencer to infer the type of M in C. Since we are interested in the type of M itself together with the types of its free variables, we also write it using the standard notation $\Gamma_0, x : \mathtt{int} \vdash x + 1 : \mathtt{int}$.

$$Judge[\![(C, M)]\!] = \text{let } M' = C[M] \text{ in}$$
$$\text{let } \tau = \textbf{typing } M' \text{ in}$$
$$\text{let } (\gamma, \tau') = Collect_C[\![\tau]\!][] \text{ in}$$
$$(\gamma, \tau')$$

Fig. 7. The function $Judge$ to obtain typing for $\lambda_\rightarrow$

3   The Decomposition Property

In our type debugger, the most general type tree is constructed by first decomposing an expression into subexpressions and then inferring their types using the compiler's type inferencer. The shape of the tree is determined by how we decompose an expression. However, it does not mean that we can use any arbitrary decomposition. We require that the decomposition satisfies the following necessary property:

Definition 1 (The Decomposition Property). *The decomposition function Dec should satisfy the following property for any context C and term M:*

$$T(C[M]) \Rightarrow \forall(C', M') \in Dec[\![(C, M)]\!], T(C'[M'])$$

where T is a predicate stating that a given expression is well typed (under the compiler's type inferencer).

The decomposition property states that if a program $C[M]$ is well typed, all of its decomposed subprograms are also well typed. Although this property looks trivial, it does preclude $x + 1$ as a decomposition of $\lambda x.x + 1$, because the latter is well typed, but the former is not typable with unbound x. In the next section, we will see how this property guides us to define decomposition that is suitable for type debugging.

This property is essential for our type debugger. Since the source of a type error is detected by tracking conflicts between inferred types and intended types, we can no longer continue type debugging into subexpressions if their inferred types are not available from the compiler's type inferencer. Therefore, we design decomposition carefully so that it satisfies the property and thus keeps the typability of expressions. In the following sections, we sketch why the presented decomposition satisfies this decomposition property. For the simply-typed lambda calculus, we reason as follows.

Decomposition for $\lambda_\rightarrow$ Satisfies the Decomposition Property. We need to show that for each case of the definition of Dec in Fig. 5, all the subexpressions in the right hand side are well typed if the left hand side is well typed. For constants and variables, it is satisfied vacuously. For abstraction, because the expression in the left hand side $C[\lambda x.M]$ is identical to the expression in the right hand side $C[\lambda x.[M]]$, the decomposition property is satisfied. For application, we notice that if $C[M_1 M_2]$ is well typed, $M_1 M_2$ is also well typed in a type environment consistent with C (formally proven by induction on C). Hence, both M_1 and M_2 are well typed in the same environment. Since C has all the necessary bindings for M_1 and M_2 and C simply adds binding to them, both $C[M_1]$ and $C[M_2]$ are well typed as required.

4   Let Polymorphism

In this section, we extend our idea to let polymorphism.

The Language. We show the syntax of λ_{let} in Fig. 8. It extends the simply-typed lambda calculus with pairs, fixed points, and let expressions. Types are also extended accordingly. Unlike the standard let-polymorphic calculus, we do not introduce type schemes. Type schemes are required only for inferring types. Once the type inference is done (in the compiler), all the expressions in the most general type tree are given mono types (possibly containing type variables).

Naive Decomposition. To support a let expression in the type debugger, we first need to define its decomposition. Because a let expression contains two subexpressions, the let-bound expression and the main body, we are tempted to define its decomposition as these two subexpressions. However, straightforward decomposition leads to violation of the decomposition property (Sect. 3). Let us consider the following program:

$$1 + (let\ id = \lambda x.x\ in\ (id\ id)\ 2.0)$$

Since *id* in the second subexpression $(id\ id)\ 2.0$ is free, we need to supply its context. If we naively follow the previous section, however, we end up with the following tree:

$$
\begin{array}{c}
\boxed{\begin{array}{c}
\vdash [\lambda x.x] : \text{'}a \to \text{'}a \quad \vdash (\lambda id.[(id\ id)\ 2.0]) \cdots \texttt{Type Error} \\
\hline
\vdash [let\ id = \lambda x.x\ in\ (id\ id)\ 2.0] : \texttt{float}
\end{array}} \\
\end{array}
$$

$$\vdash [1] : \texttt{int} \quad [+] : \texttt{int} \to \texttt{int} \to \texttt{int}$$

$$\vdash [1 + (let\ id = \lambda x.x\ in\ (id\ id)\ 2.0)] \cdots Type\ Error$$

Although the bottom expression in the boxed part is well typed, one of its subexpressions is not well typed. Thus, this decomposition does not satisfy the decomposition property.

$$
\begin{array}{rll}
(M : term) &::= \dots \mid (M_1, \dots, M_n) & \text{(tuple)} \\
&\mid\ fix\ f\ x \to M & \text{(fixed point)} \\
&\mid\ let\ x = M_1\ in\ M_2 & \text{(let expression)} \\
(\tau : typ) &::= \dots \mid \tau_1 * \dots * \tau_n & \text{(product type)} \\
(C : context) &::= \dots \mid fix\ f\ x \to C & \text{(fix context)} \\
&\mid\ let\ x = M\ in\ C & \text{(let context)}
\end{array}
$$

Fig. 8. The syntax of the let-polymorphic language λ_{let} (new cases only)

The reason why $(\lambda id.[(id\ id)\ 2.0])$ is not typable is clear. In the original expression, id is used polymorphically, while in the decomposed subexpression, id is bound by λ and thus monomorphic. From this example, we observe that we need to preserve the polymorphic types of let-bound variables, when decomposing expressions.

Decomposition with let Context. To preserve polymorphic types of let-bound variables, we extend the context with a let context (Fig. 8). We also extend it with a fix context since it is a (monomorphic) binder. Using the let context, the above tree changes as follows, satisfying the decomposition property:

$$
\frac{
\begin{array}{c}
\dfrac{
\dfrac{\vdash [\lambda x.x] : \text{'a} \rightarrow \text{'a} \quad \vdash (let\ id = \lambda x.x\ in\ [(id\ id)\ 2.0]) : \texttt{float}}{\vdash [let\ id = \lambda x.x\ in\ (id\ id)\ 2.0] : \texttt{float}}
}{}
\end{array}
}{\vdash [1 + (let\ id = \lambda x.x\ in\ (id\ id)\ 2.0)]\ \cdots\ \texttt{Type Error}}
$$

$$\vdash [1] : \texttt{int} \quad [+] : \texttt{int}\rightarrow\texttt{int}\rightarrow\texttt{int}$$

Construction of the most General Type Tree. To enable inspection of the definition of let-bound variables, we change the decomposition function as shown in Fig. 9. The definition is the straightforward extension of the previous definition except for the variable case. When we decompose a variable, we search for its definition using *Get* defined in Fig. 10. When the variable is bound by a let expression, *Get* returns its (inner-most) definition as the decomposition of the variable. Otherwise, the variable is bound by lambda or fix, so *Get* returns no decomposition. Using this decomposition function, we can further debug into the definition of let-expressions to identify the source of a type error.

Since the context is extended with a let context and a fix context, the definition of *Collect* is extended accordingly as shown in Fig. 11. It collects types for

$$
\begin{aligned}
Dec : &\ context * term \rightarrow (context * term)\ list \\
Dec[\![(C, x)]\!] &= Get(C, x, \Box, None) \\
Dec[\![(C, (M_1, ..., M_n))]\!] &= [(C, M_1); ...; (C, M_n)] \\
Dec[\![(C, fix\ f\ x \rightarrow M)]\!] &= [(C[fix\ f\ x \rightarrow \Box], M)] \\
Dec[\![(C, let\ x = M_1\ in\ M_2)]\!] &= [(C, M_1); (C[let\ x = M_1\ in\ \Box], M_2)]
\end{aligned}
$$

Fig. 9. *Dec* for λ_{let} (new cases only)

$$
\begin{aligned}
Get : &\ context * var * context * \\
&(context * term)\ option \rightarrow (context * term)\ list \\
Get(\Box, v, C, p) &= \begin{cases} [\,] & \text{if } p = None \\ [(C', M)] & \text{if } p = Some(C', M) \end{cases} \\
Get(\lambda x.C', v, C, p) &= \begin{cases} Get(C', v, C[\lambda x.\Box], None) & \text{if } x = v \\ Get(C', v, C[\lambda x.\Box], p) & \text{if } x \neq v \end{cases} \\
Get(fix\ f\ x \rightarrow C', v, C, p) &= \begin{cases} Get(C', v, C[fix\ f\ x \rightarrow \Box], None) & \text{if } v \in \{f, x\} \\ Get(C', v, C[fix\ f\ x \rightarrow \Box], p) & \text{if } v \notin \{f, x\} \end{cases} \\
Get(let\ x = M\ in\ C', v, C, p) &= \begin{cases} Get(C', v, C[let\ x = M\ in\ \Box], Some(C, M)) & \text{if } x = v \\ Get(C', v, C[let\ x = M\ in\ \Box], p) & \text{if } x \neq v \end{cases}
\end{aligned}
$$

Fig. 10. The function *Get* to search definition of variables for λ_{let}

$$env = (var * typ) \; list$$
$$Collect : context \to typ \to env \to (env * typ)$$
$$Collect_{fix \; f \; x \to C}[\![\tau_1 \to \tau_2]\!]\mu = Collect_C[\![\tau_2]\!]\mu[f \mapsto (\tau_1 \to \tau_2); x \mapsto \tau_1]$$
$$Collect_{let \; x=M \; in \; C}[\![\tau]\!]\mu = Collect_C[\![\tau]\!]\mu$$

Fig. 11. *Collect* for λ_{let} (new cases only)

lambda- and fix-bound variables and discards let-bound variables since they do not appear in the type returned by the compiler. (We assume that the compiler's type inferencer returns $\tau_1 \to \tau_2$ as the type of $fix \; f \; x \to M$ (and hence of f) where τ_1 is the type of x and τ_2 is the type of M.)

As the program to be debugged becomes larger, the number of let-bound variables increases. Since we can debug into the definition of let-bound variables when their types conflict with the programmer's intention, we can skip asking for the type of let-bound variables as an oracle each time. (For example, in the previous tree, the type debugger can skip the node $\vdash [\lambda x.x] : \text{'a} \to \text{'a}$). Rather, we only ask for variables in a context that are bound by lambda or fix. This is consistent with Chitil's approach that maintains an environment for polymorphic variables separately.

Decomposition for λ_{let} Satisfies the Decomposition Property. We can confirm that the decomposition property is still satisfied. The interesting case is for variables. (Other cases are similar to the reasoning shown for $\lambda_\to$.) Assume that $C[x]$ is well typed. We first observe that $Get(C_1, x, C_2, p)$ maintains an invariant that $C_2[C_1]$ is always the same across the recursive call, because at each recursive call, the topmost frame of C_1 is simply moved to the hole of C_2. This ensures that all the contexts appearing in the definition of Get are well typed (as contexts), because the initial context $[C[x]]$ with which Get is called from Dec is well typed. Next, the returned expression $C[M]$ is collected only from the let case. Because $C[let \; x = M \; in \; C']$ is well typed, we hence have that $C[M]$ is also well typed as required.

Observe how the decomposition property serves as a guideline for what we have to do and what we can do to incorporate let expressions. We have to define the decomposition function so that the let polymorphism is preserved. On the other hand, as long as the decomposition property is satisfied, we have the liberty of defining the decomposition in a way the debugging process becomes easier for programmers to understand. By defining the decomposition of let-bound variables as their definition, the debugger's focus moves from the use of variables to their definition.

5   Objects

So far, we have seen that interactive debugging is possible for various language constructs by suitably defining a Dec function that satisfies the decompositon property. This idea extends to advanced language constructs. In this section, we introduce objects and see how they can be supported in a similar way.

$$
\begin{array}{lll}
(L : classobj) ::= & inherit\ x & \text{(inheritance declaration)} \\
\quad\ | & method\ x = M & \text{(method declaration)} \\
\quad\ | & val\ x = M & \text{(value declaration)} \\
(M : term) ::= ...\ | & x_1 \# x_2 & \text{(method invocation)} \\
\quad\ | & new\ x & \text{(object creation)} \\
\quad\ | & class\ x\ v_1...v_n = object(v')\ L_1...L_n\ end\ in\ M & \text{(class definition)} \\
(\tau : typ) ::= ...\ | & obj & \text{(object type)} \\
(C : context) ::= ...\ | & class\ x\ v_1...v_n = object(v')\ L_1...L_n\ end\ in\ C & \text{(class context)}
\end{array}
$$

Fig. 12. The syntax of the object language λ_{obj} (new cases only)

$$
\begin{array}{l}
Dec : context * term \rightarrow (context * term)\ list \\
\quad Dec[\![(C, x_1 \# x_2)]\!] = SearchObj(C, x_1, \square, [\,]) \\
\quad Dec[\![(C, new\ x)]\!] = SearchObj(C, x, \square, [\,]) \\
Dec[\![(C, class\ x\ v_1...v_n = object(v') \qquad = [(C[class\ x\ v_1...v_n = object(v') \\
\qquad L_1...L_n\ end\ in\ M)]\!] \qquad\qquad\qquad L_1...L_n\ end\ in\ \square], M)]
\end{array}
$$

Fig. 13. Dec for λ_{obj} (new cases only)

The Language. We show the syntax of the object language λ_{obj} in Fig. 12. It models OCaml-style objects where an object is defined using a class (in which single inheritance is allowed) and is created by the *new* construct. Besides the inheritance declaration, an object can contain method and value declarations. In OCaml, class names (to be more precise, the object structures denoted by the class names) are used as types. We use them as is in our type debugger, abbreviated as *obj* in Fig. 12.

Construction of the most General Type Tree. The decomposition function Dec is extended with the new constructs and the Get function used in the variable case is extended with the class context (Figs. 13, 14). The interesting cases are for *new* and method invocation of Dec. In both cases, we need to identify the object mentioned in the expressions (in case their types contradict with intended types, so that we can debug into the object). For this purpose, the function $SearchObj$ in Fig. 15 is used. Its behavior is similar to that of Get, but differs in that $SearchObj$ collects *all* the method declarations in the designated object. In particular, if the object contains inheritance declaration, those method declarations are collected, too (see $SearchObj'$).

We collect all the declarations in an object because types of declared methods in an object are mutually dependent. Thus, we need to ask for the types of

$$
\begin{array}{l}
Get : context * var * context * \\
\qquad (context * term)\ option \rightarrow (context * term)\ list \\
Get(class\ x\ v_1...v_n = object(v') \qquad = Get(C', v, C[class\ x\ v_1...v_n = object(v') \\
\qquad L_1...L_n\ end\ in\ C', v, C, p) \qquad\qquad\qquad L_1...L_n\ end\ in\ \square], p)
\end{array}
$$

Fig. 14. Get for λ_{obj} (new cases only)

$$SearchObj' : classobj \; list * context \rightarrow (context * term) \; list$$
$$SearchObj'([], C) = []$$
$$SearchObj'((inherit \; x) :: r, C) = SearchObj(C, x, \Box, [])@SearchObj'(r, C)$$
$$SearchObj'((method \; x = M) :: r, C) = (C, M) :: SearchObj'(r, C)$$
$$SearchObj'((val \; x = M) :: r, C) = SarchObj'(r, C[let \; x = M \; in \; \Box])$$

$$SearchObj : context * var * context *$$
$$(context * term) \; list \rightarrow (context * term) \; list$$
$$SearchObj(\Box, v, C, p) = p$$
$$SearchObj(\lambda x.C', v, C, p) = SearchObj(C', v, C[\lambda x.\Box], p)$$
$$SearchObj(fix \; f \; x \rightarrow C', v, C, p) = SearchObj(C', v, C[fix \; f \; x \rightarrow \Box], p)$$
$$SearchObj(class \; x \; v_1...v_n = object(v') \; L_1...L_n \; end \; in \; C', v, C, p) =$$
$$if \; x = v \; then$$
$$SearchObj(C', v, C[class \; x \; v_1...v_n = object(v') \; L_1...L_n \; end \; in \; \Box],$$
$$SearchObj'(L_1...L_n, C[\lambda v_1...\lambda v_n.\lambda v'_v.\Box]))$$
$$else \; SearchObj(C', v, C[class \; x \; v_1...v_n = object(v') \; L_1...L_n \; end \; in \; \Box], p)$$

Fig. 15. The function $SearchObj$ to search for the definition of objects for λ_{obj}

all these method declarations to locate the source of type errors. For example, consider the following program:

```
class counter = object (self)
                val mutable n = 0
                method incr = n <- n+1
                method get = n
            end
let t = (new counter) in
t#incr; ("now, the conter is" ^ t#get)
```

The last line results in a type error, because t#get returns an integer, which is in conflict with the intended type (i.e., string). To find the source of this type error, we first look up t's class definition counter and search for the definition of the get method. However, we find here that the get method itself does not force the type of n as an integer. It simply returns a value of n. Instead, n is an integer because it is assigned 0 and n+1 elsewhere in the class. Thus, we need to examine all the declarations in an object to find the source of type errors.

Since any method declarations can be the source of type errors, we collect all the method declarations in a class definition, and return them as decomposition of the object reference. Although this strategy is necessary in general, it could lead to a large number of questions. Its practical implementation is future work.

Decomposition for λ_{obj} Satisfies the Decomposition Property. We can confirm that *Dec* satisfies the decomposition property as follows. First, *Get* will return a list of well-typed subexpressions only, using the similar argument we described in Sect. 4. For *new* and method invocation, we have to show that *SearchObj* returns a list of well-typed subexpressions. It can be proved by observing that *SearchObj* simply collects subexpressions in an object in a suitable context. The only interesting case is for a class declaration, where we have to properly insert bindings for the arguments to the class and the self variable v'. Note that declared values are put into let contexts in *SearchObj'*.

6   Implementation

We have implemented a type debugger for OCaml 3.12.1. To minimize the implementation efforts, we utilize the following components from OCaml as is:

- the abstract syntax tree for structures, expressions, and types (together with the lexer, the parser, and the pretty printer)
- the type inferencer `typing` (that accepts an expression and returns its type, both expressed using the above abstract syntax tree)
- the `is_expansive` function (that accepts an expression and returns a boolean to judge whether the given expression needs to be kept monomorphic or not)

By using exactly the same abstract syntax as OCaml, we can not only avoid reproducing the same abstract syntax but also utilize OCaml's own lexer, parser, and pretty printer. In addition to the type inferencer, we utilize the `is_expansive` function. Although OCaml has its own criteria for weak polymorphism [2], we can stay away from it by using OCaml's `is_expansive` function as is. Furthermore, this approach is robust to updates of OCaml: if the syntax and the interface of the two functions are the same, we can use the same debugger.

A slight complication is that OCaml treats a let expression without in differently from the one with `in`: the former is a structure, while the latter is an expression. We support both styles by splitting the context into two: the structure part and the expression part.

Another complication is the use of patterns in place of a variable declaration. For example, instead of `fun lst ->`, one can write `fun (first :: rest) ->`. Because patterns have type constraints, they may be the source of a type error. To make such an error detectable, we included patterns as the decomposition of the expression.

The rest of the language constructs are supported without requiring any special treatment. For each new construct, we define its decomposition and show that it satisfies the decomposition property. Our type debugger supports all features of OCaml including weak polymorphism and modules.

To construct the most general type tree, we use the compiler's type inferencer many times. Although it appears that our type debugger incurs significant overhead, this is not the case, because we do not have to construct the whole tree beforehand. Instead, the most general type tree is constructed as we debug: after the root node is constructed, the rest of the tree can be constructed during the interaction with the programmer.

7   Related Work

The typical approach to improving type error messages is to design a new type inference algorithm. Wand [16] keeps track of the history how type variables are instantiated and shows the conflicting history when a type error arises. Lee and Yi [6] present the algorithm M that finds conflict of types earlier than the algorithm W and thus reports a narrower expression as an error. Heeren and Hage [5] use a constraint-based type inference for improving type error messages. Although these improved type error messages are useful for programmers, it is in general not possible to identify the source of type errors by a single error message.

To locate the source of type errors, Chitil [1] uses compositional type inference and constructs an interactive type debugger for a subset of Haskell. Based on his work, we designed a type debugger for OCaml using the compiler's own type inferencer rather than a tailor-made type inferencer. The use of the compiler's type inferencer enables us to build a type debugger for a larger language easily. Stuckey, Sulzmann, and Wazny [14] find the source of type errors using type inference via CHR solving. They implement a type debugger called Chameleon, which can explain why an inferenced type is derived by searching. Tailor-made type inference is used for this purpose.

As different approaches, Haack and Wells [3] use slicing with respect to types to narrow the possibly erroneous parts of programs. By extracting the slice related to type errors, they help the programmer to identify the source of type errors. The advantage of this approach is that the process is automatic and the programmer does not have to answer questions. Schilling [10] obtains slices using the compiler's type inferencer. We share the goal of reusing the available resources in the compiler.

Lerner et al. [7] propose automatic type-error correction. They replace the erroneous part with various syntactically correct similar expressions, and see if they type check. If they do, they are displayed as the candidates for fixing the type error. Since the system automatically shows us possible fixes without intervention, the system is useful if the programmer's intended fix is shown. Unfortunately, it does not always produce the intended program.

As visualizing tools of types, Simon, Chitil, and Huch [13] show TypeView that allows programmers to browse through the source code and to query the types of each expression. McAdam [8] displays types as graphs and extracts various facts from them that are useful for debugging. Our previous Emacs interface [15] inspired by these works, and we will continue to build such interface.

8   Conclusion

In this paper, we have fleshed out our thesis that it is possible and also practical to write a type debugger by piggy-backing on the built-in type inferencer of an existing compiler. The key observation is that we only need the most general type tree with the decomposition property; such a tree can be constructed using the compiler's type inferencer. The decomposition property guided the design of our type debugger: we maintained contexts so that the property is satisfied all the time. We have illustrated the thesis with OCaml, and we have described how to handle a number of issues: simple types, let polymorphism, and objects. Our design is in use in our laboratory and in our classrooms.

We plan to continue the present line of work as follows. First, we want to explore how far the idea presented in this paper scales. In particular, we are interested in supporting type classes [4] in Haskell and GADTs introduced in OCaml 4.0. We will investigate how we can define decomposition of a program with type classes or GADTs and see if it satisfies the property (Sect. 3). Secondly, we want to perform thorough user tests. We have built an Emacs interface based on our previous work [15] and the type debugger is in use in several courses in our university. From user tests, we plan to obtain various feedback including usefulness and how to effectively show the type information to novices. Finally, we want to establish some kind of correctness criteria of the type debugger. By considering the most general type tree, it might become possible to formally state a property such as the type debugger would always find the source of a type error.

Aknowledgements. We would like to thank Olaf Chitil, Olivier Danvy, Ian Zerny, IFL participants, and anonymous reviewers for valuable comments and discussions.

References

1. Chitil, O.: Compositional explanation of types and algorithmic debugging of type errors. In: Proceedings of the Sixth ACM SIGPLAN International Conference on Functional Programming (ICFP'01), pp. 193–204 (2001)
2. Garrigue, J.: Relaxing the value restriction. In: Kameyama, Y., Stuckey, P.J. (eds.) FLOPS 2004. LNCS, vol. 2998, pp. 196–213. Springer, Heidelberg (2004)
3. Haack, C., Wells, J.B.: Type error slicing in implicitly typed higher-order languages. In: Degano, P. (ed.) ESOP 2003. LNCS, vol. 2618, pp. 284–301. Springer, Heidelberg (2003)
4. Hall, C., Hammond, K., Jones, S.P., Wadler, P.: Type classes in Haskell. ACM Trans. Program. Lang. Syst. (TOPLAS) **18**(2), 241–256 (1996)
5. Heeren, B., Hage, J.: Parametric type inferencing for Helium. Technical Report UU-CS-2002-035, Utrecht University (2002)
6. Lee, O., Yi, K.: Proofs about a folklore let-polymorphic type inference algorithm. ACM Trans. Program. Lang. Syst. **20**(4), 707–723 (1998)
7. Lerner, B.S., Flower, M., Grossman, D., Chambers, C.: Searching for type-error messages. In: Proceedings of the 2007 ACM SIGPLAN Conference on Programming Language Design and Implementation (PLDI'07), pp. 425–434 (2007)
8. McAdam, B.J.: Generalising techniques for type debugging, chapter 6. In: Trinder, P., Michaelson, G., Loidl, H.-W. (eds.) Trends in Functional Programming, pp. 49–57. Intellect, Portland (2000)
9. Nilsson, H.: Declarative debugging for lazy functional languages. Ph.D. thesis, Linköping, Sweden (1998)
10. Schilling, T.: Constraint-free type error slicing. In: Peña, R., Page, R. (eds.) TFP 2011. LNCS, vol. 7193, pp. 1–16. Springer, Heidelberg (2012)
11. Shapiro, E.Y.: Algorithmic program debugging. MIT Press, Cambridge (1983)
12. Silva, J., Chitil, O.: Combining algorithmic debugging and program slicing. In: Proceedings of the 8th ACM SIGPLAN International Conference on Principles and Practice of Declarative Programming (PPDP'06), pp. 157–166 (2006)

13. Simon, A., Chitil, O., Huch, F.: Typeview: a tool for understanding type errors. In: Draft Proceedings of the 12th International Workshop on Implementation of Functional Languages, pp. 63–69 (2000)
14. Stuckey, P. J., Sulzmann, M., Wazny, J.: Interactive type debugging in Haskell. In: Proceedings of the 2003 ACM SIGPLAN Workshop on Haskell (Haskell'03), pp. 72–83 (2003)
15. Tsushima, K., Asai, K.: Report on an OCaml type debugger. In: ACM SIGPLAN Workshop on ML, 3 p. (2011)
16. Wand, M.: Finding the source of type errors. In: Proceedings of the 13th ACM SIGACT-SIGPLAN Symposium on Principles of Programming Languages (POPL86), pp. 38–43 (1986)

Pure and Lazy Lambda Mining

An Experience Report

Nicolas Wu[1]($\boxtimes$), José Pedro Magalhães[1]($\boxtimes$), Jeroen Bransen[2]($\boxtimes$), and Wouter Swierstra[2]($\boxtimes$)

[1] Department of Computer Science, University of Oxford, Oxford, UK
{nicolas.wu, jose.pedro.magalhaes}@cs.ox.ac.uk
[2] Department of Computer Science, Utrecht University, Utrecht, The Netherlands
{j.bransen, w.s.swierstra}@uu.nl

Abstract. This paper discusses our entry to the 2012 ICFP Programming Contest, written entirely in Haskell. Our solution uses many features of Haskell: pure immutable data structures, laziness, higher-order functions, concurrency, and exception handling. Each of these features plays an essential part in our overall solution, and we demonstrate how these key elements can be composed together. In this exposition, we stress the importance of how the code was structured in such a way that made safely refactoring and extending the model a relatively easy task, and how Haskell's strong type system made it possible for our team to remain agile under changing specifications.

1 Introduction

In the classic paper *Why Functional Programming Matters*, Hughes [3] argues that functional programming in Miranda provides two kinds of glue that enable the modular construction of programs: lazy evaluation and higher order functions. To drive this point home, Hughes presents several small and elegant example programs that rely on precisely these features. But how useful are laziness and higher order functions in larger developments?

This paper investigates this question and aims to provide further evidence supporting Hughes's claim. We describe a solution to the 2012 ICFP programming contest.[1] This programming contest allows participants to write solutions in any language, or combination of languages, in a time frame of 72 hrs. Our solution was entirely implemented in Haskell [4]. We describe our solution as it was developed in the 72 hours of the contest, plus some later refactoring for readability and bug fixing. Crucially, the solution we present uses many different Haskell features: pure immutable data structures, laziness, higher-order functions, concurrency, and exception handling.

Nicolas Wu and José Pedro Magalhães have been funded by EPSRC grant number EP/J010995/1.

[1] The official task description is available at http://icfpcontest2012.wordpress.com/task/. A video presenting the task and announcing the winners can be seen at https://www.youtube.com/watch?v=5TCqUU3-GT0.

R. Hinze (Ed.): IFL 2012, LNCS 8241, pp. 207–223, 2013.
DOI: 10.1007/978-3-642-41582-1_13, © Springer-Verlag Berlin Heidelberg 2013

Fig. 1. Graphical representation of a mine

1.1 Problem Description

The ICFP programming contest has been run every year since 1998. This year, participants were invited to program a virtual mining robot to collect resources called 'lambdas' while avoiding falling rocks, getting trapped, or drowning. The overall score of a route was determined by the number of lambdas collected and the number of moves required to collect those lambdas. Figure 1 shows a graphical depiction of a game in progress. The goal is to compute a sequence of moves for the robot to collect as many lambdas as possible, without being crushed by falling rocks. If all the lambdas are collected, reaching the exit gives an extra score bonus.

The problem specification was extended four times over the course of the competition, demanding efficient and correct code to be produced under tight deadlines. This provided an excellent means of substantiating the claim that functional programming languages help to produce code that is both modular and reusable. In the remainder of this paper, we describe our solution and how it relies on several key Haskell features. The precise description of the problem will become clear from the presentation of our solution.

We begin by describing pure models of both the mine (Sect. 2) and the search space (Sect. 3). Our solution uses a combination of search strategies (Sect. 4), that traverse the shared search space. The main program then applies these strategies in parallel (Sect. 5), returning the best result. Section 6 describes the changes necessary to adapt our solution to each of the problem specification extensions. We conclude in Sect. 7 with a summary of our experience, including a number of practical guidelines for code development in a situation similar to ours.

2 Pure Modelling

In this section we describe how we model and simulate the problem in Haskell.

2.1   Model

The model represents the entire state of a mine at any given time, and forms an important interface for the rest of the system: the simulator (Sect. 2.2) takes one state of the model to the next, the parser must produce a value of this type, the visualiser outputs a visual rendering of the model (Sect. 2.3), and various strategies can be employed based on the state held within the model (Sect. 4).

The basic building block of a mine is a *Tile*, which holds information about what exists at a particular coordinate:

$$\textbf{data } \textit{Tile} = \textit{Robot} \mid \textit{Wall} \mid \textit{Rock Bool} \mid \textit{Lambda} \mid \textit{Earth} \mid \textit{Empty} \mid \textit{Exit}$$

Note that rocks are parameterised by a Boolean which indicates whether or not a rock is falling: when the robot is directly beneath a falling rock, it is crushed.

Each tile in the mine is given a specific coordinate, which is simply a pair of *Int* values named *Coord*. Putting these elements together, we are interested in an array that is indexed by *Coord*s and contains *Tiles*. This describes the layout of the mine:

$$\textbf{type } \textit{Layout} = \textit{Array Coord Tile}$$

Using an array for this representation is appropriate, since we need to perform lookups of elements at coordinates very often, and arrays have constant time lookup.

It is useful to define a function that checks the value of a tile in the layout at a particular coordinate, by dereferencing the appropriate location in the array:

$$\textit{isTile} :: \textit{Layout} \rightarrow \textit{Coord} \rightarrow \textit{Tile} \rightarrow \textit{Bool}$$
$$\textit{isTile } l \; xy \; t = l \, ! \, xy \equiv t$$

There is an important caveat to using this function and others like it which make use of (!), the unsafe indexing operator. This operator is efficient, but makes no effort to ensure that the coordinates being sought are within the bounds of the array, and this is a danger which could easily result in an exception being thrown at runtime.

Another utility function finds the coordinates of all the tiles which satisfy a given predicate:

$$\textit{findTiles} :: (\textit{Tile} \rightarrow \textit{Bool}) \rightarrow \textit{Layout} \rightarrow [\textit{Coord}]$$
$$\textit{findTiles } p = \textit{map fst} \circ \textit{filter } (p \circ \textit{snd}) \circ \textit{assocs}$$

This works by getting a list of all the associations in the array and representing these as a value of type $[(\textit{Coord}, \textit{Tile})]$. This list is then filtered by the predicate, before the coordinates are extracted.

While the *Layout* structure holds much of the information required during the game, some essential features are lacking, such as the number of moves that have passed since the beginning of the game. The whole state is saved in a structure named *Mine*, which contains all the information required for assessing the current score:

```
data Mine = Mine { layout   :: Layout
                 , robot     :: Coord
                 , lambdas :: Int
                 , moves    :: Int }
```

In particular, *Mine* stores the current position of the robot along with the number of remaining lambdas and the number of moves it has taken to reach this point, since this is an important part of calculating the score.

When the robot has finished collecting all the lambdas, the exit opens and the robot is allowed to leave the mine. Our representation indicates that the robot has exited when the robot's coordinates correspond with the *Exit* tile in the layout:

```
isDone :: Mine → Bool
isDone mine = isTile (layout mine) (robot mine) Exit
```

The task of ensuring that the robot can only enter an exit when all lambdas have been collected is left to the simulator, which we explain in the next section.

2.2   Simulation

The simulation code determines how the system responds to the robot's actions: each time the robot makes a move the world is updated and a new *Mine* value is calculated.

The robot can perform several moves: moving up, down, left, right, waiting, or aborting the mission. For brevity, the data constructors that represent these moves contain only the initial letter of each action:

```
data Move = L | R | D | U | W | A
```

We often calculate coordinates based on a sequence of moves; the following function returns a coordinate that has been shifted by some movement value:

```
(⤳) :: Coord → Move → Coord
(x, y) ⤳ L = (x − 1, y      )
(x, y) ⤳ R = (x + 1, y      )
(x, y) ⤳ D = (x     , y − 1)
(x, y) ⤳ U = (x     , y + 1)
(x, y) ⤳ _ = (x     , y      )
```

For example, this operator is used to verify whether the robot has been crushed by a rock, which happens whenever the tile directly above the robot is a falling rock:

```
isDead :: Mine → Bool
isDead mine = isRockFalling (layout mine ! (robot mine ⤳ U))
```

The function *isRockFalling* distinguishes rocks that are falling.

The score is calculated by multiplying a constant factor per collected lambda minus the number of moves the robot made. The constant depends on how the game ended, and is 75 when all lambdas were collected, 25 when the robot dies, and 50 if the robot aborted (which is the default action when no more moves are made).

The central function used to simulate the robot's progression through a mine is *step*, which takes a current mine, a move, and steps the simulator through that move:

$$
\begin{aligned}
&step :: Mine \rightarrow Move \rightarrow Mine \\
&step\ mine\ A \quad = mine \\
&step\ mine\ move = mine'\ \textbf{where} \\
&\quad (layout', robot') = stepRobot\ mine\ move \\
&\quad layout'' \qquad\quad = array\ ((bounds \circ layout)\ mine)\ \$ \\
&\qquad concat\ [\ updRocks\ (mine\ \{layout = layout'\})\ (x, y)\ (layout' \, !\, (x, y)) \\
&\qquad\qquad |\ y \leftarrow [1 \mathinner{.\,.} h], x \leftarrow [1 \mathinner{.\,.} w]] \\
&\quad moves' \qquad\qquad = 1 + moves\ mine \\
&\quad lambdas' \qquad\quad |\ isTile\ (layout\ mine)\ robot'\ Lambda = lambdas\ mine - 1 \\
&\qquad\qquad\qquad\qquad\ \ |\ otherwise \qquad\qquad\qquad\qquad\ = lambdas\ mine \\
&\quad (w, h) \qquad\qquad = (snd \circ bounds \circ layout)\ mine \\
&\quad mine' \qquad\qquad\ \ = mine\ \{layout \quad = layout''\ , robot \quad = robot' \\
&\qquad\qquad\qquad\qquad\qquad\ , lambdas = lambdas', moves = moves'\}
\end{aligned}
$$

When a move other than A is requested, the simulator returns the result of the updated record *mine'*. The *layout* field is updated in two stages. First the value of the layout is calculated after the robot has made its step and stored in *layout'*, and then this value is used in creating a new array, *layout''*, that contains the state of the mine after all the falling of rocks has been calculated. This follows the problem specification.

Updating the robot is left to the *stepRobot* function, which returns the layout after the robot has moved, and gives the new coordinate of the robot:

$$
\begin{aligned}
&stepRobot :: Mine \rightarrow Move \rightarrow (Layout, Coord) \\
&stepRobot\ mine\ move = \\
&\quad \textbf{case}\ l\ !\ xy'\ \textbf{of} \\
&\qquad Earth \quad\ \rightarrow (l\ /\!\!/\ [(xy', Robot), (xy, Empty)], xy') \\
&\qquad Empty \quad \rightarrow (l\ /\!\!/\ [(xy', Robot), (xy, Empty)], xy') \\
&\qquad Lambda \quad \rightarrow (l\ /\!\!/\ [(xy', Robot), (xy, Empty)], xy') \\
&\qquad Exit \quad\ \ |\ lambdas\ mine \equiv 0 \\
&\qquad\qquad\qquad\quad \rightarrow (l\ /\!\!/\ [(xy', Robot), (xy, Empty)], xy') \\
&\qquad Rock\ \_\ \ |\ (move \equiv L \vee move \equiv R) \wedge isTile\ l\ (xy' \rightsquigarrow move)\ Empty \\
&\qquad\qquad\qquad\quad \rightarrow (l\ /\!\!/\ [(xy', Robot), (xy, Empty), (xy' \rightsquigarrow move, Rock\ False)], xy') \\
&\qquad\quad\ \_ \qquad\qquad \rightarrow (l\ /\!\!/\ [(xy, Robot)], xy) \\
&\quad \textbf{where}\ l \quad = layout\ mine \\
&\qquad\qquad xy \quad = robot\ mine \\
&\qquad\qquad xy' \quad = xy \rightsquigarrow move
\end{aligned}
$$

Moving towards earth, an empty tile, or a lambda simply updates the robot position, leaving an empty space behind. Moving towards the exit is only allowed if all the lambdas have been collected. Moving towards a rock is possible if the movement is sideways, and there is empty space next to the rock being pushed. All other movements are invalid, and the robot remains in the same position.

Another crucial function is *updRocks*, which is responsible for updating the position of rocks after the robot has moved:

$$updRocks :: Mine \rightarrow Coord \rightarrow Tile \rightarrow [(Coord, Tile)]$$
$$updRocks\ mine\ xy\ (Rock\ \_)$$

$$
\begin{aligned}
&|\ isFallDown \quad\ l\ xy = [(xy, Empty), (xy \rightsquigarrow D \qquad\ , Rock\ True)] \\
&|\ isFallRight \quad\ l\ xy = [(xy, Empty), (xy \rightsquigarrow D \rightsquigarrow R, Rock\ True)] \\
&|\ isFallLeft \qquad l\ xy = [(xy, Empty), (xy \rightsquigarrow D \rightsquigarrow L, Rock\ True)] \\
&|\ isFallLambda\ l\ xy = [(xy, Empty), (xy \rightsquigarrow D \rightsquigarrow R, Rock\ True)] \\
&|\ otherwise \qquad\quad = [(xy, Rock\ False)]
\end{aligned}
$$

$$\textbf{where}\ l = layout\ mine$$
$$updRocks\ \_\ xy\ tile = [(xy, tile)]$$

The functions *isFallDown*, *isFallRight*, *isFallLeft*, and *isFallLambda* determine whether the rock will fall in a particular direction. These are all predicates that take a *Layout* and a *Coord*, and simply output the appropriate *Bool*.

Keeping the entire state of a mine as a single value of type *Mine* enables the definition of *step* to remain relatively simple, since all of the required data for an update is held in a single structure. This complete encapsulation of state means that there are no implicit outside dependencies to handle when trying to evaluate a particular mine.

2.3   Input and Output

The input maps are supplied in text format. To read these into our model, we wrote a text parser using Attoparsec,[2] working on *ByteStrings* for efficiency reasons. The input format is simple, so the parser is unsurprising and therefore omitted in this presentation.

Visualising the maps in a user-friendly way was not a requirement of the contest. However during development it was helpful to visualise maps and generated solutions, and to be able to manually play each mine. Due to time considerations we developed only a simple ANSI text-based visualiser, which was enough for our testing purposes.

3   The Game Trie

One of the key benefits of Haskell is its purity, allowing game states to be shared across different solvers. Our strategy for exploiting this was to spawn a number of different agents that explore a shared data structure that holds paths to different game states together with their scores.

---

[2] http://hackage.haskell.org/package/attoparsec

3.1 Tries

The structure we use to encode paths through the mine is a non-empty trie [2]:

data *Trie k v* = *Trie* { *root* :: *v*, *branches* :: *Map k* (*Trie k v*) }

An important aspect of a value of type *Trie k v* is that it can behave like a map of type *Map* [*k*] *v*, and this forms the basis of an intuitive interface with a number of well-understood standard functions. These standard functions on *Trie* will prove useful in the strategy code (Sect. 4), since the entire search space of a game can be encoded as a trie, mapping sequences of moves to a game state:

type *GameTrie* = *Trie Move GameState*
data *GameState* = *GameState* { *gameStateMine* :: *Mine*
                                            , *gameStateScore* :: *Score* }

For instance, we can lookup the *GameState* associated with a certain path by using the familiar *lookup* function:

lookup :: (*Eq k*, *Ord k*) ⇒ [*k*] → *Trie k v* → *Maybe v*
lookup []   (*Trie v* _)   = *Just v*
lookup (*k* : *ks*) (*Trie* _ *kvs*) = *Map.lookup k kvs* ≫= *lookup ks*

A *Path* is represented by a list of moves:

type *Path* = [*Move*]

The type *GameTrie* operates much like the type of *Map Path GameState*, but its encoding is very efficient; each branch of the tree encodes one possible move, as illustrated in the following figure:

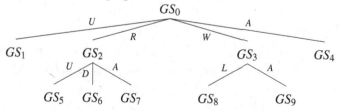

In this example, starting from some initial game state GS_0, the robot can move up and die, resulting in game state GS_1, with no further paths. Alternatively, the robot can go right, and then proceed either up, down, or abort. A *GameTrie* is computed by starting with an initial state (of score zero), and considering only valid moves from the current position:

mkTrie :: (*Eq k*, *Ord k*) ⇒ *v* → (*v* → [*k*]) → (*v* → *k* → *v*) → *Trie k v*
mkTrie v f next = *Trie v* (*Map.fromList* [(*k*, *mkTrie* (*next v k*) *f next*) | *k* ← *f v*])
gameTree :: *Mine* → *GameTrie*
gameTree $mine_0$ = *mkTrie* (*GameState* $mine_0$ 0 (*hash* $mine_0$))
                        (*goodMoves* ∘ *gameStateMine*)
                        (*mkGameState* $mine_0$ ∘ *gameStateMine*)

We omit the function *mkGameState*, which simply computes the current *GameState*, and function *goodMoves*, which returns the valid moves for the robot. One of the key features of our solution is that the *GameTrie* represents all the paths in the mine, and this trie is shared over the different robot strategy algorithms. This means that states are never computed twice; if strategy one already went down a particular path, the next strategy can immediately get the corresponding game state for that path, without having to step through each move. In addition, equivalent states that are reachable through different paths are not recomputed, and this is achieved through the use of hashes, described in more detail in Sect. 3.3.

Another useful property of values of type *Trie k v* is that they behave like trees of type *Tree* $([k], v)$, which brings another family of standard functions that are well understood. In particular, a tree can be traversed in breadth-first order in order to compute all possible paths in increasing length:

$$flatten :: Trie\ k\ v \rightarrow [([k], v)]$$
$$flatten = concat \circ levels$$

$$levels :: Trie\ k\ v \rightarrow [[([k], v)]]$$
$$levels\ tree = (map\ extract \circ iterate\ expand)\ [([], tree)]$$
  where
$$\quad expand :: [([k], Trie\ k\ v)] \rightarrow [([k], Trie\ k\ v)]$$
$$\quad expand = concatMap\ (\lambda(sk, Trie\ \_ kts) \rightarrow map\ (first\ (:sk))\ (Map.toList\ kts))$$

$$\quad extract :: [([k], Trie\ k\ v)] \rightarrow [([k], v)]$$
$$\quad extract = map\ (\lambda(sk, Trie\ v'\ \_) \rightarrow (reverse\ sk, v'))$$

In Sect. 3.2 we will use variations of these functions to build efficient pathfinding algorithms that are used to search for solutions within the *GameTrie*.

3.2   Pathfinding

The key to our strategy is to navigate the *Trie* structure, and identify a path that leads to a high score. The following function, for example, finds the paths to the exit:

$$solve :: Mine \rightarrow [(Path, GameState)]$$
$$solve\ mine = (filter\ (isDone \circ gameStateMine \circ snd) \circ flatten \circ gameTree)\ mine$$

Since *flatten* produces a breadth first traversal of the tree, we know that the result at the head of the list will have the shortest path. Furthermore, since the predicate applied is *isDone*, we know that the solution found is for a completed mine. Therefore, the head of this list will contain a solution with the maximal score for a completed mine! However, while this strategy would eventually find such a solution for completable mines, it is prohibitively inefficient. In addition, since the tree is potentially very large, and not all mines are necessarily completable, an exhaustive search will generally not be possible. In order to solve this, we break the problem down into finding paths to a number of intermediate states given by some predicate: the basis for the searches will still be variations on breadth first search, but the goal is different. Rather than finding paths to different values of type *GameState*, we will seek values of type *GameTrie*, so that we can search for new paths based on the returned tree, thus giving us more sophisticated searching strategies, where intermediate goals are reached and further analysis is performed on the trees that follow on from the paths to those goals.

A useful utility function along these lines is *findPaths*, which looks for paths to a particular coordinate:

$$findPaths :: GameTrie \rightarrow Coord \rightarrow [(Path, GameTrie)]$$
$$findPaths\ tree\ dest = bfs\ ((\equiv)\ dest \circ robot \circ gameStateMine)\ tree$$

This can be used, for example, to find a path to the *Exit* once the task of collecting all the lambdas is complete:

$$findExits :: GameTrie \rightarrow [(Path, GameTrie)]$$
$$findExits\ tree = findTiles\ (\equiv Exit)\ (layout\ (getMine\ tree)) \ggg findPaths\ tree$$

This works by first finding the appropriate tile, and, if such a coordinate is found, then it is used by *findPath* to calculate a path.

At the heart of *findExits* is an efficient breadth first search algorithm, with a more general interface than that of *solve*. A naive breadth first search that operates on the *Trie* structure can be described as follows:

type $KTrie\ k\ v = ([k], Trie\ k\ v)$

$bfsNaive :: (v \rightarrow Bool) \rightarrow Trie\ k\ v \rightarrow [KTrie\ k\ v]$
$bfsNaive\ p\ tree = (filter\ (p \circ root \circ snd) \circ stems)\ [([], tree)]$

This makes use of the function *stems*, which is similar to *flatten*, but returns a list of paths with corresponding subtrees:

$stems :: [KTrie\ k\ v] \rightarrow [KTrie\ k\ v]$
$stems\ [] \qquad\qquad = []$
$stems\ ((sk, t@(Trie\ \_\ kts)) : skts) = (reverse\ sk, t) : stems\ skts'$
   where $skts' = skts + [(k' : sk, t') \mid (k', t') \leftarrow Map.toList\ kts]$

The *stems* function produces a breadth-first traversal of the tree, but is certainly not optimal: this function makes no effort to ensure that some common state has not been investigated several times: certain paths lead to exactly the same state, and we have no reason to assume that there will be any implicit sharing of these states.

3.3   Hashing

During the lazy construction of the tree structure, sharing is not exploited between nodes that are equal. As a result, a search of the tree will likely result in repeated inspections of equal nodes and their children: this happens whenever there is more than one path to a particular state. To avoid this expensive recomputation, the breadth first search algorithm is modified to contain an accumulator that keeps track of the nodes visited so far, and will not queue nodes whose values have already been visited elsewhere.

Rather than have the accumulator store the entire state of each visited mine, and have to perform an expensive equality operation, a hash of the mine is stored instead. We therefore extend the type of a *GameState* so that it contains a *Hash*:

```
type Hash = Int
data GameState = GameState { ...
                           ; gameStateHash :: Hash}
```

An instance of *Hashable* is provided, giving us a means of obtaining the hash of a *Mine*:

```
instance Hashable Mine where
    hash mine = hash ((hash ∘ assocs ∘ layout) mine
                     , (hash ∘ robot) mine
                     , (hash ∘ moves) mine)
```

An accumulator, which is a set of hashes, is then added to the machinery of *stems* that allows states which have already been visited to be pruned:

```
stemsPrune :: Hashable v ⇒ Set Hash → [KTrie k v] → [KTrie k v]
stemsPrune _        []                          = []
stemsPrune visited ((sk, t@(Trie v kts)) : skts) = case insertM (hash v) visited of
    Nothing      → stemsPrune visited skts
    Just visited' → (reverse sk, t) : stemsPrune visited' skts'
    where skts' = skts ++ [(k' : sk, t') | (k', t') ←  Map.toList kts]

insertM :: Ord a ⇒ a → Set a → Maybe (Set a)
insertM x xs | Set.member x xs = Nothing
             | otherwise       = Just (Set.insert x xs)
```

The idea is to keep an accumulator that checks if the value of the tree being examined has been visited before. If it has been visited, then this value is rejected by the function *insertM*, and the next candidate for traversal is considered. If the value has not yet been visited, then the tree that contains it is added to the output of the search, its content is added to the set of visited values, and children are scheduled for traversal.

This lets us define a breadth first search that does not visit the same subtree twice:

```
bfsPrune :: Hashable v ⇒ (v → Bool) → Trie k v → [KTrie k v]
bfsPrune p t = filter (p ∘ root ∘ snd) ∘ stemsPrune Set.empty $ [([], t)]
```

The beauty of this solution is that it requires only the values v of the *Trie k v* structure to be *Hashable*. However, this does not come without its cost: the hashing itself is not perfect, and so it is possible that two different states hash to the same value. If this were to happen, then not all unexplored states will be visited, since we would incorrectly discard states that collide with already visited states that a hash. In practice, this does not turn out to pose a problem, since the hash space is large enough.

Another performance issue is that *stems* uses a list to hold the queue of subtrees left to visit: the performance of appending to the end of a list is poor, and this can be easily improved by using a queue structure instead, and replacing the call to *stemsPrune* with an adequately instantiated call to *stemsPruneQ*.

```
stemsPruneQ :: Hashable v ⇒ Set Hash → Seq (KTrie k v) → [KTrie k v]
stemsPruneQ visited q = case Seq.viewl q of
  Seq.EmptyL         → []
  (sk, t@(Trie v kts)) :< q' → case insertM (hash v) visited of
    Nothing       → stemsPruneQ visited q
    Just visited' → (reverse sk, t) : stemsPruneQ visited'
      (foldr (flip (|>)) q' [(k' : sk, t') | (k', t') ← Map.toList kts])
bfsPruneQ :: Hashable v ⇒ (v → Bool) → Trie k v → [KTrie k v]
bfsPruneQ p t = (filter (p ∘ root ∘ snd) ∘ stemsPruneQ Set.empty ∘ return) ([], t)
```

This is a relatively straight-forward transliteration of the list based version into one that uses a *Seq* datastructure instead.

On a final note about pathfinding, the *findPaths* function takes a destination coordinate as an argument, and filters out the results of a breadth-first traversal until a state is found where the robot is at the coordinate. A heuristic for possibly improving the search is by using a distance metric which determines how close a given point is to the destination, and using this information to give priority to certain elements within the queue. This is the basis of the well known A* algorithm [1], which is widely used in path finding and graph traversal.

To implement this algorithm, much of the structure present in *bfsPruneQ* can be reused, where *Seq* is replaced by a *MinQueue* structure which orders the elements according to some comparison function. For brevity, these details are omitted, but the development revolves around choosing an appropriate comparison function: a valid option would be to use the well-known Manhattan distance between two points, although there are other possible options. This function is then used to form the priorities of elements within the *MinQueue*, which arranges its elements so that those which are closest to the destination are favoured when considering the next value to explore in the search.

4 Robot Strategy

Our solution relies on using a portfolio of simple strategy algorithms competing for finding the best solution. A strategy takes a *GameTrie* and computes possible paths through the mine, together with their score:

```
type Strategy = GameTrie → [(Path, Score)]
```

We can now write a variation of the *solve* function (from Sect. 3) that produces a *Strategy* using *bfsPruneQ*:

```
solveS :: Strategy
solveS = map (second getScore) ∘ bfsPruneQ (const True)
```

This encodes the strategy of trying all possible paths, in a breadth-first manner. Naturally, this strategy is not very efficient, and will only work on very small maps. We also have a variant strategy that looks ahead only a number steps, and then takes one step along the best path found so far. This strategy finds locally optimal solutions.

An alternative strategy orders the remaining lambdas, tries to reach each one of them, and then walks towards the exit:

```
cmpS :: Comparison → Strategy
cmpS cmp tree
   | lambdas (getMine tree) ≡ 0 = case listToMaybe $ findExits tree of
       Just (p, tree') → [(p    , getScore tree')]
       Nothing       → [(([A], getScore tree )]
   | otherwise = case pathToLambda cmp tree of
       []            → [(([A], getScore tree)]
       ((p, tree'): _) → (p, getScore tree') : map (first (p++)) (cmpS cmp tree')
```

We omit functions *getMine* and *getScore*, which are simple accessors of the *GameTrie* data structure. Function *pathToLambda* takes a ranking function for lambdas and returns a list of paths:

```
pathToLambda :: Comparison → GameTrie → [(Path, GameTrie)]
pathToLambda cmp tree = concatMap snd (sortBy cmp dests)
   where dests = map (λcoord → (coord, findPaths tree coord))
                 (findTiles (≡ Lambda) ((layout ∘ getMine) tree))
```

We can now define multiple strategies simply by instantiating the comparison function of *cmpS*:

```
eqCmpS, lowCmpS, highCmpS :: Strategy
eqCmpS   = cmpS (λ _ _ → EQ)
lowCmpS  = cmpS (cmpCoords (λ( _, y) ( _, y') → compare y  y'))
highCmpS = cmpS (cmpCoords (λ( _, y) ( _, y') → compare y' y))
```

Strategy *eqCmpS* treats all lambdas equally, while *lowCmpS* prefers lambdas located the lowest in the mine. This strategy might make sense when the lower parts of the mine become harder to access as time goes by (see Sect. 6.1).

We also have more complicated strategies involving *cmpS*, such as preferring lambdas that are part of large clusters.

5   Concurrency and Exception Handling

Strategies turn the representation of a game tree into a list of paths with their corresponding score. By sharing the game tree structure, a number of concurrent worker threads using different strategies can compete with one another to find an optimal solution. The communication between these threads occurs through the use of Haskell's *MVar* values: these are mutable variables which can be shared and synchronised between threads. Initially, a trivial solution is put in *mvBest*. The task of each worker is to improve this solution with whatever they might encounter in their list of candidate answers.

$$improve :: (Ord\ s, NFData\ s, NFData\ a) \Rightarrow MVar\ (a, s) \rightarrow [(a, s)] \rightarrow IO\ ()$$
$$improve\ mvBest = mapM\_\ (\lambda x \rightarrow x\ `deepseq`\ modifyMVar\_mvBest\ (cmpBest\ x))$$
$$\textbf{where}\ cmpBest\ x\ best = return\ (\textbf{if}\ snd\ x > snd\ best\ \textbf{then}\ x\ \textbf{else}\ best)$$

Here, each solution x is a tuple of type (s, a), where s is a score that will be maximised, and a the answer itself. We require s and a to have an *NFData* instance to be able to force evaluation using *deepseq*, since the entire computation of the value of x should occur before blocking on the *mvBest* variable. The *MVar* is a reference to the best solution found so far; *improve* updates this *MVar* whenever a better solution is found. As this worker might be interrupted before the list is fully evaluated, it is important that *modifyMVar_* is an atomic operation: if the worker raises an exception while it is modifying *mvBest*, then the value is restored to its original state.

The workers are spawned by *spawnWorkers*, which creates a new asynchronous thread for each of the answers returned by the strategies, and then waits for all the threads to finish.

$$spawnWorkers :: (Ord\ s, NFData\ s, NFData\ a) \Rightarrow MVar\ (a, s) \rightarrow [[(a, s)]] \rightarrow IO\ ()$$
$$spawnWorkers\ mvBest\ xss = \textbf{do}\ workers \leftarrow mapM\ (async \circ improve\ mvBest)\ xss$$
$$mapM\_\ waitCatch\ workers$$

An important feature of this function is that the failure of one worker does not affect the others, since *waitCatch* will silently ignore any worker which has thrown an exception. While deceptively succinct, these two functions provide a powerful mechanism by which multiple concurrent workers can be spawned to improve the value of a solution, all the while dealing with exceptions in a safe way by allowing the best known solution to prevail in the case of failure.

Since we can rely on the fact that the best solution will not be lost when the workers fail, we can make use of this mechanism to allow the system to demand an immediate answer at any point during the computation. This fits nicely into the framework of the contest, where programs are given a set amount of time within which to find a solution, and then given a signal which raises an exception when time is up and an answer is required. To exploit this, the function *run* is used, which spawns the workers to perform the task of finding the best solution, and provides a callback that should be executed whether the computation terminates naturally, or an exception is thrown.

$$run :: (Ord\ s, NFData\ s, NFData\ a) \Rightarrow$$
$$(a, s) \rightarrow [[(a, s)]] \rightarrow ((a, s) \rightarrow IO\ ()) \rightarrow IO\ ()$$
$$run\ best\ xss\ callback = catchUserInterrupt\ \$$$
$$bracket\ (newMVar\ best)$$
$$(\lambda mvBest \rightarrow takeMVar\ mvBest \ggg callback)$$
$$(\lambda mvBest \rightarrow spawnWorkers\ mvBest\ xss)$$

The function $bracket :: IO\ a \rightarrow (a \rightarrow IO\ b) \rightarrow (a \rightarrow IO\ c) \rightarrow IO\ c$ takes three arguments: the initial computation, which initialises the best result found so far, the final computation, which reads the best result found and calls the callback, and the intermediate computation, which spawns the workers and waits for all threads for finish. The final computation of a $bracket$ is performed even if an exception is raised, which is precisely the behaviour required here when the callback is an action which outputs the best known solution.

One problem remains: if an exception is raised within a $bracket$, then after the final computation has been executed the exception will be re-raised so that it can be handled elsewhere in the system. If left unhandled, the program would exit and indicate that there was an error. The $catchUserInterrupt$ function is a helper which allows the program to gracefully exit when the interrupt signal which is expected from the judging environment is received.

$$catchUserInterrupt :: IO\ () \rightarrow IO\ ()$$
$$catchUserInterrupt = handle\ (\lambda e \rightarrow \textbf{case}\ e\ \textbf{of}\ UserInterrupt \rightarrow return\ ()$$
$$- \qquad\qquad \rightarrow throwIO\ e)$$

Note that if the exception received is not one that is expected, then the exception is thrown again and allowed to propagate further.

For testing purposes it is convenient to be able to kill worker threads after a particular amount of time, in order to simulate the judging environment. This is implemented using the $timeout$ function which runs an IO computation within a thread and kills the thread if no result is returned within a given time limit.

$$runWithTimeout :: (Ord\ s, NFData\ s, NFData\ a)$$
$$\Rightarrow Int \rightarrow (a, s) \rightarrow [[(a, s)]] \rightarrow ((a, s) \rightarrow IO\ ()) \rightarrow IO\ ()$$
$$runWithTimeout\ t\ best\ xss\ callback = timeout\ t\ (run\ best\ xss\ callback) \ggg return\ ()$$

This works as expected since exceptions are used to kill a thread that has expired.

6   Changing Specifications

One of the challenges was to deal with changing specifications. This was very easy to cope with in our model, and only minor extensions were required, mostly confined to the $Mine$ and $Tile$ datatypes, and the $stepRobot$ and $updRocks$ functions. On average, about 20 lines of code were added for each extension. The construction of the $GameTrie$ structure relies on the $step$ function to generate its branches, and so the changes in the specification are automatically reflected in the tree. As a result, all the strategies are also updated to reflect the change in specifications, since strategies use the $GameTrie$ to explore possible moves.

6.1   Flooding

The first extension was to add flooding to the mines. In certain maps, there is a rising level of water. The robot operates normally underwater, but it gets destroyed if it spends too many turns underwater. Modelling flooding requires changing the *Mine* data structure, extending it to contain additional information:

data *Mine* = *Mine* { ...
        , *flood*   :: *Int*
        , *waterproof* :: *Int*
        , *water*   :: *Int* }

These fields store the rate of flooding, how long the robot can last underwater, and the current level of water.

6.2   Trampolines

The second extension introduces trampolines, which act like teleporters. Once entering a trampoline, the robot gets instantly moved to a fixed destination location, and the trampoline disappears.

Similarly to flooding, trampolines requiring adding extra information to the *Mine* data structure:

data *Mine* = *Mine* { ...
        , *trampolines* :: *Set Coord*
        , *targets*   :: *Set Coord* }

These fields store the current position of trampolines and their associated targets. Additionally, the *stepRobot* function has to consider the case of moving into a trampoline, and we need two new tile types: trampolines and targets.

6.3   Beards and Razors

The third extension introduces beards. Beards are a new type of tile, that expand into the surrounding empty spaces in a fixed number of turns. The robot cannot traverse beards, but can collect and apply razors, which eliminate all beards surrounding the robot.

Again, the *Mine* structure has to be extended, this time with a growth factor and the number of available razors:

data *Mine* = *Mine* { ...
        , *growth* :: *Int*
        , *razors* :: *Int* }

Two new tile types are added (beard and razor). A new robot "movement" is to apply a razor, and the *updRocks* function now needs to update the tiles adjacent to beards as well.

6.4 Higher Order Rocks

The last extension introduces higher order rocks, which are rocks that upon impact (from falling) transform into a lambda. Each higher order rock counts as a lambda for the purpose of determining whether all lambdas have been collected.

We add a second Boolean to the *Rock* constructor to distinguish higher order rocks from normal rocks:

data *Tile* = ... | *Rock Bool Bool*

The *updRocks* function now treats higher order rocks just like ordinary rocks, apart from a small special case to check if a higher order rock should be transformed into a lambda. Additionally, the calculation of the number of lambdas after a step (*lambdas′* in Sect. 2.2) becomes more complicated. Two falling rocks can fall into the same spot, with one disappearing. If the rock that disappears is a higher order rock, then there is one fewer lambda in the mine. For simplicity, we calculate the number of remaining lambdas by traversing the entire layout:

$$lambdas' = length \; \$ \; findTiles \; (\lambda t \rightarrow t \equiv Lambda \vee isRockLambda \; t) \; layout''$$

7 Conclusion

We have described our solution to the 2012 ICFP programming contest, and seen how Haskell's features are useful during fast paced prototyping. Both low-level features (such as concurrency and exception handling) and high-level features (such as purity and laziness) are key ingredients in our solution. Haskell is a mature language, with both a stable compiler and high-quality libraries. We now give some general advice for code development in similar situations, based on our experience, and reflect briefly on possible improvements to our solution.

7.1 Practical Guidelines

Testing Even though Haskell's strong type system caught many common programming errors, we still had several bugs in our code. In particular, our submitted version often returns rather poor solutions because of bugs in the simulator. We focused our development in supporting the extensions and improving the strategies, but it would have been more effective to find and eliminate bugs.

Communication Our team was split into two groups in different locations. We found that frequent short meetings were helpful to keep the team up-to-date with the whole development, while allowing individual team members to work on separate parts of the program. Video communication, and screen/application sharing is useful for distance communication, but whiteboard brainstorming is invaluable, and hard to mimic in a distance communication.

Model first We started developing our solution by writing the model (Sect. 2.1). With this in place, different team members could develop the surrounding infrastructure more or less independently. Changes to the model were discussed with everyone before being implemented, and applied as soon as possible. This helped to minimise the mismatch between different components, and to allow development in parallel effortlessly.

Pair programming We have alternated our development between whole team discussion, individual coding sessions, and pair programming. We found pair programming to be an effective way of coding the more challenging parts of our solution, with the advantage that both team members become familiar with the code.

With regard to possible improvements to our solution, while the pathfinding algorithms take care to avoid going back to the same state several times, it would be nice to have this built into the tree structure itself. However, this would mean not using a tree structure, but rather some kind of directed graph. The lazy construction of such a graph requires the use of an appropriate constructor function to be called when elements are missing in a node lookup. The details of such an implementation are beyond the scope of this paper.

We have no regrets about our choice of programming language: we found Haskell to be suitable for developing a solution to this programming contest. We had no need for features or libraries that were not available, and our solution really played to Haskell's strengths. Haskell's type system helped catch bugs early on, but we failed to test our solution against a number of simple scenarios. These bugs (all minor and easy to fix, but nonetheless present), cost us a lot of points on a number of maps, and we failed to enter the last round of the competition. In that sense, dozens of submissions outperformed ours, but our development tried to find an elegant, functional solution to the problem that was easy to adapt to changing requirements. We feel that we achieved this goal, and despite our poor final results, the sheer fun of competing in such a contest using Haskell is hard to beat.

References

1. Hart, P., Nilsson, N., Raphael, B.: A formal basis for the heuristic determination of minimum cost paths. IEEE Trans. Syst. Sci. Cybern. **4**(2), 100–107 (1968)
2. Hinze, R.: Generalizing generalized tries. J. Funct. Program. **10**(4), 327–351 (2000)
3. Hughes, J.: Why functional programming matters. Comput. J. **32**(2), 98–107 (1989)
4. Peyton Jones, S. (ed.): Haskell 98, Language and Libraries. The Revised Report. Cambridge University Press, Cambridge (2003). Journal of Functional Programming Special Issue 13(1)

Decomposing Metaheuristic Operations

Richard Senington and David Duke[✉]

University of Leeds, Leeds LS2 9JT, UK
richardsenington@gmail.com, d.j.duke@leeds.ac.uk

Abstract. Non-exhaustive local search methods are fundamental tools in applied branches of computing such as operations research, and in other applications of optimisation. These problems have proven stubbornly resistant to attempts to find generic meta-heuristic toolkits that are both expressive and computationally efficient for the large problem spaces involved. This paper complements recent work on functional abstractions for local search by examining three fundamental operations on the states that characterise allowable and/or intermediate solutions. We describe how three fundamental operations are related, and how these can be implemented effectively as part of a functional local search library.

Keywords: Search · Optimisation · Stochastic · Combinatorial

1 Introduction

Metaheuristics (also known as local search) refer to a collection of methods for tackling combinatorial problems which are ubiquitous in areas including the sciences, engineering, economics, business and logistics [1]. These methods stand in contrast to "exhaustive" (global) search (such as Branch & Bound (B&B) which explicitly and/or implicitly examine all candidates in the solution space), in that they do not guarantee to find an optimal solution to the problem.

In many tasks however time is limited, and finding a high quality solution quickly is more important than finding a provably optimal solution. When problem sizes become large enough, global methods are unable to complete in practical time limits and in these cases metaheuristics have been shown to give better solutions to the same problems in practical time bounds.

Metaheuristics are iterative algorithms that operate through the transformation of a solution or group of solutions into new solutions, before taking these new solutions and transforming them again. They are abstract search methods, in that the basic search logic can be applied to many different problems. For example the hill climber, or iterative improver, works by only moving to new solutions that improve upon the old solution, a concept that can be applied to any problem that has a way to generate new solutions from old, and a way to decide which of two solutions is *better*. The interaction with specific problems is handled by *low level, problem specific operators*, defined with the problem. Three types of operator are commonly used and are described in Sect. 3; perturbation, neighbourhood and recombination. Low level operations on problems are usually

R. Hinze (Ed.): IFL 2012, LNCS 8241, pp. 224–239, 2013.
DOI: 10.1007/978-3-642-41582-1_14, © Springer-Verlag Berlin Heidelberg 2013

implemented in singular *monolithic* functions. This paper contributes the first analysis of these low level operators for metaheuristics, breaking them down into smaller, more generic components whose various combinations illuminate the design space of the operations.

While metaheuristics have been found to give very strong results they are not a "Silver Bullet" for optimisation. Each algorithm has a number of parameters which must be *tuned* to the problem, to allow the metaheuristic to perform well. The parameters traditionally tuned are scalar types such as the size of a population in a genetic algorithm, however the low level operators themselves are functional parameters which can be tuned. The break down of the low level operators into composable components supports a mechanism for subtle tuning of functional parameters, which is not possible in a monolithic approach.

A more complex approach to creating a metaheuristic for a problem is known as *hybridisation*. This is where either several metaheuristics, or components of metaheuritics are combined together to give a new algorithm that is better suited (or can be better tuned) to the specific problem that is being considered. Some hybrid methods will include other search methods as components, such as exhaustive search [2, 3].

Toolkits to aid in metaheuristic design, tuning, hybridisation and research have been created, however they are complex, frequently (though not by design) obscuring their inner workings. By analogy with crafting wood, these tools are adequate when one works 'with the grain' defined by the tools' abstractions and interfaces, but their limitations [4] are painfully exposed when a new problem requires working 'against the grain'.

One solution is to build tools from finer-grained components, and we have previously argued [5] that functional abstractions provide a powerful substrate for developing metaheuristics from combinators. Functional languages like Haskell, and implementations like the Glasgow Haskell Compiler, contribute layers of mechanism for the translation of these high level abstractions into efficient low level code, thus helping to resolve the tension between expressiveness and efficiency.

The paper is structured as follows. Section 2 reminds the reader of the Travelling Salesperson Problem (TSP), a well known and intensively studied problem that is used as an example in this paper. Section 3 provides a brief description of the library that is used in this paper, and how the low level operations for interaction with combinatorial problems interact with it. Section 4 describes perturbation and neighbourhood methods, and shows how higher order functions can facilitate the easy conversion between these two.

Section 5 decomposes Perturbation methods, providing finer grained operators for the design of low level interactions with problems. Section 6 describes Recombination methods and shows how they have elements in common with some perturbation methods. Section 7 Uses the decomposition to investigate a broad range of different perturbation operations for the TSP. Section 8 details conclusions further work.

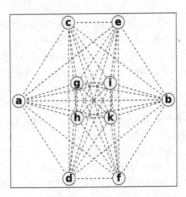

Fig. 1. The example TSP problem that will be used in this paper.

2   Example Problem: TSP

The Travelling Salesperson Problem (TSP) is a combinatorial problem that is often used as an example and for testing optimisation algorithms. The TSP is defined as finding a Hamiltonian cycle (a tour of a graph going through each node exactly once), of minimum *cost*, in a complete graph with an edge of known cost connecting every pair of vertices.

A TSP may be symmetric, where the cost of an edge is the same whichever way it is traversed, or asymmetric where this constraint does not necessarily hold. This paper will use the TSP as the example problem for illustrative purposes though other combinatorial problems will also be mentioned.

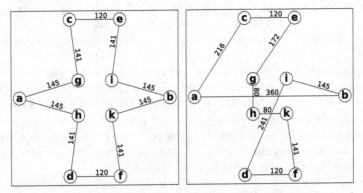

(a) The optimal solution for the example TSP, with a value of 1384.

(b) The solution that will be used for demonstrations in this paper, with a value of 1675.

Fig. 2. Example solutions to the illustrative TSP problem.

Figure 1 gives the complete graph of the TSP that will be used in diagrams throughout this paper. The optimal solution to this problem can be computed using an exhaustive search and is shown in Fig. 2, however to illustrate the actions of search operators a non-optimal solution will be used and is included in the same figure. Where code is shown we will assume that there is a data type called *TSP*, which supports equality testing and ordering based upon the relative quality of the solutions.

3   Combinators for Metaheuristics

This paper uses an experimental library [5] for the expression of metaheuristic algorithms in the pure functional language Haskell. Metaheuristics are iterative, and work by transforming one (or more) solutions into new solutions that are fed back into the process and form the basis for the next iteration. We capture this as a *stream transformation*, that is a function that takes a stream of solutions and yields a stream of solutions that are one step forward in the metaheuristic process. Metaheuristics expressed in this way may be created and manipulated using higher order functions, and composed with other transformations to create more complex search logic.

A metaheuristic iterates from an initial *seed* that must be provided externally. To achieve this using stream transformations, the function that represents the search process is *looped* using the following function, which represents infinite streams using lazy lists.

$$loopS :: ([s] \to [s]) \to [s] \to [s]$$
$$loopS\ f\ seeds = \textbf{let}\ as = seeds \mathbin{+\!+} f\ as\ \textbf{in}\ as$$

The library frequently uses finite lists to represent collections or groups, in addition to their use as streams of unlimited length. This can cause confusion, so to distinguish between the uses of lists we define the following type synonyms:

```
type Stream a = [a] --always of unlimited length
type Group a = [a] --promises to always be finite
```

The various well known metaheuristic algorithms (Iterative Improvement, TABU search, Simulated Annealing, Genetic Algorithms) all interact with the underlying problem through one of the three basic operations described below. Within the functional toolkit, these generic operations will be expressed as forms of stream transformation:

type *Perturbation s = Stream s → Stream s* — a single solution is changed to yield a different, but similar, solution. This can be seen in algorithms such as random walk and simulated annealing.

type *Neighbourhood s = Stream s → Stream (Group s)* — a single solution is used as the seed to generate a group of similar solutions. This can be seen in iterative improvement and TABU search.

type *Recombination s = Stream (Group s) → Stream s* — a group of solutions are merged in some way to yield a new solution sharing characteristics of the *parents*. Genetic algorithms are the classic example of this type.

Problem-specific specialisations are then used to realise these operations in metaheuristic algorithms, providing the low level interactions with the problem data. This paper explores higher order functions to aid in the expression of these different classes of interaction function.

To further illustrate how the library is used to combine logic to implement metaheuristics we will use the first-found iterative improver. The search process of this algorithm is to select the first solution in a neighbourhood that improves upon the solution used to construct that neighbourhood. This can be implemented using a higher order function called *improvement* to transform a neighbourhood function into an improving neighbourhood, and then composing this with a selection method. Below is the implementation of improvement, an example of the completed algorithm, and a how the completed algorithm can be *looped* at the ghci prompt. In these examples nF is the problem specific neighbourhood function, and *seed* is an initial solution for the program to iterate from.

$$improvement :: Ord\ s \Rightarrow Neighbourhood\ s \rightarrow Neighbourhood\ s$$
$$improvement\ nF\ xs = zipWith\ (\lambda\ x \rightarrow filter\ (< x))\ xs\ (nF\ xs)$$
$$ffii :: Ord\ s \Rightarrow Neighbourhood\ s \rightarrow Stream\ s \rightarrow Stream\ s$$
$$ffii\ nF = map\ head \circ improvement\ nF$$

```
> loopS ffii nF [seed]
```

4   Perturbation and Neighbourhoods

Both perturbation and neighbourhood functions can be defined as specialized, problem specific functions for any given problem. A common example neighbourhood function for the TSP is the *adjacent swap* neighbourhood. In this function a group of new solutions are defined as the exchange of adjacent cities in the original, and an example of this can be seen in Fig. 3.

We will assume a function called *swap*, which works with the previously defined *TSP* data type. *Swap* will take two indices and an instance of a TSP solution and returns a new TSP solution with those indices swapped. The adjacent exchange function, taking the number of cities as a constant parameter, can then be implemented as follows:

$$adjNeighbourhood :: Int \rightarrow Neighbourhood\ TSP$$
$$adjNeighbourhood\ nCities = map\ (\lambda t \rightarrow map\ (\lambda i \rightarrow swap\ i\ (i+1)\ t)\ [0 .. nCities])$$

However this hides a general relationship between perturbation and neighbourhoods, which permits each to be described in terms of the other:

– A Neighbourhood is the application of a perturbation function to a solution many times and gathering up the results into a group of solutions.

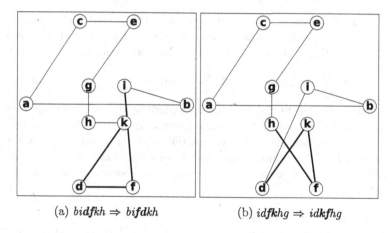

(a) *bidfkh* ⇒ *bifdkh*   (b) *idfkhg* ⇒ *idkfhg*

Fig. 3. The solutions resulting from applying two adjacent swapping transformations to the base solution.

- A Perturbation function can be implemented as the composition of a selection operation with a neighbourhood function, where the selection operator selects one element from the group.

4.1   Neighbourhood to Perturbation

A neighbourhood function can be adapted to become a perturbation function through the composition of the function with some form of selection function. The selection function, operating over streams, will have the type[1]:

$$\textit{type Selection } s = \textit{Stream (Group s)} \to \textit{Stream s}$$

The methods that may be used for selection are numerous and fall into two major categories:

Deterministic: such as selecting the *first, last, maximum or minimum* valued solutions from each neighbourhood. Of these, *first* might be used because in combination with lazy evaluation it will limit the runtime requirements of the program; where as *minimum* might be used to move towards a local minima in the shortest number of iterations. Deterministic operations can be lifted to operate over streams using the standard *map* function.

Stochastic: while uniform likelihood selection is the most obvious concept here, other options include stochastic selection with varying likelihood based upon quality of the solutions in the underlying group. A function with the type:

$$\textit{System.Random.Random } r \Rightarrow r \to \textit{Group s} \to s$$

---

[1] Note that this is also the type of recombination, so any recombination method could be used at this point, if it was felt that it was appropriate to do so.

may be lifted to operate over streams using the *zipWith* function, and the *randoms* function from the System.Random package, which produces a stream of random values from a random number generator.

> zipWith selectFunction (randoms g) :: Selection s

The *selectFunction* in this example is a place holder for functions that perform a single selection from a single group. Since such stochastic selection functions may make use of any probability distribution it is not possible to enumerate all possible examples. A selection method using a uniform distribution will be shown as an example of how these functions can be implemented.

$$uniformSelect :: double \rightarrow Group\ s \rightarrow s$$
$$uniformSelect\ d\ xs = xs\ !!\ (floor\ .\ (d\ *)\ .\ fromIntegral\ .\ length\ \$\ xs)$$

4.2   Perturbation to Neighbourhood

The repeated application of a perturbation operation to elements of an underlying stream, and the subsequent collection of these results into a group can be achieved using a function called *doMany* from the local search library. This is defined as follows:

$$doMany :: Int \rightarrow (Stream\ b \rightarrow Stream\ s) \rightarrow Stream\ b \rightarrow Stream\ (Group\ s)$$
$$doMany\ n\ f = chunk\ n\ \circ\ f\ \circ\ stretch\ n$$

The *doMany* combinator works by duplicating the underlying elements creating a stream that is *n* times longer than the original (*stretch*), and when the function *f* is applied to this it is equivalent to applying it many times to each value in the underlying stream. *chunk* is then used to divide the output of this process into a stream of regularly sized blocks, gathering the results back together into a new group.

Using *doMany*, different forms of neighbourhood can be created from a single perturbation function. For example, using the *swap* function for TSP,

- a *deterministic* neighbourhood which performs the same operation on each seed can be created by cycling a specific pattern of cities to be exchanged, for example:

$$tspDNF :: [(Int, Int)] \rightarrow Neighbourhood\ TSP$$
$$tspDNF\ p$$
$$= doMany\ (length\ p)\ (zipWith3\ swap\ (cycle\ pA)\ (cycle\ pB))$$
$$where\ (pA, pB)\ =\ unzip\ p$$

This allows the previous *adjNeighbourhood* for TSP to be implemented as

$$adjNeighbourhood\ nCities = tspDNF\ (zip\ [0..nCities]\ [1..nCities\text{-}1])$$

- *stochastic* neighbourhood functions are implemented by parameterising *do-Many* with a stochastic perturbation function. In the example of swapping cities, this can be achieved by creating two streams of random city indices (integers in the range 0-*nCities*) to indicate which cities should be swapped, rather than a cycling pattern as was seen in the deterministic approach.

$$stocSwap :: RandomGen \; g \Rightarrow \; g \rightarrow \; Int \rightarrow \; Perturbation \; TSP$$
$$stocSwap \; g \; numCities = zipWith \, 3 \; swap \; r \; r'$$
$$\textbf{where} \; r = randomRs \; (0, numCities\text{-}1) \; g$$
$$r' = randomRs \; (0, numCities\text{-}1) \; \circ \; snd \; \circ \; split \; \$ \; g$$

This can then be used to implement a stochastic neighbourhood function.

$$tspSNF :: RandomGen \; g \Rightarrow \; g \rightarrow \; Int \rightarrow \; Int \rightarrow Neighbourhood \; TSP$$
$$tspSNF \; g \; numCities \; nSize = doMany \; nSize \; (stocSwap \; g \; numCities)$$

5 Decomposition of Perturbation

The swapping operation for TSP, which has been used so far as the most basic operation in these examples, is known not to be particularly effective. A better method is to model a solution as a collection of edges, rather than a sequence of cities, and make changes by deleting edges and then reconnecting the resulting fragments. The swapping of cities can be seen as a very restricted configuration of functions that manipulate the edge set of a solution, where the cities being swapped determine exactly which edges are to be removed and inserted.

More generally this gives rise to two different activities, which when paired give rise to a perturbation technique, *damage and repair*. In this general pattern the damage phase removes something from the solution, leaving a data structure that is no longer a valid or complete solution to the combinatorial problem. The repair phase is then required to create a completed solution from the incomplete data structure.

The *damage/repair* model of perturbation is also more effective when considering more general models of combinatorial problems than the specific TSP example, for example when modelling problems using constraints. A constraint model provides a solution as a collection of constraints, generated through a constructive search process. Once a completed solution is achieved, what does it mean to *swap* or otherwise make changes to the constraints. In many cases arbitrary changes to the constraints will make them inconsistent, however using a damage repair model to define methods for deleting and reconstructing from the remaining constraints can give rise to effective algorithms.

5.1 Damage Methods

Damage methods have two dimensions and a rough diagram of how these overlap can be seen in Fig. 4. All decisions in the damage method are made with respect

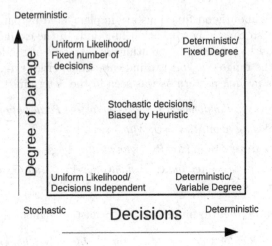

Fig. 4. Characteristics of damage methods, where a decision is an action upon a solution, for example the removal of an edge from a TSP solution. The degree of damage refers to the number of changes that will be made at once, for example the number of edges to remove.

to some problem specific valuation mechanism, for example in the TSP edge length is a simple way to evaluate the quality or usefulness of any give edge. A decision can be made in an entirely stochastic way, ignoring this valuation mechanism (usually resulting in each edge having a *uniform likelihood* of selection), or can be made with no stochastic element, resulting in a *most likely* or *greedy* deletion method. Between these extremes is an approach where decisions involve a stochastic element, but it is biased with respect to the value of the decisions, so that worse decisions are less likely. For example, in the TSP the selected edges could be ordered by length and then selected from based upon a probability distribution. Two possible example distributions are seen in Fig. 5.

On the other axis is how the scale of damage to be done will be selected. At the deterministic end is a fixed level of damage, for example three or six edges to be deleted from each solution. At the stochastic end is that any number of edges can be deleted and how many will be chosen with uniform likelihood.

In the centre of Fig. 4 is a situation where each decision is made stochastically, but with a reasonable respect for the valuation mechanism for the decisions. Each decision is independent of the others, so that any number of edges might be deleted, but it is unlikely it will be all, and the number is dependent upon the qualities of the edges in the solution at the time.

Implementation of the damage methods are required to operate over streams, giving rise to a transformation from a stream of solutions, to a stream of damaged solutions. Internally stochastic elements and logic can be threaded using *zipWith* and *map* as with the previous combinators.

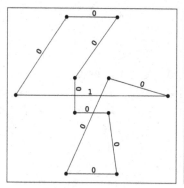 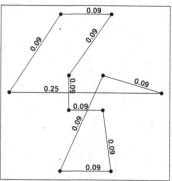

(a) Greedy probability distribution, where only the longest edge can be chosen.

(b) Uniform distribution, with bias on longest (worst) edge, so that it has the highest likelihood of being chosen for removal, but if it is not selected the other edges all have an equal chance of being removed.

Fig. 5. Two probability distributions for managing how edges are selected for deletion.

5.2   Repair Methods

Unlike damage methods, repair methods cannot easily vary how far they repair a solution, so there is only one dimension that can be varied, the level of stochastic computation involved in each decision. Like damage methods a valuation system for potential choices is used to guide decisions, and at one end of the spectrum is uniformly random likelihood of any *legal*[2] decision being made, at the other a greedy process that always chooses the cheapest option. Figure 6 shows two possible probability distributions for repair after three edges were removed from the example solution.

Repair methods can make use of a further style of operation, exhaustive search. Due to the level of repair usually being limited, exhaustive methods such as *Branch & Bound* can be used with confidence that they will complete. This can be seen as a variant on a neighbourhood, where a number of solutions are considered, and only the best is accepted, however it is more simply defined at this time as a separate operation, rather than breaking it down into the generation of solutions and selection.

In Sect. 4.2 we saw how neighbourhoods could be created through the repeated application of a perturbation operation. The decomposition of perturbation operations allows for an alternative form, where damage is carried out only once, and a stochastic repair procedure is then used several times to yield

---

[2] An illegal decisions would result in an invalid solution, for example sub-loops in a TSP.

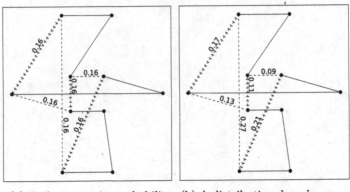

(a) Uniform repair probability distribution.

(b) A distribution, based upon a geometric progression.

Fig. 6. Two probability distributions for managing how edges are selected for insertion. The edges that were removed from the original solution are indicated by crosses rather than dashes.

a neighbourhood. The reverse of this, where damage is carried out many times and then each is repaired is the equivalent of a neighbourhood built from a perturbation operation.

6   Recombination

As with neighbourhoods and perturbation, recombination can be defined mono-lithically, and often is. When considering problems such as Boolean Satisfiability (SAT), a simple recombination method is to cut two lists of boolean values at the same point and concatenate the sublists, for example see Fig. 7. However such an approach is not effective for the TSP, because it tends to result in duplicated cities. This issue can be fixed by creating the second part of the solution through filtering the second solution, removing any city found in the first part created through cutting the first solutions string, hence preserving some sense of the order of the original solutions.

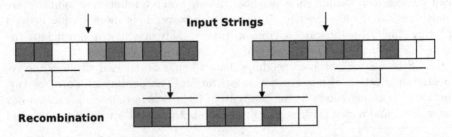

Fig. 7. Illustration of a simple crossover mechanic in SAT

However, as with perturbation methods, the most effective recombination algorithms for TSP consider the solutions in terms of the edges they use, rather than the order of the cities. The most effective genetic algorithm for the TSP [6], made use of a recombination method that was *maximally respectful* of the edges in the parent solutions. This meant that it identified edges common to both parents and ensured that they were present in the new solution. Each other edge in each parent was then selected probabilistically, on the condition that the result was not invalid. Any final gaps were filled in using a greedy repair algorithm.

These examples of the TSP and SAT do not provide guidance on creating recombination techniques for other problems. For example, the recombination of a problem modelled using constraints, where constraints are simply selected from the parents, once again runs a considerable risk of having irreconcilable conflicts. The final example of TSP recombination, using a greedy algorithm to complete a solution legally does however provide inspiration for an approach which can be explored; selecting some constraints from the parents and then using a greedy approach to insert new constraints until the solution is completed.

The process of recombination can be described as following a pattern of analysis of the parents, followed by the construction of a new solution based upon the analysis. The construction process has a strong similarity to repair concepts seen in perturbation, as in the TSP example already seen. This suggests that analysis forms a new class of operations, but that the repair operations can be reused.

7   Which Perturbation Algorithm?

The *No Free Lunch Theorem* [7] says that there is no one metaheuristic, nor perturbation method that is best for all problems. So it is of value to be able to experiment with specific problems and see how different perturbation algorithms compare.

This paper has proposed a collection of building blocks, specifically related to the TSP, which may be used to construct perturbation methods. To demonstrate their effectiveness, and requirement with relation to the No Free Lunch Theorem, we built a simple program to test a number of perturbation methods in the context of a single problem and metaheuristic. The problem chosen was *fl417* a symmetric TSP problem drawn from the TSPLIB [8] and the metaheuristic was simply the repeated application of the perturbation method to the last solution seen.

The program combined various damage and repair elements to generate different perturbation methods. In the event that uniform likely hood damage and uniform likely hood repair are used, this results in a form of random walk of the solution space. Damage levels of three edges and six edges were used, to compare the result when different degrees of damage occurred, and how this affected the performance of each metaheuristic. The results of each metaheuristic were processed to preserve only the best solution seen at that point, and were

Table 1. Results of an iterated damage-repair perturbation with various combinations of selection methods for each phase. Lower scores indicate better solutions and the optimal for this test problem has been previously found : *11861*. In the table each name indicates a way of selecting edges for either damage or repair. In general these are distributions over the edges ordered by length, with the following meanings; **Geo** is a distribution created from a geometric progression, **Uniform** is a uniform distribution, **Greedy** is a distribution where only one edge can be chosen (the longest available for damage, the shortest for repair), **BU 0.05** is the *best* edge has a likelihood of 0.05, and all others are uniformly distributed, and **Exhaustive** is where every combination is considered and the best solution created is chosen.

Repair	Damage			
	Geo	Uniform	Greedy	BU 0.05
Deleting and inserting 3 edges				
Geo	32200	183000	172000	152000
Uniform	31500	191000	175000	156000
Greedy	32000	85400	175000	53400
Exhaustive	34400	32400	188000	25400
Deleting and inserting 6 edges				
Geo	25300	183000	63300	151000
Uniform	25400	195000	61500	158000
Greedy	24500	84000	56100	54700
Exhaustive	29200	19600	254000	16700

sampled at 10,000 iterations. Each test was run 25 times and the average, to 3 significant figures, is presented in Table 1.

Table 1 does not contain all the results that were generated, only a cross-section including the most interesting or illustrative results. Other distributions that were tried included varying the parameters to the geometric progressions, changing the parameter of the biased uniform strategies and normal distributions. Similarly other combinations were tried that are not listed here. An exhaustive strategy' for damage is not practical because there is no way to know, before repair has begun, which set of edges is *best* to remove.

These results exhibit some broad patterns which are consistent with the expected characteristics of the combinations, but also some interesting diversity worth deeper consideration. The worst results are seen in algorithms which are highly stochastic, such as uniform likelihood of damage and repair, or purely deterministic such as greedy damage with exhaustive repair. This is correct for both three and six edge experiments, however there is a particularly interesting result, the high weakness of greedy damage, combined with exhaustive rebuild over this shift. This suggests that, rather than the increased size of damage improving performance through widening the options that might be considered, for this algorithm the change causes it to more rapidly find and become stuck in a local minima.

The geometric damage patterns perform consistently well at both levels, with any form of repair technique, however the best perturbation method uses the Biased Uniform damage strategy, with an exhaustive repair technique. This pattern of successful algorithms also supports common wisdom, that the best results come from a careful marriage of the level of damage, stochastic and deterministic components. However these results also show the significant variances that occur as components are exchanged, and how other parameters, such as the level of damage can change the apparent performance of particular combinations on particular problems.

This all supports the idea that flexibility and ease of experimentation are important characteristics of any library or toolkit for metaheuristic implementations. Our library, and this approach to the construction of new low level operators, provides this flexibility to the metaheuristic designer and enables rapid experimentation upon new problems with minimal programming cost.

To further investigate the use of these combinators a test was built using a Set Covering problem, drawn from train scheduling algorithms. Integer Linear Programming (ILP) provides the most effective tool for tackling these problems, providing the best known solutions though it suffers the usual limitations of an exhaustive search, that it cannot complete for most problem instances.

The Hypermutation metaheuristic [9] is also known to give interesting results, though not actually able to compete with ILP on the scale of problems that have been used in this study. Hypermutation works through an iterated perturbation, where the perturbation is achieved through the composition of a stochastic damage method, biased towards components with a worse value, and a greedy repair strategy. An exhaustive repair strategy has not, to the authors knowledge, been tried in the context of Hypermutation.

The TSP experiments had suggested that using an exhaustive repair strategy, in combination with a highly random damage strategy could provide better results. The damage process that was chosen was to select a finite number of components in a solution using a uniform likelihood selection method, rather than biasing it with respect to an valuation function.

Repair was carried out using an ILP solver, with the elements of the previous solution designated for preservation *fixed* in the constraints of the ILP model.[3] This more constrained problem could be completed at each iteration, though a search on the problem instance in general would not complete (though would yield some solutions). The ILP system used was the GNU Linear Programming Kit Version 4.25[4] and linked to Haskell using *glpk-hs*,[5]

The solutions found were good, superseding the Hypermutation previously described, and over runtimes of between 15 minutes and 2 hours the metaheuristic gave stronger results than the ILP method alone over the same time limit. We were pleased that the use of concepts from the previous TSP study gave such promising results, however they do not equal results yielded from a commercial solver, based upon ILP methods using specialised extensions.

---

[3] Other uses of ILP as a component in the construction of metaheuristics may be seen in [2,3].

[4] GLPK may be found at http://www.gnu.org/software/glpk/glpk.html

[5] glpk-hs is written by Louis Wasserman and may be found in the Haskell libraries at http://hackage.haskell.org/package/glpk-hs

8   Conclusion

This paper has used functional programming techniques to examine perturbation, recombination and neighbourhood methods, used as the low level interaction operations in metaheuristics. This has resulted in the creation of combinators for moving between these various methods and the decomposition of the monolithic functions into three alternative classes of function; analysis, damage and repair. A number of types and variations upon each these have been proposed.

This decomposition into smaller building blocks makes visible a broad range of alternative perturbation, neighbourhood and recombination methods, through picking and choosing from the options available. The visibility of the elements being used in each composition allows for clearer comprehension of how they interact and how larger methods operate, aiding in the design of new variations.

This was demonstrated using a short investigation of a specific TSP problem, mixing and matching across a range of both well known and less frequently seen operations, yielding some useful results. The results of the investigation into the TSP provided inspiration for a new variation of a known metaheuristic for a large real world problem, which when tested was found to be similarly successful. We see that the right set of abstractions, here as elsewhere, can provide powerful tools to aid in the investigation of problems and the construction of algorithms.

Haskell's expressiveness aids in these forms of investigation, with the type system providing clues and pointers as to how components may be combined. This in turn proposes lines of investigation, sometimes unconsidered, or shows where more sophisticated conversion techniques will be required to facilitate a desired line of research.

The next stage in this investigation is the further hybridisation of these operations. At present damage and repair alternatives have been created, but a more complex approach might use a number of damage and repair strategies in a single perturbation method. For example, fixing one part of the solution using a greedy method, another part of a solution using a uniform likelihood and finally an exhaustive technique. This suggests a new range of combinators that can be explored to improve the expression of these hybrids.

We see this work as moving in the direction of superior methods for investigating metaheuristic methods, and automated experimentation through combining well understood building blocks. This places the work in the realm of hyperheuristics [10], a branch of metaheuristic research that attempts to automate the design of algorithms for specific problems.

Acknowledgements. The authors would like to thank Tim Sheard for all his advice in the final stages of writing this paper.

References

1. Hoos, H., Stützle, T.: Stochastic Local Search: Foundations & Applications. Morgan Kaufmann Publishers Inc., San Francisco (2005)

2. Contardo, C., Cordeau, J.-F., Gendron, B.: A grasp + ilp-based metaheuristic for the capacitated location-routing problem. Technical report (2011)
3. Prins, C., Prodhon, C., Ruiz, A., Soriano, P., Calvo, R.W.: Solving the capacitated location-routing problem by a cooperative lagrangean relaxation-granular tabu search heuristic. Transp. Sci. **41**(4), 470–483 (2007)
4. Masrom, S., Siti, A.Z., Hashimah, P.N., Rahman, A.A.: Towards rapid development of user defined metaheuristics hybridisation. Int. J. Softw. Eng. Appl. **5**(2), 1–12 (2011)
5. Senington, R., Duke, D.: Combinators for meta-heuristic search. J. Funct. Program. (2012, Submitted)
6. Merz, P., Freisleben, B.: Memetic algorithms for the travelling salesman problem. Complex Syst. **13**(4), 297–345 (2001)
7. Wolpert, D.H., Macready, W.G.: No free lunch theorems for optimisation. IEEE Trans. Evol. Comput. **1**(1), 67–82 (1997)
8. Reinelt, G.: TSPLIB - a traveling salesman problem library. INFORMS J. Comput. **3**(4), 376–384 (1991). http://comopt.ifi.uni-heidelberg.de/software/TSPLIB95/
9. Li, J., Kwan, R.S.K.: A fuzzy genetic algorithm for driver scheduling. Eur. J. Oper. Res. **147**(2), 334–344 (2003)
10. Burke, E., Hart, E., Kendall, G., Newall, J., Ross, P., Schulenburg, S.: Hyperheuristics: an emerging direction in modern search technology. In: Glover, F., Kochenberger, G. (eds.) Handbook of Metaheuristics. International Series in Operations Research & Management Science, pp. 457–474. Kluwer, Dordrecht (2003)

Author Index